THE COURAGE OF SIMPLICITY

NEW INTERNATIONAL LIBRARY OF GROUP ANALYSIS

Series Editor: Earl Hopper

Other titles in the Series include:

THE COURAGE OF SIMPLICITY

Essential Ideas in the Work of W. R. Bion

Hanni Biran

KARNAC

First published in English in 2015 by
Karnac Books Ltd
118 Finchley Road, London NW3 5HT

British Library Cataloguing in Publication Data

A C.I.P. for this book is available from the British Library

ISBN 978 1 78220 142 7

Edited, designed and produced by The Studio Publishing Services Ltd
www.publishingservicesuk.co.uk
e-mail: studio@publishingservicesuk.co.uk

www.karnacbooks.com

CONTENTS

PART I
INTEGRATIVE CONCEPTS

For Hanan, Lior, and Yoav
with all my love and gratitude

ACKNOWLEDGEMENTS

My most profound gratitude goes out to Earl Hopper, without whom this book would not have been published. Thank you, Earl, for countless hours spent reading these chapters, for your ideas, your words, and your creative thoughts, and for making such an enriching and broad minded contribution to each and every chapter of this book.

Thank you, my beloved spouse, Hanan Shafir, for supporting, encouraging, and helping me in so many ways, with much love and patience. And thank you again, Hanan, for the wonderful photo on the cover of this book.

I am indebted to two psychoanalysts, Naomi Huller and Yolanda Gampel, for opening the door for me to psychoanalytic thinking and for always encouraging me to contemplate the elusive and the invisible. I consider you both my very significant psychoanalytic mothers.

I am grateful to my beloved brother Doron B. Cohen, for his translation, advice, and support.

I dedicate the chapters concerning the unconscious in the context of society at large to my friend and mentor Gordon Lawrence, who inspired me in my writing. Gordon passed away recently (2014) leaving an immense void in my life. As my psychoanalytic father, he taught me how to linger in a state of not-knowing and let thoughts find me, and to look at dreams as bearing social messages.

ABOUT THE AUTHOR

Hanni Biran, MA, is a clinical psychologist, a trainee psychoanalyst, and lecturer and supervisor at Tel Aviv Institute of Contemporary Psychoanalysis, where she is a member of the committee for social involvement of the Institute. A group analyst, she is also a lecturer at The Israeli Institute of Group Analysis, and supervises many teams and staff members in public clinics and hospitals involved in group psychotherapy. She has also been trained according to the group relations tradition of Tavistock Institute, and conducts small and large groups and role analysis workshops in Israel and abroad. She is a lecturer in the programme for psychotherapy at Tel Aviv University and in the programme for psychotherapy at Magid Institute, The Hebrew University.

She has worked in private practice since 1978. She also works with underprivileged populations in Tel Aviv, where she has hosted many social dreaming matrixes with citizens of several generations. She is a member of "Psycho-Active", a movement of mental health professionals against the occupation and for human rights, and is involved in projects promoting dialogue between Jewish Israelis and Palestinians. Her main interests are Bion's theory, the social unconscious, social dreaming, and individual psychoanalysis. She is the author of numerous papers and book chapters published in both Hebrew and English.

In a way, psychoanalysis is extremely simple, but like every simple thing, for some reason it is awfully difficult to carry out

W. R. Bion, (1987), *Clinical Seminars and Other Works*, p. 5

Simplicity is rarely simple. It is based on the sense that the perception of a phenomenon is neither more nor less complex than the perception needs to be in order for it to be as accurate and truthful as possible. This applies to all our perceptions of the world, but perhaps to the socio-cultural and psychic realms in particular. The great challenge to the achievement of simplicity lies in the conceptualisation of our perceptions and the communication of them to other people. This is made even more difficult by the fact that we are intrinsically interwoven into the fabric of the objects that are of interest to us.

The courage of simplicity is a function of our willingness to free ourselves from the restraints and constraints of the determinants of our perceptions. We must allow ourselves to become unfettered from the sources of our security and safety and from all that is familiar to us. Such courage demands flirtation with madness and the experience of psychotic anxieties, including the fear of annihilation caused by failures of dependence, and perhaps above all the experience of profound loneliness. Such courage also depends on finding one's own voice and one's own vision of what is true and what is real. This requires a readiness to withstand the dismissive indifference of others, which can be more painful than direct and open expressions of their envy of individuality. This demands that we are able and willing to speak truth to power while at the same time to avoid the corruption of arrogance.

It is always necessary to learn from experience. Individually and collectively we must relinquish our oedipal configurations, both those that are internal and those that have been and continue to be external. We must also try to enter into the protectorate of the Sphinx. Other mythical territories and their icons are especially pertinent to such quests. For example, the myth of Osiris offers the insight that both in the beginning and the end there was One. We can hardly apprehend our own individualities without an appreciation of the Oneness from which we have originated and to which we will return.

Bion understood this, almost from the beginning of his professional life, when he was influenced by his collaboration with Rickman (2003), who was also his mentor. Analysed by Klein, Bion became a Kleinian. Clearly, he continued to be a Kleinian, as he from time to time acknowledged. This was based on the axiomatic importance that he continued to give to the death instinct, the power of innate malign envy, psychotic anxieties, and the assumption of an innate ego of adaptation as well as agency. Yet, he became the most creative and independent of Klein's offspring. Bion understood that although Klein was one of Freud's heirs, Anna Freud inherited an equally important, compelling, and truthful ladleful of her father's potage.

Bion became what Lewin termed a "field" theorist (the dimensions of which ranged from the mathematical probabilities of quantum mechanics, to the realities of the socio-cultural world, to the uncertainties of the spiritual universe), sharing the insights of Einstein with those of Jung. His conceptualisation of the "proto-mental" evolved from its sole emphasis on the psyche-soma to include its socio-cultural context, in full recognition that its contextual "envelope" is both inside and outside the epistle of its own contents. Appreciating both paradox and the dialectics of hope and envy, Bion's work forms one of the banks of the river that we all must cross. Of course, the opposite bank is the home of Foulkes and his colleagues, where it can be said that colleagues such as Yalom also reside (Hopper, 2009).

Hanni Biran is one of the few of us who are able and willing to bridge this eternal river. Like a deeply religious person who prays each day through reading a portion of one of the Great Books, Biran reads "Bion". She interprets the meaning of his words in a very personal way, while always attempting to apprehend his intentions.

However, she fully understands that the work of Bion must be read alongside the work of Foulkes. She understands that the social unconscious in the context of field theory is at the heart of the project of Foulkesian Group Analysis (Hopper & Weinberg, 2015). Whereas the work of Foulkes overlaps and inter-penetrates with the work of Bion, Foulkes draws his inspiration from an alternative, additional set of intellectual sources, namely European sociology, anthropology, and political philosophy, which developed in parallel with the work of Freud. Although Foulkes was not politically active, perhaps because of his forced emigration to England, his work had a political quality. Almost from the beginning he was concerned with the elucidation of the psychodynamics and group dynamics of the world and its groupings with and of which we are intrinsically interwoven. This went beyond the phenomenon of valence, and the projection of inherent phantasies and anxieties, and defences against them. Foulkes' interest in trauma was not based on an appreciation of the life of a team leader encapsulated within a tank under attack, as much as it was based on an understanding of failed dependency in the external world, breakdowns of systems of communications, and an inability of political systems to withstand their psychotic personification and inadequate leadership. Aware of the unconscious transgenerational repetition of social trauma, Foulkes realised that human experience is itself always Janus-faced, directed inwards to the mysteries of the soma-psyche and outwards to the mysteries of socio-cultural political life.

In addition to many books about Foulkesian Group Analysis, two books about Bion and his work were included in the original International Library of Group Analysis: *W R Bion and Group Psychotherapy* edited by Malcolm Pines (1985); and *Building on Bion: Roots* and *Branches*, each edited by Malcolm Pines and Robert Lipgar (2003a,b). I am very pleased to be able to include in the New International Library of Group Analysis this book of Hanni Biran's selected papers concerning Bion's ideas and their many applications in psychoanalysis, group analysis, and political activity. Although it is a very academic book, it is also a very personal one. Generous in its intellectual style, it is not driven by the length of its bibliographies and the esoteric quality of its citations. It embraces both art and poetry, novels and films, the connotations of which are seen in Biran's clinical work as well as in her subtle appreciation of the nuances of Bion's ideas, which are often penetrating in a quiet and indirect way.

Beautifully organised, this book starts with several key integrative concepts from Bion's work over several decades. It then turns kaleidoscopically to the study of people, groups, and society itself. I personally was especially struck by the clarity and power of Biran's discussions of alpha and beta elements and their social manifestation. Also important to me is her analysis of terrorism, deeply personal sources of it interwoven with the relational dance of the terrorist with his enemies. Although this work has been forged in the passion of the present, subtle distinctions are made between myths and collective memories, and between cultural transmissions and the individual discovery of personal pain. She discusses the vicissitudes of sibling rivalry with great sensitivity.

For the time being Hanni has had to put aside a number of papers that are in various stages of completion. We are working together on a number of projects that I hope will see the light of day. For example, we have begun to discuss a project on anti-Semitism based on the dynamics of the "no-thing", acknowledging that very few Israelis seem to appreciate the nature of anti-Semitism, perhaps because they are first and foremost Israelis and only secondarily Jews, although of course these two complex aspects of their identities are completely interrelated. We are also writing a paper on the dynamics of incohesion in Israel as a traumatised society, mainly in terms of an illustration of my theory of the fourth basic assumption of Incohesion: Aggregation/Massification of (ba) I:A/M. I have deeply appreciated Hanni's willingness to read my work and discuss it with me in depth and in detail, on the basis of which I have often been able to understand more clearly what I have really meant—if not exactly what I have written.

Hanni has provided a great deal of entirely relevant information about herself. I will add only a little to what she has deemed to be important for her readers. A good and loyal friend, she is also a stimulating colleague. She is honest and straightforward, and, therefore, very "difficult". She takes no prisoners in the game of the politicised intellectual activities of our profession in Israel. She is compelled to go against the grain, to resist the winds of popularity. A fearless critic of the intellectual work of others, she is much less gentle with regard to her own, constantly striving to express what she feels to be true and what needs to be said. As she herself has begun to acknowledge, her real *métier* is the study of social dreaming and the hosting of social dreaming matrices in order to discover more about the unconscious common preoccupations of the members of a particular social system. Hanni inherited her passion for this work directly from Gordon Lawrence, with whom she worked and by whom she was influenced and inspired. The study of social dreaming will almost certainly provide a further opportunity for personal growth and integration from which we will all benefit. This book will be of value to colleagues and students alike, not only in Israel, but also throughout our international network of psychoanalysts, group analysts, and organisational consultants.

Earl Hopper
Series Editor

Introduction

I was born in Jerusalem, around the time the state of Israel was established. Ever since, as a citizen of Israel, I have lived in a land of conflict, war, terror, and occupation. The work of Wilfred R. Bion has helped me realise both how blind leadership can be, and how much a society can need an enemy.

The need for an enemy defies logic and stems from the world of instincts and anxieties. Bion (1958), like Klein (1975b), accepts Freud's (1915c) thinking about the life and death instincts. While many psychoanalytic schools have turned away from the theory of the death instinct, I personally believe that this theory is of value, especially in the context of so much continuing destruction, bred by hatred and evil.

I find the term "social texture" to be most vital, because it allows me to observe the society in which I grew up. As a child, I took part in two annual national ceremonies, one on Holocaust Memorial Day and the other on Memorial Day, in memory of the Israeli soldiers who died in war and civilian casualties of terror actions, and I still stand to attention when the siren sounds. As early as kindergarten, our children and grandchildren learn to stand to attention on these two days. Then and now, a child growing up in such a socio–cultural–political context learns that the only way to survive is through war. When this is the prevailing perspective, the Palestinian people might well not exist.

Bion's work on the existence of the "vertex" (1967), however, allows a shift from one perspective to another. In order to see a complex picture, I must observe social reality from various positions, stepping beyond the place allotted to me by the society in which I grew up. It is thus that I discovered the suffering of the Palestinian people and the inherent cruelty of the occupation.

I feel obliged to take a moral stand supporting the rights of the two peoples who live in and who share this land. Human life is more important than soil.

The Jewish society living in Israel was built on the backs of refugees, but in constructing itself, it has caused another people to become refugees. We must study and explore the life circumstances leading to the perpetual, dead-end relationship between victim and victimiser. When Israeli society was being formed, its leadership was not mature enough to acknowledge this complexity. It was difficult for it to perceive its others, those who were different, who did not belong. Naturally, an emerging society needs absolute values that are both clear and resolute, but this comes with a high price. National identity, which had to be concise and uniform, gave birth to the proud, warrior-like "Sabra" ("prickly pear" in Hebrew). Pushed to the fore by the trauma of the Holocaust, this image of the warrior-like Sabra became idealised. The Sabra is the new Jew, prickly on the outside, soft and sweet in the inside. A yearning for heroism swept over the people, and courage was heralded as the supreme virtue. With this state of affairs, any attempt at dialogue or even contact with the other peoples of the Middle East was out of the question. I grew up in a young society that cultivated fear of the other. This society placed itself under a mental siege in which the other was not an interlocutor but a menacing enemy, dehumanised and demonised, surrounded by fantasies of evil, barbarity, monstrosity. I would ask, however, whether at this present time, where Jewish society in Israel is a given, unquestionable fact, can we shift from the sense of being dead-ended to an experience of creative dialogue? Can we shift from a sense of helplessness to hopefulness, from existential anxiety to a belief in co-existence?

Before describing each of the chapters in this book, I would like to comment on its title, although the epigraph, quoting Bion, speaks for itself. The title was suggested by Earl Hopper, during a conversation we had about Bion. We were saying that, paradoxically, behind his enigmatic writings are some very simple issues. I have a clear sense of this simplicity, and this is how I transmit Bion to my colleagues and students. In teaching, I employ the Talmudic method of reading each paragraph together and then discussing it. I have never yet taught the same text twice, thus allowing those studying with me to join me in becoming a team of scholars, collectively deciphering the text. This act of deciphering never fails to bring us face to face with simple life facts. Bion needed great courage to formulate the three universal assumptions outlining the life of every group in such simple terms. Their clarity and simplicity made them into paradigms, serving to advance the study of groups by light-years. Moreover, in reading *Learning from Experience*, we come to realise that Bion conceives of psychoanalysis as a methodical observation of plain human wisdom. Later in this book, I quote from his *Clinical Seminars* held in Brasilia. This quote shows Bion discussing the simple human wish to be born, to be oneself. The need is simply for someone intuitive enough, equipped with enough common-sense, to be able to discover the singular patient, enabling them to be born.

Relying on and developing the ideas of W. R. Bion, this book observes psychoanalytic thinking through three prisms: person, group, and society.

It is divided into four parts:

The first part revolves around some integrative concepts of Bion's theory. It elucidates key concepts in Bion's thinking, such as container and contained, the selected fact, and the caesura. It is also clinically oriented, demonstrating how these concepts can shape interventions and interpretations in our work with patients.

The second part focuses on the person. Clinical in its emphasis, it discusses Bion's theory of thinking and his reading of the Oedipus myth. These are illustrated by vignettes highlighting the emotional aspect of thinking.

This part is concerned with processes of the inner world of the individual person, and the way he interprets and understands the reality in which he is living. In fact the person, group, and society are inextricably interlaced. However, focusing on the person allows us to delve deeper into Bion's unique contributions to the theory of thinking: how do thoughts come to be? What is the emotional component of thinking? The answers to these questions can be illustrated through psychoanalytic practice. Bion dealt extensively with the boundary between clinical work and theory. His thinking opened up many spaces for exploring both the way analysts think and the various kinds of linking between patient and analyst.

The myth of Oedipus is explored as a crucial layer of human life. The journey of King Oedipus to reveal the truth of his life was for Bion a metaphor for the wish of human beings to know themselves.

The third part discusses the small group and its unconscious processes. Although Bion's paradigms have greatly influenced psychoanalytic conceptions of small group processes, this section integrates the thinking of Bion with that of Klein.

Small group processes are more or less universal. Their structure and processes are similar throughout different cultures. This universality provides a broader perspective to the study of the effect of myths on human culture.

I am referring mainly to the myths analysed by Bion: eating from the tree of knowledge, the tower of Babel, King Oedipus (Bion, 1970). These myths are ingrained in human culture all over the world, recurring on social, group, and personal levels. All three share a similar structure, featuring the human desire for knowledge and the punishment meted out to men who challenge divine mastery by trying to become omnipotent and omniscient.

The small group exhibits obstructions and weaknesses that originate in the unconscious. This provides an opportunity to explore what the group rejects and excludes, for instance, prejudice and racism.

I attempt to integrate several theories and concepts:

1. The phases and the positions in Kleinian theory (Klein, 1975a)
2. Bion's basic assumptions (Bion, 1961)
3. My own thinking and learning from experience.

In another chapter, I attempt to integrate some of the ideas of Bion with those of Foulkes (1973) concerning the concepts of link and matrix.

What is the meaning of the term *link*? It first appeared in a paper (Bion, 1959) and again in *Learning From Experience* (Bion, 1962a, p. 42). According to Bion, the link is the space where an emotional experience occurs. Such an experience is only possible within a relationship. The link is the space in which the meeting of two entities causes something new to be born. These two entities can be two ideas, or two people, or a person and a group, or two sub-groups.

Bion also used these links in his study of cultural myths (Bion & Bion, 1992), and he found them interwoven into the central myths that interested him.

While Bion was developing his work on links, Foulkes developed the concept of the group matrix. Behr and Hearst (2005) reviewed Foulkes' work, showing that the basic concepts of his theory are surprisingly similar to Bion's thinking. His matrix, which includes the notions of the *nodal point*, the *mirror reaction*, and *resonance*, is based on principles closely resembling Bion's thoughts on linking. Foulkes' basic assumption is that human beings are primarily social creatures. The group precedes the individual, because the individual is born into the group. Foulkes believes that the infant is born into a network of communication, which determines his identity from the start. According to him, the group is the basic psychological unit. A person in isolation is like a fish out of water.

If we try to integrate Foulkes' and Bion's thinking, we find that Foulkes' network of communication is indeed made up of links. The matrix develops gradually, and enables us to map the patient's difficulties as they become re-enacted in the context of the group.

Foulkes, like Bion with his notion of catastrophic change, was interested in changes and how they come about. Foulkes wrote (1971) that the purpose of group therapy is to lead to insight and adjustment. By using the term adjustment he emphasised the internal psychological change and the rebuilding of the inner world. Adjustment, according to Foulkes, is not submission to authority or compliance with group norms, but rather self-discovery through the processes of communication taking place in the group. In this Foulkes resembles Bion. However, unlike Bion, Foulkes does not emphasise the pain entailed in growth, nor does he focus on psychotic anxieties. Unlike Bion, he does not stress the disintegration that precedes integration. Foulkes underlines the links rather than attacks on linking.

The fourth part, focusing on the feelings of despair and helplessness in the face of repetitive, unending war, is inspired by the author's life in Israel. It relates to society at large and the traumatic history of the Jewish people: the Holocaust is still inscribed in the Israeli social–unconscious and this social trauma has considerable impact on the Jewish Arab conflict.

This part focuses on society at large, drawing on insights from sociology and anthropology. The Israeli–Palestinian conflict is described by applying Bion's theory of thinking. The difficulty to transform from possessing to belonging is analysed as a barrier in the way of peace dialogues. The split between clinical thinking and the social unconscious that is presented intensively to the outside world, shown to be responsible for misunderstanding the patient's life. The unconscious emergence of identity is explained by analysing the inevitable connections between the person and his social environment.

In this part I also explore the influence of some social and historical processes of which I was not conscious but were manifested in the life of my analytic group.

I have concluded the book with an essay about several events in my personal history. I want the reader to understand the sociocultural context in which I grew up, and my own process of becoming a psychoanalyst and group analyst.

The central theme of this book is the elaboration and application of Bion's thinking as I employ and develop it in my observation of unconscious processes in society at large, in small groups, and in the individual person. Bionian theory helps us explore the limitations of human life. Bion often mentions the fact of human transience, of our limitations in terms of time, space, and knowledge. In this context, how human beings live a full life while acknowledging death is a key question. The book as a whole is about unconscious processes as they are realised in a person's life and in society.

It is inevitable that some ideas are repeated several times throughout the book. Without such repetitions, which are necessary for the development of ideas, some chapters might be either unclear or incomplete.

PART I

INTEGRATIVE CONCEPTS

CHAPTER ONE

The concepts of the container and contained in Bion's thought

I n this chapter I will attempt to understand the meaning of the concepts of the container and the contained, first formulated by Bion (1956) and developed (1970, pp. 72–83) in *Attention & Interpretation*, and elaborated in a further chapter in the same book (1970, Chapter Twelve, pp. 106–125). My arguments are grounded in Bion's (1962b) and (1967, pp. 106–125) theory of thinking and in his various statements regarding the concepts of the container and the contained that are scattered throughout his work.

I am aware of the writings of theoreticians such as Ogden, Eigen, Symington, and others, that rely on and develop Bion's conceptualisations. Nevertheless, in this undertaking, I have endeavoured to return to the Bionian source, presenting it through my own world of experience and my clinical practice.

I will begin by describing several different aspects of the container, as I experience them.

The primary container is the mother. She is the one who provides the infant with her non-verbal emotional presence. She is attentive to this pre-verbal infant, who still cannot express himself in words. She grasps his being, his temper, his unique presence, his distress. This process takes place through two main functions (Bion, 1967).

The first function is translation. The mother receives the infant's β-elements, elements the infant cannot yet think but only act. Bion paradoxically refers to these elements as "unthinkable thoughts".

The infant, in himself, is helpless, able only to signal his distress to the mother. Some cries speak of hunger, others of cold. The body expresses different kinds of tension—stomach aches, and so on. According to Bion's depiction, it is not easy being an infant. Without language, the infant has no other choice but to send such un-deciphered signals to his mother. These are all β-elements, which the mother receives and thinks. Inside herself, she transforms them and names them. This translating function is the most vital containing faculty; Bion calls it "the α-function": the mother is internally giving words to the infant's distress. His message is being transformed, inside her, into verbal thinking—she is doing the thinking for her baby, transforming the messages she received from him into α-elements, or "thinkable thoughts". The more she is able to translate correctly, the more the infant is likely to be mentally healthy. When she is emotionally unavailable, anxious, or confused, she may leave the infant without her translation, or provide him with a confounded one. For instance, the infant is signalling that the room is too cold, but the anxious, inattentive mother shoves a bottle in his mouth. This is a confounding translation that only increases the infant's distress, creating the grounds on which future thought-disorders and mental ailments may grow. When the mother provides a correct translation, she is thinking for her baby. Later on, he will learn, through her, how to think verbally on his own. She is helping him to acquire this important function and to learn to deliver his messages to the world in a clear way, leading to joy and satisfaction. The mother's α-function is vital for the development of emotional life and the ability to think. This function shows us the extent to which Bion conceives of the container as a thinking container, which does not simply absorb, but also thinks and transforms, endowing the material entrusted to it with verbal meaning. Bion believes this manner of thinking is an action; therefore, the container is seen as an active agent, rather than a passive absorber, as it is often mistakenly depicted. A container with the capacity to contain is an active, dynamic, seeking, wondering, examining, and questioning container. This means that thinking is an act, an action. Thinking through the process of finding the right word is a complex, subtle, and devoted activity. The α-function has to do with creativity; the creativity of the mother thinking for her baby. This creativity increases when the mother is free to contemplate her own motherhood. When she actively forms her mothering experience she is creating a beneficial environment for her baby.

In summary, the container is the mother's area of creation, that gradually turns into a shared area of creation, for both her and her infant. Finally, it will become a container for the child, a benevolent container that generates thought and feels emotional freedom and active curiosity, which is growing and becoming throughout its life, and in which motherhood is sustained without the need for the mother's concrete presence. It is important to add that β-elements are the most primordial form of raw material. They are not yet transformed into thinking and at times retain their raw form. Bion (1970, pp. 22–41) often refers to them as "the thing in itself".

In his chapter about the theory of thinking, Bion depicts the process of the growth and development of the ability to think: the first stage of thinking is the appearance of a preconception. The primary and most important preconception is the infant's anticipation to encounter the mother's nourishing and emotionally present breast. If this encounter takes place, it becomes what Bion calls a *realisation*. The encounter will thus lead to the development of a conception, that is a key element of the ability to think. As mentioned before, β-elements remain beyond the ability to think, appearing as they are (for instance, as a psychosomatic illness).

The second function performed by the mother as the primary container is her capacity for reverie. Bion sees this in terms of the mother's capacity to daydream forward (Bion, 1967). I believe that the reverie is the mother's ability, in times of great difficulty, distress, and falling apart, to daydream inside herself, to conjure up a complete image that keeps her looking forward. She is imagining that all the bad, difficult, confused, and broken things now overwhelming her will develop into benevolent being. She is daydreaming toward the horizon from which something good will be born, from which growth will surely arrive. What now seems like a catastrophe will turn out to be a catastrophic change bringing forth renewed growth. Reverie gives one the ability not to fall apart or lose one's way. It is a non-verbal emotional presence. Still, it too is not passive, but a form of action. I think that the capacity for reverie lies in a world where the mother or the analyst are capable of performing what Bion (1970, pp. 6–26) calls an "act of faith".

This aspect of daydreaming forward, in which the mother or analyst daydreams a benign future image, is implicit in Bion's formulations. Most interpreters of his work consider reverie a form of meditation that entails renouncing logical thinking. It is commonly portrayed in analytic literature as the ability to tap into one's intuition and perceive an unseen, non-verbal being, here and now. This interpretation sees the analyst, who is dreaming for the patient, as performing a containing function. However, I also see in reverie the ability to daydream forward into a better future for the patient who is now in misery.

As his clinical work develops, Bion makes things more complex. Through his profound research and the questions he poses to himself, he grants the contained an ever increasing role. As we move on to his later writings, the mother seems more and more to be part of the container–contained equation, meaning that the infant plays a central role in the performance of the containing function. Container and contained are developing a kind of interrelation, in which the infant has considerable influence over the mother's ability to contain. The infant may be born with a restless temper, making him harshly demanding. The more the infant is dissatisfied, irritated, and misunderstood, the less the mother is able to contain him. The more he is responsive, calm, smiling, and content, the more the joy of giving and creativity grows. Therefore, according to this perspective, the contained also creates its container. When the infant extorts the container, giving nothing in return, the container is diminished. When the contained uses the container to fill itself up, their roles may become reversed: the contained containing the container and vice versa. This is a subtle, yet important, shift. A misunderstood or very passive infant reduces the mother's capacity for creativity. A happy, responsive infant increases her capacity to give and create. The dramatic area of growth is therefore the mother–infant link (Bion, 1967, Chapter Eight).

The following vignette illustrates this matter. A patient tells me that her mother said to her that as a baby, she suckled very slowly, so that each feed took a long while. The mother told her grown up daughter: "you suckled so slowly, that I had time to read all of Agatha Christie while breastfeeding you". This infantile situation, which I could vividly imagine, shed light on the patient's work in group therapy, specifically regarding her difficulties in establishing emotional intimacy with other members. Our initial tendency might be to be angry at the mother, blaming her for not being emotionally present, for looking for the thrill of figuring out "whodunit", while her daughter is suckling in her lap. On second thoughts, however, it will be wrong to judge only the mother, without considering the role of the contained in this constellation. We might find it more accurate to say that the mother–infant communication was disrupted, and this disruption had various implications for the grown up psyche. Such an event is certainly registered in the emerging psyche, but there are no guilty parties: it took place in the space between container and contained. The more the mother became withdrawn and preoccupied with her books, the slower the infant suckled. And Bion would say, "wait, the opposite is also true". This is the Bionian perspective, always pointing out the reversible perspective, the "vice versa" (Bion, 1963, pp. 48–53). The opposite is also true: the slower the infant suckled, the more the mother found refuge in her book. She may not have known any other way to handle the situation. Such events should be examined carefully, we should study their effect on the patient's relationships while constantly rethinking and avoiding clichés such as the automatic accusation directed at the emotionally absent mother. The key is observing the space formed by the mother–infant link.

I will now turn to a second aspect of the container as conceptualised by Bion: the intricate analyst–patient relationship. The analyst, like the mother, is the container and the patient is the contained. The functions of translation, reverie, creativity, innovation, and discovery are evident here, and there is great importance to what is going on in the space between both parties. Some patients hinder our ability to give, and some patients expand and enrich our joy of creation and discovery. In analysis, the patient brings forth obscure fragments or particles as well. These frightening β-elements, which the patient cannot think verbally, are residues of material that were left untranslated in infancy and have now come back to attack the inner world. The patient acts them and the analyst translates them, internally, into verbal thinking. Beta-elements can take many forms: acting out, psychosomatic pains, sleep disorders, attention deficit disorder, and other similar manifestations. The analyst, through her emotional presence, is re-enacting the role of the mother, providing, by means of her thinking, the translation of unthinkable elements into thinkable elements. This is the essence of containing. Those of us who are experienced clinicians know well how different patients are contained in various and distinct ways. There are those who are easily contained, containing us as well and contributing to our growth and capacity; then there are those who are grumpy, dissatisfied, demanding, passive, giving little, and asking plenty, hindering our containing ability. A good example of this is boredom in analysis. When it is boring, we might find ourselves following our thoughts elsewhere, drifting after thoughts that run away from the office toward our daily matters and concerns. This is not uncommon, it happens to many of us and it is not always easy for us to admit it. Still, this is clearly a red light: I need to check why I am absent, why is the patient putting me to sleep, what must I do to change the quality of our relationship, and so on. We must ask questions that would help awaken us, putting us back in tune with the patient. Bion's working assumption is that the analyst–patient link is under attack. An attack carried out by two parties.

Analytic containing is an intricate craft, a form of art even, and Bion devoted much of his writing to this subject. He claims that for such growth-promoting containment to exist, the analyst must subject herself to a state that resembles dreaming or daydreaming. This state prepares the analyst for the moment in which the patient is perceived as an original and unique being and to the reception of the patient's signals. This requires the analyst's container to be free and vacant, much like the mother's freedom to form her own motherhood. The analyst must create herself as an analyst for the patient.

What is the meaning of a "vacant container"? First of all, it must be vacant of the dozens, even hundreds, of psychoanalytic theories. One must forget, for a while, all that one knows so as not to arrive in the analytic session with a container that is saturated and overflowing with theory. This might create a session filled with analytic jargon but lacking any authentic dialogue, as the analyst is unable to see the unique patient and hear her unique story. A vacant container is a container that never knows right away, that never understands too quickly, that does not label or categorise. It is a container that is not saturated with pre-existing knowledge. This vacancy has an active aspect as well—that of clearing away those elements within the container that obscure the patient's unique presence. The vacant container enables the analyst to summon up those images that the patient evokes in her.

This begs the question, regarding the clinical application of this theory, of whether the experience of reverie is spontaneous or is it an artificially conjured image. Bion does not elaborate on this technique, leaving it open to our clinical insight. I believe that while spontaneous reverie is more faithful to the patient's needs, in states of helplessness, pessimism, or failure in the analyst–patient relationship, a conjured image is both needed and appropriate. Thinking in images is much more "experience-near" than intellectual interpretations, and therefore capable of helping the analyst find a hidden channel of communication into the patient's inner world.

The second aspect of the analytic container has to do with Bion's famous saying that the analyst must come to the session without desire or memory. Bion kept coming back to this issue, which recurs throughout his writings. When the analyst is preoccupied with desire, she is not here. She may desire to cure the patient, to see some results, to see the patient get married, finish her studies, etc. She is harbouring some expectation that might hinder the attention she must employ. Memories are also a source of deception and disruption. Engaged with the past, memories derail the analyst into irrelevancies. She finds herself struggling to remember the previous session, the story the patient told when she first came to analysis, etc. This means that she is trying hard not to be here. Something important is happening here. It might be difficult. It might be frightening, causing the analyst to run away, to grasp at familiar material in the attempt to bridge the emerging gap. Avoiding the use of memory is also an active effort, that cannot happen on its own. The container must be cleared. It should be noted that Bion distinguishes memory from remembering. The latter is a welcome, spontaneous occurrence—"I suddenly remembered something that is related to what is happening now". Remembering contributes to analysis, unlike memory. Memory fills the container with deceptive material. Bion illustrates this very well by saying that one cannot analyse one's family members because one's container is full of memories that prevent the discovery of the patient's personality.

In discussing containing, we should note that Bion did not consider psychoanalysis in terms of the medical model. He saw it as dealing with evolution, development, and growth. The analyst performs a function that is much more mothering than medical—she is there for the patient in order to perceive and encourage her growth process. In other words, the analyst is a container that cannot operate by itself; it needs a growing, developing contained—a contained that sometimes switches roles, containing the container through a fruitful dialogue, through an interesting dream, through its fertilising creativity. Such growth cannot take place without the occasional crisis, setback, or even catastrophe. These difficult experiences slowly give rise to developmental change (Bion, 1970, pp. 87–92).

I will now turn to a third aspect of the container and the contained: the container exists as an internal function. The infant, with the help of the mother, and the patient, aided by the analyst, will eventually develop an internal container. This internal container arranges our world, distinguishing inside from outside, and possible from impossible. It is involved with acknowledging limitations, which, in turn, generates creative freedom. Attention deficit disorders, for instance, indicate the lack of a container that could enable one to focus and concentrate. About two years ago, a daily Israeli paper published a story about a sixteen-year-old boy who won a gold medal at the Physics Olympics. This boy told the reporter:

> You don't start learning physics at any given point. Even a year-old baby sees the objects it's dropping falling down. That's a physics lesson like any other. Learning is a gradual process. I didn't learn physics through the public education system.

This is an adolescent with a strong internal container. A curious boy who, from a very young age, was free to observe the laws of nature. He acquired a vacant container and the joy of discovery as an infant— he had taught himself to learn.

It is important to stress that the internal container expresses a kind of ability that differs from person to person. This ability has to do with curiosity and learning from experience. It is not an interpersonal faculty but a capacity to observe the world as a source of knowledge, play, and pleasure.

A fourth aspect of the containing function is found in the containing function of the "word". The word gives shape to things that are shapeless; it has an organising, clarifying, and calming function. The word provides meaning but it is also limited—some things cannot be expressed in words and must remain outside this container. According to Bion, we have to keep in mind that certain things, even very important things, remain non-verbal. When describing our experiences, we sometimes use the expression "words cannot say"—referring to emotional or spiritual occurrences that cannot be depicted in language. Wordless experiences exist on both the positive and negative poles of the spectrum. At the negative pole, we find the psychotic dissolution that cannot find any containing word. The psychotic person may cut herself or jump to her death; she is experiencing something unbearable—a nameless dread. The negative aspect of uncontained material can also be found in the social domain. For instance, no words can depict the atrocity of genocide. Can the world "Holocaust" capture the Holocaust? Apparently not. For example, Claude Lanzmann (2012), in his autobiographical *The Patagonian Hare* (2012), relates that when his *Shoah* was screened in China or Japan, no suitable title could be found in either language. At the positive pole of material that words cannot contain, we find strong emotional experiences, spiritual experiences, in which some hidden divine quality has been encountered. Similarly, Gershom Scholem (1974) tells that Isaac Luria, the "Holy Lion", the founder of the Lurianic Kabbalah, declared that he would not write a book, as the insight that overwhelmed him could not be contained in a book:

> Luria acknowledges his inability to present his teachings in written form since the overflow of his ideas did not lend itself to systematization. Nor did he select the various subjects for study in his doctrine in a logical sequence but at random. He guarded the secrets of his system and did not permit its propagation during his lifetime, therefore becoming celebrated at first mainly for his conduct and saintly qualities. (p. 422)

A fifth aspect of the containing function is that of the group, the organisation or the society. (Bion, 1970, pp. 77–83) devotes an entire chapter of his *Attention and Interpretation* to this idea. In this chapter, entitled "Container and contained", Bion explains, in great detail, his notion of the dynamics between the contained, the genius that he calls "the mystic", and the container, that is the society or "the establishment". This key chapter was pushed aside in post-Bionian thinking, that was mostly concerned with studying the inner world and the analyst–patient relationship. Bion uses the term "establishment" to describe the social container that human beings require. People are essentially social beings and they need to belong. They may belong to various establishments, whose rules they accept, such as a country, a work-place, a professional union, etc. These perform a containing function by providing frameworks and rules. The establishment is supposed to foster the growth of a person with exceptional abilities as its contained. According to Bion, Freud was such a person or "genius". But he would have surely failed if it were not for the considerable group of people that followed him. The establishment is always in conflict with the genius. At first, the creative and innovative genius terrifies the establishment and is rejected by it. Then, a new establishment is formed around this new idea. Any group is always in danger of halting all innovation and preventing the growth of new genius. An establishment without a genius atrophies; a genius with no establishment becomes psychotic. This is another example of the importance of container–contained relatedness to the possibility of growth. The good social container is that which can contain difficult material without falling apart. It also entails the capacity of its leadership to contain differences and to allow these differences to co-exist.

I witnessed the epitome of the ability to contain difference on memorial day in 2011, when I took part in an alternative commemorative ceremony, conducted by the organisation "Combatants for Peace", in which we grieved for casualties from both peoples. I was astounded to see an impressive man, dressed in the style of the national-religious movement, come up on stage. Earlier, I had seen him standing with his children, all wearing kippas, and his wife, whose head was covered. He introduced himself as part of the Fogel family—he had lost his brother, sister-in-law, and nephews in the horrible murder of the Fogel family in Itamar, a settlement in the West Bank. He spoke with great pain about the murder of his brother and his brother's family, while maintaining the brave and uncompromising willingness to acknowledge the suffering of the other people. He said that he did not judge his brother for choosing to be a settler, as that was his belief and the essence of his being, but he also refrained from judging the tormented Palestinian people. He emphasised that he had no political affiliation and that he did not wish to mix politics with human suffering. It was a moment of human greatness. We sometimes forget, or find it difficult to believe, that human beings are human beings, wherever they are. It is surprising to discover just how similar the human container is, throughout all cultures and societies. For example, Amos Oz (2002), the renowned Israeli author, expressed great wonder when his *A Tale of Love and Darkness* became a best-seller in China. He was certain that the novel would only be of interest to readers who grew up in the Jerusalem neighbourhoods described in it. But what he saw as provincial was, in fact, at the very heart of human experience. This was made possible by an emotional auto-biography that reaches out to people everywhere.

It is important to remember that the containing function, so vital to development, often becomes hindered or obstructed by anxiety, constant demands, or envy. Envy is one of the main factors disrupting the containing function. The container's envy of the contained or vice versa curtails the development of the containing function. In order for containment to develop, one must first deal with envy. The idea based on the phases and the positions of Klein. Envy is central in the schizo-paranoid phase and it destroys the ability for integration. Only in the depressive phase is containment possible due to the ability to inte-grate contradictions and to come to terms with weaknesses and faults.

I will now move on to a clinical illustration, presenting a vignette from an analysis.

This patient has prominent verbal abilities. He speaks fast, racing from issue to issue, leaving me a bit dizzy. At the last minute of the session, I suddenly hear myself saying: "you're filling the room up with speech; you're overwhelming me. I feel 'flooded', I can't think."

Two days later, in the following session, pauses began to appear between sentences, there were even some short moments of silence here and there. I felt good, pleased with having mentioned my feeling of being overwhelmed. Quite content, I told him what good progress he was making and "how good it is to have moments of silence".

My intervention angered him. He said: "This is a controlled, arti-ficial silence. I've been pausing intentionally so as not to overwhelm you, not to 'flood' you. This is not my silence. I have been forcing it for your sake."

I panicked. I did not answer. I did not know what to say. I under-stood that something about my containing went wrong. I could not find any words to reply. An awkward, irritating silence came over us. I felt completely empty. I tried summoning up an image—the image that surfaced was a difficult one. I saw myself as a kind of animal trainer, rather than an analyst. I asked myself—what am I doing here, analysis or taming?

I said: "You're angry at me for having to be compliant here as well, like you are outside analysis".

Silence, then he said: "I was very offended when you said I overwhelmed you. You told me I was filling up the room with speech. I am disappointed in you. Maybe you just can't stand my overwhelming you. From now on, make no mistake, I am a manipulator, I know how to please, and this is what I will be doing here from now on; trying to adapt myself to you."

Long silence. I do not really know what to say. I feel pain.

Happily, he kept talking.

> I feel with you just like I did with my mother when I was little. I lived with my grandmother and every Thursday, mother would come to visit. She sat in her car and gave me a toy through the window. I just wanted to throw the toy back into her car and make her go away with her stupid toy. But I never did. I behaved myself. I was a good boy, I did what was best for her. Now you want me to do what's best for you, too. What, you think that I don't know that I am overwhelming? And now you're telling me you can't take it anymore. I came to you with a fantasy, I thought I could bring up everything here, and have it my way. I came to be given unconditionally. But you can't be overwhelmed by me. Now I'm trying to adapt to holding things in again, trying to be a good boy. I'm turning fake for your sake.

I felt that I had no idea what to say, that nothing I could say would make sense. The session ended with his anger and pain. Afterwards, I was upset. How can I reach out to him? It suddenly occurred to me that what he was telling me was actually very important: he was trying to contain my inability to contain. He was brilliantly pointing out the dangers in our relationship. Once more, I tried summoning up an image—I saw him as a crying baby and me as the mother who was letting him fall through her hands. I knew that his mother was handicapped and I could imagine the feelings of a little boy whose mother had never hugged him.

In the following session, I said: "You helped me see something I didn't see before. It was wrong of me to tell you that you were overwhelming me. By doing so, it was as if I was letting you fall from my arms. I am taking responsibility for my mistake."

After a moment of silence, he cried, for the first time in analysis. "This is very moving for me. No one has ever talked to me like that. You suddenly realised it. I want to thank you for what you said."

In terms of container–contained relations, two things had happened. There was a breaking point, when my container was fractured.

But this fracture led to a moment of growth. He repaired me, and thereby contained me. After he did that, I was able to acknowledge my mistake. Acknowledging my mistake led to his growth. His ability to allow me to make mistakes helped me develop a bigger container for him. I appreciated his ability to help me become a better analyst for him. When he felt certain that I was tuning myself to him, he naturally became less and less overwhelming.

This example illustrated the intricacies of the reverie function. It seems to me that this function oscillates between the experience of here and now and a historical–biographical story that paints significant childhood images. The image could come to the surface as living material because of the frustration that occurred in the session, and which was shared by both patient and analyst.

After it was worked through and finished, it brought the patient significant relief and made his dialogue less overloaded and overwhelming. Afterwards, a new phenomenon appeared in analysis. The patient declared that he was just "whining", that he was pretending to be the victim. After all, his childhood was not all that bad . . . He told me I should watch out, that he was a master with words:

> You get all compassionate about me, but how bad was it, really? I am telling you that when I was four I came back to living with my mother, and then, every now and again, I would go back to grandma's. The thing is, I'm not telling it like that—I'm using words that evoke your compassion. I am saying "they tossed me from one home to the next like I was some bundle", sometimes I tell you they "threw me around like I was a ball". What's the big deal? Why am I choosing words that elicit such strong feeling in you?

This kind of statement came up again and again, and still does every now and then. It is not right for him to be "whining", it is wrong for me to be impressed by his tear-jerking vocabulary. I gave this much thought. I understood this manoeuvre as expressing a kind of shame he was feeling. He was ashamed of the little boy he used to be and was calling him names. This time, I refused to join this perspective, to take the side of the part he called the "cry-baby". I refused to accept that his pain was a pretence or a charade. I realised that a certain aspect of his personality stepped out of the container and was observing analysis from without, mocking him for crying and me for being so gullible as to believe his pain. I was finally able to identify this mocking figure through its vocabulary. This was the vocabulary of mother's new husband, who brought him back from his grandmother's to his mother house, but kept mocking him, calling him a "cry-baby" and abusing him in other ways. Following this abuse, his grandmother took him back in, this time into another kind of hell, as all his memories of her house were of loud, frightening arguments between her and his grandfather. They argued about his mother's illness, which kept her from taking care of him physically, and about other unresolved issues, such as where should this child live. His biological father abandoned his sick mother and him, his only son, remarried, and had a new family, completely detaching himself from the patient. I refused to see this childhood reality as inconsequential. I understood that he was feeling humiliated, so much so that it was still hurting him. I decided to tell him so and did. I tried showing him that he is not that omnipotent and that he could not choose how to make me feel and always keep the analysis under control. I had to work hard to separate the truth from the lie. He was lying to himself and to me, he wanted us both to believe that "it was nothing". I adamantly refused to accept the words "whining" and "nothing". The maltreatment and abuse he experienced took place due to harsh circumstance and the lack of a containing figure. Certain people, especially his mother's husband, wanted him to think it was nothing and to stop whining. Now, it was up to us to contain that little child inside him, to understand what he wanted to tell the grown-ups around him, who would not listen. Instead of mocking him our task was to stop being ashamed of this child and ease his pain.

By saying that the patient was lying to himself and to me, I try to illustrate the distinction between a lie that results from emotional distress, which is activated like an unconscious defence, and a fiction that is consciously fabricated. A lie is the result of not being able to bear the truth, while a fiction is the invention of one who already knows the truth (Bion, 1970, pp. 97–105). The lie employed by this patient belongs to the first kind—it is a lie stemming from the emotional pain of learning the truth.

In summary, I have reviewed five different aspects of the concepts of the container and the contained, which, although they are linked, are actually scattered throughout Bion's writings: the mother as a container, the analyst as a container, the internal container, the word as a container, the social and cultural container. I presented a clinical example that poses questions about containment that I had to answer in each session anew. This case also highlighted the five aspects of containment that I reviewed:

1. We have no accessible material regarding the patient's pre-verbal infancy. Still, in light of his history, we may develop a working assumption about the significant disruptions occurring in early life, due to his mother's disability and his father abandoning him.
2. Childhood scenes were re-enacted in the container–contained relations manifest in the analytic relationship.
3. The patient was a child with a well-developed internal container that enabled him, under very difficult conditions, to cultivate his curiosity, playfulness, and joy of knowing.
4. The word, as a container, had served him well in establishing his sanity in a fragile and unstable world. We developed a sophisticated vocabulary, his profession involves writing and he often invents interesting and unexpected idioms.
5. While we are often preoccupied with the inner world, Bion reminds us of the social world and the culture in which we live. Therefore, the broken familial container and the mother's disability that singled her out in society, also had a tremendous effect on the patient's ability to feel part of an establishment. This difficulty is manifest in his being divorced for many years as well as in his work as a freelancer, dealing with establishments that hire his services for limited periods of time, leading to permanent financial insecurity.

In conclusion, in this chapter I tried to illustrate some different facets of the concept "container and contained" and to look at the vivid relationship between the container and the contained. I emphasised the activity of the container and its engagement with the contained. Containment is not a passive entity. It is an act of emotional involvement. The container not only responds to the contained but also develops by it. Today this concept is crucial in psychoanalytic thinking.

CHAPTER TWO

The selected fact

This chapter will focus on Bion's term "selected fact". In it, I will attempt to demonstrate how it helped me to think freely, and how I allowed myself to use it in my clinical work.

Characteristically, Bion does not elaborate or explain the term. He speaks abstractly, leaving it to each of us to translate it into clinical practice. References to the selected fact are scattered throughout his various books, as are many of his other creative concepts. His writing is a flow of thoughts and associations, evolving through his interdisciplinary freedom.

Bion (1962a, p. 72) offers a quote from Poincaré, a French mathematician and philosopher:

> If a new result is to have any value, it must unite elements long since known, but till then scattered and seemingly foreign to each other, and suddenly introduce order where the appearance of disorder reigned. Then, it enables us to see a glance of each of these elements in the place it occupies in the whole. Not only is the new fact valuable on its own account, but it alone gives value to the old facts it unites. Our mind is frail as our senses are: it would lose itself in the complexity of the world if that complexity were not harmonious: like the short-sighted, it would only see the details, and would be obliged to forget each of these details

before examining the next, because it would be incapable of taking in the whole. The only facts worthy of our attention are those that introduce order into this complexity and so make it accessible to us.

It is exciting to read this quotation, written in the early twentieth century (1904), and to realise the similarity between Poincaré's thinking and Freud's (1900a) writings about the interpretation of dreams: Freud analyses each element of the dream separately and then finds new meaning, using associations to create links, leading to the discovery of a surprising narrative.

Bion uses this quotation to describe the psychoanalytic interpretation of the psyche, that presents itself as chaotic, as analogous to the construction of a mathematical formulation. Mathematical formulations introduce order where previously there were elements that seemed scattered and foreign to each other. In other words, the formulation identifies the whole and discovers coherence where disorder reigned.

The idea expressed in the quote from Poincaré resonates throughout Bion's thinking. He takes it into the depths of communication between patient and analyst. The patient may seem disintegrated, parts of him appearing in confusion in the analytic session. The patient presents disorder. The situation requires an analyst capable of reverie. The hallucinating and dreaming analyst, coasting through the world of associations, is an analyst who can imagine that this disintegrated patient will one day be whole. Reverie is the ability to hold on to a picture of something whole even when the patient has fallen apart, become confused and become lost. Often, when the patient is at sea, there seems to be no connection between the various contents of his speech.

The analyst who is capable of seeing a whole picture will find a connecting thread, a single idea underlying the patient's words. This idea is the "selected fact". It is the thing the analyst has chosen to say so the patient will feel contained and may sense some degree of cohesion. It is a situation in which the analyst has solved a riddle the answer to which was obscured and had been waiting to be discovered. Cohesion appears, not because the analyst proposed a brilliant idea; it materialises as a result of the analyst's emotional presence. The analyst need say no more than one short sentence. For instance: "What's common to everything you're saying is a powerful emotion of anger that's overwhelming you." One need not be a mathematical wizard to solve the riddles of the mind, although the metaphor of a formula originates in mathematics. Bion searches the various sciences for a path to the mind, but his translation of them is unique and surprising.

In *Cogitations* (1992), published thirteen years after his death, Bion elaborates the notion of the selected fact, emphasising the emotional experience of discovering it. This experience occurs suddenly, accompanied by the feeling of being creative. The psychoanalyst discovers a synthesis that binds together unconnected elements. These are moments of illumination, which happen only when the analyst allows himself to be in a state of not knowing. These moments of discovery strengthen our curiosity, and curiosity, in turn, strengthens the life instinct. The most surprising lines about this issue are on page 275:

> The fear and intolerance of the selected fact ultimately contribute to increasing attacks on the individual's equipment for feeling and satisfying curiosity, and therefore contribute to the forces operating in producing senility. Senility is a process analogous to destruction of the ego and of alpha function. It contributes to the shortening of physical life.

The selected fact is different from a cause. A cause is essentially related to time, but the selected fact is timeless: its elements can manifest simultaneously or in a jumble of different times.

The selected fact is associated with a point of view; with what the analyst sees before the patient can see it. This is often the situation in therapy. The patient sees a flat picture and the analyst searches for depth in the picture. However, the analyst can only discover the selected fact once he has entered the consulting room and after he has had an emotional experience.

It should be noted that, although Bion turns to mathematics, he is not searching for logic in the common scientific sense, but for a different mathematics—one could say, for a mathematics of the mind. The question is, how do various elements of the mind connect? How does one see a picture when the patient presents an unknown? According to Bion's thinking, the psychoanalytic therapist must solve the riddle of the mind. When he does, a new riddle will appear. Bion believed that for this process to occur, the analyst must be in a position of +K (Bion, 1962a, p. 47). The selected fact is a fine thread hiding in a tangle of other threads. A +K position is an attitude of pure attention, devoid of expectations or any activity that might obstruct the patient's discourse. Bion (1962a, p. 95) also demonstrates various types of –K, and, in fact, attempts to warn the analyst of the dangers of a –K attitude, which disturbs listening. Examples of –K are listening judgmentally, listening condescendingly, listening with prior knowledge that blocks new knowledge, listening enviously, listening through one's own value system, etc. A –K attitude can occur, for instance, when a patient wants to get divorced, and this seems to the analyst to be wrong according to his own value system. Or when a patient wants to get married and the analyst considers this a hasty decision. These are examples of situations where we find it difficult to listen, because inside we are taking a stand.

To me, the advantage of the theory of –K is that it is left open, so that when we turn to practice, each of us can sense our own pitfalls leading to a biased, –K type of listening. Once we identify this, we can shift from a –K to a +K position. We can only find the selected fact from a position of +K.

Bion also turns to mathematics because mathematics are concerned with the search for and discovery of the unknown. Bion makes an analogy between this attitude and that of the analyst, because the patient speaks of unknown objects that are not present in the room. The objects spoken about in analysis have no physical presence, and for this reason the analytic discourse must discover these absent objects. Both in mathematics and in psychoanalysis, the objects are abstract. For example, when we tell the patient that he has internalised his mother's aspirations for excellence, we are saying something very abstract. Therefore, Bion is careful when entering this field. He emphasises that we are constructing thoughts and dealing with abstract signs and symbols, as in mathematics.

The selected fact is highly abstract. Its discovery may create harmony between all the elements appearing in the dialogue. It seems to me that Bion's working assumption is that in every analytic hour there is one main fact striving to be discovered.

There are other processes in an analytic session that are supposed to take place in addition to the +K position. These processes are also necessary for the selected fact to emerge. One such process is the analyst's presenting himself as a container for the patient. The containing function creates a place into which everything can be brought, including madness, perversion, etc., without breakdown having to occur.

It is important to note that the analyst's containing function determines to a large degree what will enter the therapeutic container and grow within it, and what will be rejected and thrown out of the container, and thus become lost in infinity. Bion believed that a thought without a container drifted in oblivion and was lost. This idea is closely connected with the selected fact. The analyst *chooses* which parts of the material to take up and what to ignore or marginalise. Bion showed that the analyst's function of containing was related to the "group" to which he belonged. He calls this phenomenon the Establishment. When we practice psychoanalysis, we have in our minds the school of thought to which we belong. This means that a Kleinian therapist will make different choices during an analytic hour than a Kohutian. From this follows that in each of us there resides an Establishment dictating the limits of containment. The point is to be aware of the Establishment inside oneself and to try to expand its limits. When a completely new idea, one that seems strange, emerges in the therapeutic dialogue, Bion calls it the genius or the mystic (Bion, 1970, p. 74). The question is how not to reject this idea, even though it does not fit in with the Establishment inside me. Every novel idea arouses anxiety and resistance, for it undermines the Establishment of its time. The genius who conceives it needs a group of followers in order not to be lost. Freud found followers who disseminated his theories. But it was necessary to knock repeatedly on the gates of the Establishment in order to introduce the ideas concerning childhood sexuality. It is enough to observe Breuer's inner struggle and ambivalent oscillation between Freud, his genius student, and the psychiatric and psycho-neurological establishment to which Breuer belonged. This ambivalence hurt Freud, and caused him to sever his relationship with his admired teacher. Freud needed a container. He needed a group that would contain his ideas. For a long time his friend Fliess served as such a container. From 1900 to 1909, almost nobody read *The Interpretations of Dreams*. The group of believers in Freud's theories grew slowly but steadily, and this was how his ideas took root. In order to pass on his theories, Freud needed a measure of authoritarianism. Jung admired Freud and disseminated his ideas, but when he began to think differently to Freud, it caused an irreparable rift between them. Freud divided all contemporary professionals into admirers and enemies. This division determined the limits of the container. It is at this point, according to Bion, that the container

begins to contract, so that after the new paradigm manages to penetrate and become the central axis of the Establishment, a new movement must begin that will question accepted truths in favour of new
ones. This indeed is what happened in the various transitions between
Freudian and contemporary psychoanalysis. Bion, more than any
other thinker, has caused us to think multi-dimensionally about the
container.

I now wish to return to the analytic session. So far, I have pointed
out two crucial processes necessary for the appearance of the selected
fact: the first is the containment function; the second is the +K position. A third process is the analyst's free, unfettered thinking, which
creates a spirit of freedom in the patient. One of the insights I obtained
through reading Bion's texts is that it is not only the patient who asso-
ciates freely—the analyst too must allow himself to wander and amble
through various thoughts.

For the selected fact to become known, the analyst must move back
and forth between two modes of thinking: one, which Bion (1963,
pp. 48–53) calls D, observes the whole, while the other, which he calls
PS, examines the parts. When the analyst allows himself to move
between these two phases, his thinking can be free and creative. The
movement between the whole and the partial or the fragmented leads
to the birth of a new thought. If the analyst fears fragmentation, he
will stick to the whole and block off the need to fully recognise each
separate part. Fragmentation is not bad or harmful; sometimes we
must dare to take apart an inappropriately assembled structure in
order to build a new one. If the analyst is able to contain confusion
and disintegration, a new integration will soon appear that is stronger
and truer than its predecessor. The important movement is that
between fragmentation and linking, between disintegration and integration. It is a movement that prevents fixation.

When movement such as this does not take place, thinking becomes
less and less creative, metaphors become clichés, and emotionally
infused language becomes jargon. Empty jargon appears when we
are unable to bear silence, fragmentation, confusion, and uncertainty.
The freedom of the analyst to observe from many different points of
view prevents both fixation and exhaustion.

Such blocking of analytic thinking can occur, for instance, when
a patient begins to talk about suicide. Pure attention is impossible
because of the analyst's anxiety. A less extreme example is the bias in

the analyst's thinking when a patient announces that he wants to terminate the analysis and the analyst believes the time has not yet come, and experiences this as an attack on himself. In Seminar number thirteen of his *Brazilian Lectures*, Bion (1987, pp. 67–71) shows how good parenting is a result not only of giving but also of a capacity for separateness. Sometimes it is hard for us to let go of a patient to whom we have become strongly attached, and Bion points to the permission to separate as an important ability in the analyst.

In other words, an obstruction of the analyst's freedom to think, to move freely between integration and disintegration, jeopardises his psychoanalytic thinking. When this movement is made possible, growth will take place in the patient. The movement between destruction and construction can take place within a single analytic session, but can also take years.

The following is a short clinical vignette.

> A patient who came to me at the age of twenty-two began his analysis with an incredible amount of rage and a letter he had sent to the members of his family in which he attacked and incriminated each of them and hurled vicious accusations at his divorced parents and two elder brothers. In the analysis his fury increased. Childhood memories arose depicting a lonely, sad, and strange little boy, friendless, playing alone in his room, absorbed in an imaginary world of daydreams. He became demanding towards his family, insisting they make up for all the years he felt neglected, lonely, and different. His talk had a paranoid ring to it. His grudges and complaints spread out in various directions. Finally, the entire world seemed either bad or stupid or infuriating.
>
> After a while the rage turned into depression. He gradually stopped working and studying, and spent most of his day in bed. Occasionally he had a fit of rage, during which he would throw around all the furniture, books, and other objects in his room, wreaking havoc. He would lock himself up and sleep for hours, causing his family great worry and distress as they knocked on his door.

My feeling was that this painful process was inevitable. Containment took place without words, and I felt that the whole was being held inside me. Throughout it I believed that he would make it through and build himself up. I moved between seeing him as a whole person striving to be born, and being with him while he brought himself as he was, fragmented and confused. All I did at that time in the analysis was mainly to avoid becoming frightened, and to allow him to take his world apart. During his acute depressive phase I would get phone calls from concerned family and friends accusing me of causing his depression. His mother called, worried, afraid the analysis was harming him.

The depression belonged to the paranoid–schizoid phase, because he was shattering all his internal images and all that was left was the destruction within. His thinking was PS thinking and exclusively one directional. He could only perceive the significant people in his life in a partial, distorted light. For example, he claimed he was disgusted with his brother because the latter was only interested in maintaining his celebrity status and all he cared about was famous labels. The brother was described to me in a one-dimensional fashion, a poster. It was only after a year-and-a-half of analysis that he could begin to see a whole picture. He began to see himself as a whole, and understood that he had chosen the role of a small child who longed to return to his lost childhood. He acted on his environment and filled everyone with worried feelings because he believed it was the only way he could get attention. Gradually, with the help of analysis, he became fed up with this role. It was the only role he knew that could stick the parts of his personality together and keep them from falling apart and scattering. When he began to grow in the analysis he no longer wanted to be everyone's patient, the one everyone felt must be gratified for fear he would do himself some harm. He wanted to end his dependent relations and take responsibility for his life. He began to understand that his attitude of entitlement, his demand for restitution, was keeping him weak and small. His new attitude developed slowly in the analysis—an attitude representing the D position which sees the whole. This was emotional knowledge. He felt he did not like himself in the role of the complaining and demanding victim. By the end of the third year of analysis he had reconstructed the images of his parents and brothers and acknowledged their benevolent parts. For the first time in his life he had a love relationship with a partner. He went back to school and graduated. He started to work again, and was discovered to be very talented in his profession. Thus we managed to build up together a new whole made out of the parts that had broken up and scattered. By the end of the third year, he said of this same brother: "I love him. I appreciate him. I see how he succeeded in building up an excellent office, how well he manages people. I see his many talents." Earlier he saw his eldest brother in an incomplete light and considered him a disappointing object; this changed after he managed to move towards the whole and see his brother as a subject, with strong points as well as shortcomings. Perception of the whole creates depth, a three-dimensional picture, which the partial view precludes.

Bion searched for the selected fact within the analytic hour, but at the same time he considered the analytic hour to represent an entire universe belonging to culture and society. The analytic hour reconstructs myths that exist as part of the matrix of culture. It is well known that Bion returned again and again to the myth concerning the eating of the Fruit of the Tree of Knowledge and the subsequent banishment from the Garden of Eden, to the Tower of Babel and to the myth of Oedipus (1963a, p. 46). These three texts preoccupied him, and one could say he considered they contained a common thread, which I choose to call the *selected fact*. Using these three myths he chose to address the drive for curiosity and the desire for knowledge; using all three he pointed to the limits of human knowledge; and in all three, men were punished who strove to achieve divine knowledge that would forever remain hidden from us. Man was born to live in uncertainty.

The analyst in the analytic hour must hold the uncertainty and provide a space for discovering parts of that which is not conscious. Each individual discovers his own internal drama. We will find different objects in different patients, but there is still some hidden structure that is the selected fact. It is necessary to discover each separate variation, each selected fact that solves the riddle of a particular subject's life. This riddle is based on a common universal structure. Every person was once banished from the Garden of Eden of innocent childhood, discovered the fact of death, and became disillusioned; every person has experienced the Tower of Babel, that is, the difficulty of being part of a group; and every person is born to parents and is subject to the oedipal experience.

Bion moves between the ontogenetic and the philogenetic, between observing the individual and observing the society from which he emerges. Bion (1961, p. 8) calls this "binocular vision'. He speaks of the movement between the narcissistic point of view, which focuses on the individual (symbolised by Oedipus), and the socialistic point of view, which focuses on society (symbolised by the Sphinx). We can understand this if we use the metaphor of a photographer zooming in for a close-up and out again for a panoramic view.

I will attempt to demonstrate Bion's special way of discovering the selected fact. For this purpose I have chosen Seminar number four from his *Brazilian Lectures*, in which an analyst presents a case that is continued in Seminar number eight Bion (1987).

The patient described in this seminar is a female psychologist who works as an employee in the field of psychology. She does not work as a clinical psychologist as she would have liked to. In the session described to Bion by the presenting analyst, the patient says she is afraid of her analyst, and is especially afraid to ask her whether her presence might be accepted to a seminar given by the famous analyst currently visiting Brasilia, to which she knows her analyst and other professionals are going to participate. She also says she knows her analyst will not answer her question. The patient is the mother of an eighteen-month-old baby, and is currently pregnant. The analyst says there is a distance between her and the patient, and that emotional closeness has not developed.

Bion chooses the phrase "a famous analyst" as the key to the analytic hour. He plays with it and takes it to an unexpected field of exploration. Bion says that the famous analyst is an inner aspect of the patient, which she is unable to approach and with whom she is unable to speak. It is by no means an external figure. The famous analyst inside her is actually her motherhood and her difficulties in being a mother. She is beginning to discover that her eighteen-month-old baby is becoming a person. She is afraid she will not know how to mother him. She is unable to listen either to her baby or to the pregnancy inside her. She is herself a child, surprised at her ability to produce babies. She has not worked through her feelings as a mother, and instead of focusing on her own motherhood, her mind is on the famous analyst's seminar. The emotional detachment she creates with her analyst is the same detachment she feels with regard to her baby and her pregnancy. The famous analyst is an inner part of her that she fears and with which she has formed no dialogue. The patient is in conflict between treating her baby like a doll and using psychoanalytic jargon in her analysis, and relating to her baby who is becoming a person. She is afraid of her own birth into motherhood, afraid to rejoice and to take pride in her babies. She is afraid of her analyst's envy.

It seems that in this analytic hour, Bion considers the patient's fear of being born into motherhood as the hour's selected fact. Like a true virtuoso, he manages not to say the predictable, that is, to point out the patient's envy of her analyst who is going to the seminar. Bion turns the picture upside down and speaks of the analyst's envy of the patient for the patient's nascent motherhood.

Bion's ability to move from one field of exploration to another gives the session depth, and takes us from a flat, two-dimensional picture to a three-dimensional one. Moreover, the three myths that Bion considers can all be found underlying the session. Eating from the Tree of Knowledge has to do with this patient's potential for growing from a child to a mother, for eating from the Tree of Knowledge of motherhood. The myth of the Tower of Babel can be detected in the patient's desire to belong to a privileged group, which in her mind speaks the language of analysis and to which she is not invited. The Babel myth is also repeated in her difficulty understanding the language of babies. The myth of Oedipus appears in her fear of being a mother to the baby who is beginning to grow and become a person. What will she do with the oedipal love that will soon appear between her and her son? I am mentioning the three myths mainly in order to demonstrate that they reappear in different, interesting, and complex variations in the lives of human beings. We are not searching here for the contents. The myths will not be repeated in their original form, but through the drama of each particular patient, and they can help us solve hidden riddles.

While working on the meaning of the selected fact, it occurred to me that the selected fact might appear in many families in the form of a myth passed down from one generation to another. The selected fact is the mantra, or family myth, on which a child is raised: a key phrase or sentence repeated over and over again in varying forms. I choose to call this the destructive or distorting selected fact. It occupies a place in the basic structure of the family's thinking. It is the psychoanalyst's role to replace the distorting mantra with a different key phrase, one that is comforting and growth-enhancing. I would like to give two examples.

A patient who grew up in an East European culture tells the story of her birth. Her mother is described as a beautiful woman who gave birth to a wonderful daughter, was happy with her daughter, and decided it was enough: that she did not want any more children.

When the girl was fifteen, the mother began to feel she was growing old and losing her beauty. Her friends told her that if she was pregnant again, the pregnancy would rejuvenate her. The mother became pregnant in order to preserve her youth, and had twins, a son and a daughter. The daughter is my patient. Several months after giving birth, the mother contracted an atrophying rheumatism, and was doomed to suffer for the rest of her life. This birth myth was recounted in the family and underlay the family's thinking. The mother had in fact known that she was a carrier of this disease. This makes one suspect that she had been afraid to have more children for fear that the pregnancies would precipitate the appearance of the disease—not because she did not want more children. The patient grew up with the myth that the purpose of her arrival in the world was to preserve her mother's youth, along with the myth that her arrival caused her mother's illness. I use the term "myth" because it is impossible to distinguish between truth and legend in these stories. What matters is the way they are told.

These painful facts thus recounted created a lasting emotional detachment between the mother and her twin children. This detachment also caused severe mourning, when the mother suddenly died recently. The mourning reawakened all the sorrow felt for missed opportunities. By contrast, the elder daughter was very close to her mother, or as the patient put it, "They were like best friends".

This is a tragic and painful myth, causing guilt from the outset of life. It becomes a key idea, which can oppress a person's entire life and hang like a dark cloud above his head. Such an idea must undergo transformation through analytic work, enabling rebirth by working through the tragedy and regaining the right to move about in the world without feeling destructive. It must be achieved by constructing a new key idea permitting joy in living. The new selected fact is the liberating journey, the purpose of which is to distinguish between the mother's disease and the patient's right to be born, and, moreover, to enable the patient to discover and not fear her own motherhood.

The second example is from a patient who has been in analysis for several years. His analysis began with the words: "Grandpa said to Dad and Dad said to me, if you aren't a Beethoven by the age of thirty, you have no reason to live." The patient's father committed suicide at the age of forty-three, when the patient was seventeen. The patient, the eldest of three brothers, became head of the family overnight. He

graduated with honours from prestigious schools, is highly intelligent, and is successful and acclaimed in his profession. In analysis we
discovered that it was not clear what exactly was meant by the code
called Beethoven. What and how was he to succeed in, in order to be
a "Beethoven" in the eyes of the ghosts that had become an extremely
persecuting part of his personality? The work was mainly directed
at enabling the patient to stop trying to realise the grandiose, and
at the same time ambiguous, cruel, and fatal fantasies of previous
generations.

The patient is now forty years old, and still suffers from motor
agitation and pains in the chest. His condition is improved compared
to the beginning of the analysis, but occasionally we discover that he
is still disturbed by this mantra that remains lodged in him and
becomes manifested in various somatic phenomena. He still experiences a conflict between this legacy, which he perceives as a product
of insanity, death, and terror, and which he angrily calls the family
madness, and the new mantra we managed to construct together,
according to which he is already a unique and special kind of
Beethoven, in light of his many achievements, both financial and
professional. Now, as he approaches his father's age when the latter
chose death, the patient is allowed to choose life. Through his anger
at his father, his pain over his loss, and his longing for him, he is gradually succeeding in slowing down the mad pace dictated to him in the
form of an unrealisable last will and testament, and is beginning to
treat himself more humanly. The new selected fact creates the right to
be a human being and the right to live the life he was given.

In the analytic hour it is sometimes useful to search for a main
thread connecting the parts of the session. It can be concisely formulated. It means that the session can converge into one key phrase,
containing the entire hour and also serving as a link leading to the
next hour.

Different analysts might choose different key phrases based on the
same analytic material. This may depend on the school of thinking
the analyst belongs to, on his experience, on his relationship with the
patient, and so on. Therefore, it is important to remember what Bion
says in this connection about the caesura: the interpretation is always
a caesura, for on the one hand, it is an opening move, while on the
other, it cuts out all other possibilities.

CHAPTER THREE

The caesura

I t was Freud who turned Bion's attention to the "caesura". Quoting
Freud, he wrote: "There is much more continuity between intra-
uterine life and earliest infancy than the impressive caesura of the
act of birth would have us believe" (Bion, 1989, p. 37).

The act of birth is bewildering. We stand in awe before the newborn child, complete with all its parts. This experience is so intense,
that we tend to forget that the baby was not created this instant, and
that it had already gone through nine whole months of life.

Birth is an intense caesura: the moment of birth contains both a
continuation and a break, which symbolises the end of one era and the
beginning of another. As such, the caesura always entails this double
meaning: it breaks, while at the same time it enables continuity.

Bion was enchanted by Freud's formulation, mostly because of its
duality. Bion favoured intuitive, somewhat vague concepts, which
evoke a different encounter within each of us and provoke a variety
of associations. Bion expanded Freud's term, applying it to all periods
of life. Our lives are rich in caesurae: we start things that are less a
beginning than a continuation of what was registered and accumulated in the past. The caesura is vital for development: it enables us to
make transitions, to keep on doing what we need to do, and stop
doing what we find burdensome and redundant.

In his paper "The caesura" (Bion, 1989), he is indeed inspired by Freud, but his interdisciplinary tendency leads him to touch upon philosophy, scripture, and exact sciences as well, looking for ways to link these supposedly different and distant worlds. Bion leads us into his realm of associations, exhibiting great freedom and guiding us to seek out our own associations.

In this paper Bion turns to Martin Buber, who refers to the biological womb as a caesura in itself. He claims that we are born of a greater womb, that of the universe, which he calls "the great mother", the mother of all human beings. So we are the children not only of our biological mothers; the biological womb is but a segment of the great womb of the universe. Neumann (1991) wrote about the great mother as an archetype of the goddess of earth who gave birth to mankind. This archetype dwells in the depths of the collective unconscious. This introduces us to Bion the mystic, who pursues mysteries and things unattainable by the senses. When Bion turns to the womb of the universe, we find a caesura more profound than that of birth. This is a mystic caesura, which Bion, following Buber, sees as resulting from the fact that the biological womb already manifests a kind of breaking away from the womb of the universe. A quote from Molino's (1997) interview of Michel Eigen, a psychoanalyst who is inclined towards mysticism, is relevant here:

> The age-old folklore declaring that we are the children of God was not well received in psychoanalytic thinking, which sees us, first and foremost, as children to our parents. In fact, the baby requires quite a long time to abolish its infinity. It goes through very different states, at times more finite, facing concrete and actual facts, at other times being more and more a part of the realm of infinity, or facing an infinite horizon. Acquiring the realisation that I should be where my body is, that my body is this bound and delineated package—this takes quite a long time and a certain degree of sophistication. (p. 146)

These notions of Bion, Buber, Neumann, and Eigen are thought-provoking. They lead us to contemplate the caesura between the infinite and the finite. The body is finite. Living in it, we gradually come to grasp how it breaks us away from the reaches of infinity. The great womb, infinity, mystery—these notions entail a clinical thinking that goes beyond the constant observation of the patient's relationship with her parents: the interaction of the child with her biological parents does not necessarily account for her capacity for happiness or tendency for depression, which might be entirely unrelated to the parents, involving rather the recognition of the body's finitude, and thus, of the way a certain person is torn away from infinity. For example, we sometimes find a very spiritual child with very down-to-earth parents and vice versa, a very down-to-earth, materialistic, or practical child with parents who are intellectual and spiritual. In other words, some elements are beyond what we see and understand.

While Bion was not a religious man, he still gained much from reading St John of the Cross, a charismatic priest who lived in sixteenth century Spain. As a child, St John suffered the tribulations of poverty, hunger, and homelessness. He writes that in order to achieve visions and revelations, one must liberate oneself of all memories. This notion had a profound effect on Bion's thought. Bion aspired to free the hidden core of the mind of its burden of memories that conceal the primary core of becoming. While St John of the Cross speaks of becoming one with God, Bion speaks of "becoming O" (Bion, 1989, p. 26). Both present the demand that we traverse many caesurae in order to attain a truly spiritual experience. In other words, the notion of caesura is somehow related to the notion of becoming O: if we help a patient shed the shell she has built trying to adapt herself to the demands of her environment, we are helping her reach the core of her psyche, her own truth, by which she wishes to live her life.

According to Bion, all the periods of our life, including those lived *in utero*, continue to exist within us. Remnants of these different life periods are inscribed in each and every one of us. The foetus, the child, the adolescent, etc., are all inside us. As analysts, it is important that we note that each patient also retains her problematic caesurae, for instance, when something gets lodged at an early age and persists without being fully developed. All of a sudden, such an undeveloped aspect such as this can come to the fore. For example, a highly intelligent woman patient, thirty-six years old, with an academic degree, holds a job and lives a full, independent life—yet she utterly lacks the skills required for reaching out to the other sex. In analysis, we gradually uncover a strong oedipal bond to her father, who died when she was young. The father's death had created a kind of caesura, by which certain parts of the self kept growing while others were still stuck. The father was idealised and, internalised as such, blocked any possibility for her to feel that she was a woman who was ready for intercourse.

She remained an adolescent, too immature for intimate relationships. As she was unaware of this, it took quite a bit of analytic work to acknowledge it.

Another patient, also a very intelligent woman with a capacity for abstract thinking, comes into therapy one day, speaking like a little girl who is telling mummy about her day: "I made lunch for the kids. Schnitzel and potatoes. Then, I sliced some watermelon. Then, I had to run back to the office. When I got to the office, I did all the photocopies for the staff meeting." The entire session goes on like this: trivial chatter, lacking any kind of symbolisation. This means that right now, the little girl is talking. The little girl wants mummy to listen to her detailed report. The analyst's listening allows her to see that today a little girl is in therapy, and this girl is asking for something. It is up to the analyst to discover what she is asking for, who is it that came to therapy today? Perhaps the manner of talking and describing what went on that day could make us see that part of the patient, who is a little girl, who came out in the open to talk and ask for something. This is how we find a caesura. In this example, it is clear that we are dealing with a grown woman with various responsibilities, but the little girl is also there, waiting to be noticed and acknowledged. This tells us that the adult and the child live side by side, and that sometimes, for some reason, the child comes to the fore.

In his paper about the caesura, Bion elaborates on the deceptiveness of our senses. I will illustrate this with an example regarding sight, the most deceptive of all our senses. We are sitting in front of a comely and impressive woman. The sense of hearing is also misleading: her intonation is that of an adult. Listening beyond our senses might reveal a highly fragile personality. For instance, I had a very striking patient, a forty-year-old woman who was beautiful, financially endowed, married, and a mother of one. Her life was both good and gratifying, but ever since her marriage, her career had come to a halt. She wanted to return to her work, but was unable to. Her well-furnished home and her carefree lifestyle, full of joy and travel, made it impossible to reveal any pain. I was frustrated: why would she not go back to cultivating the career that was so dear to her? I tried closing my eyes to avoid the great beauty that shone off her physical presence. I was looking for an image, but none came up. Suddenly a word popped into my mouth: vulnerability. And then I said it: "vulnerability". The patient started crying. She related an episode from her adolescence, a time when she failed an admission test to some exclusive project and was rejected. She was so ashamed that she shut herself up in her room for days. Was her vulnerability the obstacle keeping her from leaving her comfort zone and facing her challenges? How bad was the break in her confidence? Was everything that seemed so whole and beautiful in therapy no more than an illusion? Is all this abundance layered over unprocessed pain? These are key questions, waiting to be answered. However, this example demonstrates how one inner part remains damaged, while other parts keep developing. The notion of the caesura allows us to notice the places where the patient managed to keep developing, alongside those places where she became stuck. In this example I tried to depict the gap between the patient's appearance that looked strong and beautiful and her inside world that was so weak and vulnerable.

Bion argues that if something has happened to us while we were in the uterus and was registered in our bodies, we would never be able to express it verbally or even conceive of it. This would simply appear, but we would not know why. For example, the fear of elevators might be due to a suffocating sensation experienced in the womb. Although we might never know, we might still assume that something has been registered in the body. This must be treated as a β-element. In other words, when a foetal experience suddenly "pops up" and takes over, it is not easy to put this experience into words. The fear of suffocating repeats itself with no representation in verbal thinking.

In *A Memoir of the Future* (1991), Bion composes a play in which the foetus, the child at three, the young man at twenty-four, and the old man at seventy all converse with each other. These are the separate life periods of the same person in mutual dialogue. What Bion is trying to say is that everything exists simultaneously. Caesurae occur throughout life, retaining something from each period, for better and for worse. The psychotic has the worst of it: she speaks in several languages, maintaining a dialogue between different characters, dimensions, and aspects of being. She lacks the archaeological structuring of life's layers. All kinds of life jump out of her at once. She is in great pain and very confused, lacking the soothing, sorting effect of the caesura.

When treating a child or an adult, there are moments when the brilliant patient seems suddenly idiotic. Some awkwardness appears, something that got stuck and failed to develop. For instance, a woman patient who is both responsible and organised in her daily living, is constantly late in picking up her daughter from kindergarten. She has no sense of what damage her tardiness is causing the child. Her daughter sees all the other parents coming and going, while she is left alone with the teacher, who expresses her anger at the mother. Still, the patient does not feel that her being late is harming her child in any way. So much so, that the analyst sensed that she has to show this woman that her child is in danger. What we learn from this is that in one respect this person is behaving strangely, because it is unusual for such a person to ignore this kind of danger. This indicates that a highly undeveloped part of the personality has surfaced in analysis, asking to grow. Some patients simply keep accumulating experiences, refusing to let go of or to relinquish any of them. They do not know how to use the caesura to make breaks, for instance, in separating from their parents and their parental figures. Such accumulation carries with it the risk of being imprisoned in one's early childhood. As analysts, we must make use of the caesura. It is not opaque. It works both ways. Therefore, we are able to evoke a vitality that has become stuck , whose development has been halted, unable to come to light. We might even say encapsulated.

According to Bion, the foetus possesses a "proto-mind". It exhibits a "proto-mental" existence. That is, it arrives into this world with certain preconceptions. It has a preconception telling it that it will meet the nourishing breast, the containing mother. If it indeed meets the containing mother, its proto-mind will develop into a mind; its preconceptions into concepts. However, this encounter with the primary figure is often disrupted, causing certain aspects to remain without suitable concepts. These aspects will then break out as β-elements. They might do so at any age and life-periods. Bion calls these aspects "somato psyche" instead of psychosomatic. Something is first of all registered in the body, and only then grows to create a disturbance in the psyche.

In the introduction to *A Memoir of the Future* (1991) Bion writes:

> Hallucinosis, hypochondriasis and other mental "diseases" may have a logic, a grammar and a corresponding realization, none of which has so far been discovered. They may be difficult to discover because they are obscured by a "memory" or a "desire", or an "understanding" to which they are supposed—wrongly—to approximate. Unless the obscurity can be circumvented or penetrated it will remain unobserved, as the galactic centre or the origin of the universe remains unobserved. (p. ix)

We witness the caesura in transitions as well. One part talks like a little girl, the other part belongs to the grown woman who goes to work and does her duty there. Sometimes it is valuable to find out whether these parts are in dialogue or completely split-off.

We live in a world that imposes multiple roles upon us and we are often unaware of the way we take these roles on. Sometimes, someone who is no longer alive lives through us. Nina Coltart, in an interview with her by Molino (1997), told an incredible story about this. Her parents had died in a train accident when she was eleven years old. Her father was a general practitioner. I will abbreviate what she related:

> I struggled with all my might to study medicine. I found chemistry, math and physics very difficult and the first two years were a veritable nightmare. But it never occurred to me that I could fail. I knew, with absolute certainty, that I was going to be a doctor. It was only later, during my analysis, that I uncovered any kind of intimation of the fact that this was the most profound realization of my identification with my father. What's interesting is that as soon as I became a doctor, it became quite clear to me that I didn't really want to be one. I have done it, I have become him. I have brought him back to life. But it turned out that I didn't want to stare down sore throats or bandage wounds. In fact, I wanted to be a psychiatrist, which eventually happened. But I could have practiced psychotherapy without being a doctor at all. Becoming a doctor had nothing to do with my chosen profession. In a way, this whole part of my life revolved around my father, who always felt like such a stranger to me. (p. 250)

This means that her personality had a part that re-enacted the father, bringing him back to life, thus, at the same time, infringing upon hers. She might have lived an entire life that was not her own, a phenomenon that is quite familiar to us from our clinical work.

I would now like to discuss trauma as a kind of break that foils the continuity that is provided by the caesura. Michal Ben-Naftali defined trauma as:

> . . . any event which hinders our metabolism and proves indigestible , urging us rather to eject or vomit it, even, for a while, to become insensible to it in our living present, letting it exist latently, as if it was never registered in our psychic archive; in other words, we give the name trauma to any event which, as it is taking place, cannot be contained

by the psychic mechanism, let alone transformed into a testimony or a narrative. Traumatic events may occasionally sabotage the very function of memory. (Ben-Naftali, 2012b)

In her lecture, Ben-Naftali refers to a poem of Barbara, which I will quote in full:

> My Childhood
> I was wrong to return
> To this town, long since lost
> Where I once spent my childhood
> I was wrong, I would see
> Once more shadows of eve
> Blue-grey on silent hillsides.
> And I found, like before
> After So long,
> The hill, the lone-standing tree,
> just like long ago.
> I walked and my head was aflame,
> my steps overwhelming almost.
> The roads of the past come to haunt us
> And they come sounding bells.
> And under my tree I lay down
> the same scent in the air.
> And I let my weeping flow
> And flow.
> With my bare back on the tree-bark
> The tree restored my strength
> Just like it did, when I was a child.
> And closing my eyes for so long,
> To say a little prayer,
> My innocence was given back.
> Before the fall of night
> I wanted to see
> The houses all flowering roses
> I wanted to see
> The garden where our childish cries
> Flash like water running pure.
> Jean-Claude, Regina and Jean—
> everything just like before—
> the heavy perfume of red sages
> the dahlias wild on the path,
> the wells, I have found them again,

Alas.
It was war that threw us there,
More happy than others, no doubt,
In the bright days of our childhood.
It was war that tossed us there,
And we lived beyond all laws
And I loved it. When I think
Of my spring times, of my suns
Of my crazy years so lost
Of my sweet-fifteen wonders,
How dreadful it is to return—
Of the sweet-nuts of September
Of the smell crushed berries made
It's mad, I have found them again.
Alas.
One must never return,
To where memories are hiding
the blessed hours of our childhood.
Because, as memories go,
Those of childhood are the worst
Childhood memories destroy us.
Oh my mother, my dear,
Where can I find you today?
Asleep in the warmth of the ground
And me, coming all this way,
To find here again your smile,
Your anger and your youth.
And I'm all alone with my sadness,
Alas.
Why did I try to return—
back and forth, in these streets, all alone?
I am cold and afraid as night falls.
Why did I come to this place where
my past is my own torturer?
My childhood forever unsleeping.

Borrowed Memories: Barbara's poem.

Michal Ben Naftali writes movingly about Barbara's poem:

I first heard Barbara's song when I was young, in a language I knew
little at the time and that was completely unknown to me as a child—
it was not the language of my childhood. I have listened to it over and

over, then and ever since, and each time, when she reaches the final lines, describing her mother who is already gone, just hearing those words, the simple, crystal-clear words of that chanson, tears would appear in my eyes. Not because she was singing my memories, in the personal, concrete sense. My mother, may she live to a ripe old age, was, and still is, alive. But Barbara was telling me of someone I am destined to meet inside myself one day, as if she was tracing a range of memories where this song is always already sung in me, always already trembling at a memory that wasn't its own. I am not talking about autosuggestion or appropriation. Her memories did not become my possessions. Instead, they were a kind of pure potentiality which involves me, yet exceeds the biographical memories, in the narrow sense, which constitute myself. It is as if I was born into a community of memories, which relies on preexisting memory patterns, often leading to my being overwhelmed by the memories of others as if they were my own. Even though they are not memories of the past but, as paradoxical as it may sound, of what is yet to come. Could this thing pining inside me be that oedipal or, in fact, pre-oedipal, mother-daughter, mother-child pattern from which I came to be and to which I knew I must return after unraveling, one by one, all the circles of socialization I have still to traverse? Could this pattern be related to the very possibility of memories? (2012b)

In this paragraph, Michal Ben-Naftali is preoccupied with at least two caesurae. The first entails those layers of life that must be traversed in order to reach the core, the place where the soul emerged. The second lies between the world of the individual and the "community of memories", a fascinating formulation of the link between us and the cultural world that surrounded our individual development.

In this context, I would add that many people grasp the "future memory of their death", that is, imagining their eventual demise. It seems to me that, quite often, the memory of one's death is a part of life, even something that urges us to live more fully.

Encapsulated material that has been transmitted to the second generation, and from the second generation to the third, unconsciously, can be understood as a kind of social caesura. Gampel explores how traumatic events of Holocaust survivors that have never been told live again in the life of their grandchildren (2005). She discusses this phenomenon in terms of radioactive "memories" (1992).

Multiple-personality disorders that occur in response to trauma attest to a particularly severe caesura. This is a disorder. I know of an analysis in which one personality is unaware of the other, and a different one appears in each session: at times it is a joyful little girl, at times it is a man, most of the time it is the dominant personality, a damaged woman, utterly lifeless, silent, and extremely depressed. None of these characters knows of the others.

I would like to add some free associations that depict caesurae in the biographies of known writers: Kohut, Amos Oz, and Eigen.

Heinz Kohut

Late in life, Kohut told Strozier about his notion of continuity:

> I am an old man. My hair is grey. My muscles are limp. Still, I know that I am the same person that I was at eighteen, at twenty-two, at six, when I used to run and jump about. It is still inside me and it is a part of me. There is no discontinuity. I have changed completely and still, my inner consciousness of having remained the same person is consummate. (Kohut & Strozier, 1985)

Amos Oz

In an interview with Ilana Dayan:

> Nothing disappears. Every one, each of us, carries inside the child they once were. Some carry a living child and some carry a dead child. I can usually tell, almost at first glance, whether someone is carrying the living child, the child they once were, or whether they have killed this child and are still carrying it inside. I carry a living child. It may be easier for those carrying a dead child , but it is far more interesting to carry a live one.

Michael Eigen

A paragraph from "A conversation with Michael Eigen" by Kara Kaniel (2013):

> When I was a little boy I remember seeing a tree. Half of it was withered and dead and the other half was blooming. Then I realized that

one could be dead and very much alive, concurrently. We are not monolithic, and can experience vitality and life on certain levels and on others total deadness.

I found this somewhat consoling—to try to get in touch with our blooming parts, while carrying along our dead parts. Losses put death into us, then, in order to live, we must remember our bloom. As long as we are creative, as long as some part of us is in bloom, death is still bearable.

In his paper, Bion makes another use of the term caesura. He mentions that in so far as the analytic session is only fifty minutes long, the analyst cannot delay her response. The interpretation she chooses is a kind of caesura as it breaks away from all other possible interpretations. The analyst's intervention determines, to a considerable degree, the course of the session and the blocked paths where the session could not "stray".

In the conclusion to his paper, Bion notes that he recommends that the analyst study the caesurae manifest within the session: where did motion or change occur? He tells us:

> Investigate the caesura; not the analyst; not the analysand; not the unconscious; not the conscious; not sanity; not insanity. But the caesura, the link , the synapse, the counter-transference, the transitive-intransitive mood. (1989, p. 56).

Whereas the term synapse originally referred to the point of contact between two nerve cells, today, it is often used metaphorically to denote the manner in which similar materials are manifest through varying forms of expression, how the same idea runs like a thread through a film, a novel, a piece of music, a work of art. It is also used to refer to connections between disciplines. We should study this area of connection and transition: what is standing still and what keeps moving on and changing. Bion tells us that being aware of the sensitivity and vulnerability of these transitions requires the analyst to refrain from applying too heavy an instrument to such soft, tender wood, as in transition the tissues of the psyche are fragile and weak.

To summarise, I will differentiate among several kinds of caesurae:

1. We spend our entire lives enduring caesurae. The caesura is a form of transition, signifying things ended, things newly begun, and

continuity. The caesura has a two-fold nature: it breaks and cuts short, while simultaneously allowing for the continuity and growth of psychic processes. I shall call these *vertical caesurae*, as they occur chronologically, from foetal life to death. The appropriate metaphor here is that of the archaeological layers of the psyche.

2.   We also endure synchronous caesurae, that exist side by side. As we are constantly accumulating experiences, Bion claims that we always retain certain remnants of each period of life. As adults, we still carry with us traces of the foetus, the child, the adolescent, etc. A fully developed individual may acknowledge these aspects and contain them within herself. The less stable and more fragmented one's personality, the more these parts of the past resurface, erupting in various forms of early behaviour. Even with a well-organised personality, in times of duress, certain aspects of earlier periods may break out. When such aspects resurface in therapy, they are usually uncontrolled and awaiting to be healed. I shall call these *horizontal caesurae*.

3.   Trauma is an expression of a caesura that assaulted the psyche and therefore remains in the form of undigested raw material. The trauma is motionless, experienced by the analyst as an event that took place only yesterday. It is a disrupted caesura that blocks psychic development, creating a violent rupture or tear in psychic tissue, that is very difficult to heal.

4.   Bion uses the notion of caesura in reference to other fields as well. While there is a break between the individual person and her social environment, or between the individual and the cosmos, we must also keep in mind that the individual is represented by the communities and the world around her, that form a certain extension of her being. The notion of belonging enables us to understand the inescapable duality by which we are both private individuals and at the same time, belonging to and identified with the social and cultural world that surrounds us. The caesurae also entail aspects of certain figures, which the individual has internalised, and through which she expresses herself. For instance, trans-generational transmission: the individual unwittingly acts and speaks through aspects once used by her parents to address her.

5.   Bion views the analytic session as comprised of a certain kind of caesurae. For example, when the analyst chooses a certain

intervention or interpretation, she breaks away from all other possible choices, influencing the course of the session. While such choice is inevitable, Bion would like us to pay attention to it, to maintain a certain modesty, knowing that the path we chose is but one of many.

6.   Another use of the concept of caesura is found in Bion's attitude toward the great ideas that have shaped theoretical thinking. For instance, the Oedipus complex is such an astounding paradigm, that we are in awe of it, thus breaking away from other kinds of knowledge. Bion discusses this enchantment as mesmerising our thinking, keeping other ideas from surfacing. While he gladly embraced the Freudian analysis of the Oedipus myth, Bion tried to push its meaning away from sexuality, that was so central in Freud's account, toward other areas—themes in the original myth such as the desire for knowledge and the search for truth.

In Bion's thinking, the term caesura is granted a manifold nature and is used metaphorically and symbolically to denote something much deeper than the caesura of birth. There are vertical caesurae, separating one period of life from the next; horizontal caesurae, comprising periods of life that subsist side by side within us; trauma that assaults the psyche, freezing time and halting the motion from one period to another; ruptures and tears between the human being and the cosmos, and between the individual and society at large; divisions and choices within the analytic session, whenever the analyst chooses a particular interpretation; and caesura engendered by a compelling paradigm, that splits off free thinking, precluding the emergence of new ideas.

PART II

PERSON

Somewhere in the analytic situation, buried in masses of neuroses, psychoses and so on, there is a person struggling to be born.

Bion (1987), *Clinical Seminars and Other Works*, p. 45

CHAPTER FOUR

How thoughts are born in light of Bionian theory

B ion was fascinated by the question "how are thoughts born?" He came back to it again and again, each time from a different perspective. According to his theory, the core from which thinking is formed is created *in utero* and when the baby is born, the core emerges into the world as a primordial kind of thought, which Bion calls a "preconception" (1967, p. 111). The baby, Bion asserts, comes into the world with a preconception about meeting a breast. That is, the baby is born with a certain pre-verbal knowledge, that he is about to meet a breast which will nourish him and keep him alive. This encounter between the baby and the breast or between the baby and the mother-figure is crucial in determining the baby's future ability to create thoughts.

The baby's encounter with the mother in the beginning of life is the stage of fulfilment or, in Bion's terms, the stage of realisation (1967, p. 111): something that the baby has been expecting has taken place. This is an exciting event that, according to Bion, fuels the life-instinct, letting the baby know he has something to live for. The baby senses that his arrival in the world is a welcome occasion, he feels protected: he has a container. The presence of the container at the beginning of life is essential to the development of the capacity for thinking.

It is in this state, in which the baby feels contained and in which he learns to deal with frustration. Thus contained, he bears the inner knowledge that frustration is not endless. Even though the mother has not responded immediately, her containing presence is inscribed within him and he is able to wait. While waiting, he plays with his frustration, turning it into something tolerable. His ability to bear frustration is the key to the inception and development of thoughts. The baby waits; he sees images, he imagines, he plays, cultivating his capacity for thinking and creativity. He creates an entire world because the knowledge of the mother's return exists inside him. He is not alone, but one of two.

In contrast, the baby, who never encountered a containing mother, will become very anxious, restless, and confused, desperately awaiting the concrete satisfaction of his needs, unable to develop an inner world of play, imagination, and consolation. He will be tense and full of rage. Intolerably frustrated, he will try to escape frustration with all his might. As frustration grows too intense, this baby will turn indifferent, lose his curiosity and, according to Bion, develop a death-instinct that will overpower his life-instinct.

There are, naturally, many intermediate babies between the one that is able to tolerate frustration and the one whose only desire is to flee, as quickly as possible, any inkling of frustration. In any case, for thinking to develop, the life-instinct must be stronger than the death-instinct. Moreover, the development of thinking fortifies the life-instinct. The life and death instincts are very dynamic forces, constantly in motion. When a child plays with her frustration, is enriched by it and uses it to pull herself upwards, she is cultivating her life-instinct. When a child immediately voids any frustrating experience, she is unable to form thoughts, diminishing her connection to life and reality.

It is important to note that the baby's capacity for developing thoughts is not wholly dependent upon the containing mother. To a greater degree, it depends on the link between the baby as contained and the mother as a container. The essential factor is the kind of relationship formed throughout this link. Babies are born with varying measures of tolerance for frustration, different intensities of aggression, rage, and envy, different degrees of the life-instinct and the capacity for love. While a highly demanding baby, who is constantly dissatisfied, is likely impair the mother's ability to contain, a contented·

baby, who is nourished by being in touch with the mother, is likely to augment and enhance her ability to contain.

Thinking is born out of the space between mother and baby, out of the link connecting them, out of the pre-verbal communication they establish.

The essential feature of Bion's container is that it is a thinking container (1967, p. 112). In other words, it is not enough simply to take in what the baby puts into the mother, nor is it enough to take simply what the patient puts into the therapist. What is essential is to take in with the ability to think and to decipher. Thinking is crucial here: the mother's thinking enables her to conceptualise what the baby wants from her. The baby puts into the mother his raw materials: unthinkable thoughts that Bion refers to as β-elements (1967, p. 117). The mother's thinking and understanding provide the raw materials poured into her with a container and a form. These raw elements are the agonies and anxieties that the baby is still unable to express through words. By thinking, the mother is translating, transforming these impermeable materials into something that can be contained in words and concepts. This is the mother's α-function: she transforms the impermeable elements, converting them into thinkable α-elements. This allows the baby to grow feeling that he is understood. Through the mother's continual acts of transforming and her repeated displays of thinking presence, the baby learns to think. The thoughts he develops are like containers, putting his raw materials into words. Through this process, the baby is paving the way to verbal thinking.

The process I have been describing is an emotional one, as thinking, according to Bion, is always emotional, always involving encounters with reality, and learning from experience. Early in life, in order to be able to think, we need certain affectionate conditions. This holds true not only for infancy but for much later stages of life as well. Many of us recall teachers who could make the best of us and those whose strict gaze and booming voice left us paralysed before the blackboard, completely unable to think.

The mother's role is to translate the distress transferred to her sensually and pre-verbally. The more the mother excels in her role as translator, the less is the baby, and later on the child and the adult, overwhelmed by β-elements. These β-elements are all those elements that were left unnamed, without words or concepts, unaltered. Bion calls them "things in themselves" (1970, p. 87). These are the raw materials left untouched and untransformed, seen as such diverse phenomena as: rage, physical aggression, psychosomatic phenomena, acting out, substance abuse, drunkenness, insomnia, panic attacks, eating disorders, stuttering, various tics, even murder. All these phenomena attest to very powerful emotional experiences that remained without translation. They are manifest as things in themselves.

The containing function is a function of thinking. Thoughts are born within the mother, in response to her baby. She cannot think them without it. While she is thinking, all kinds of emotions are surfacing. These emotions are crucial, especially in times of distress. Bion terms this emotional-thinking process "reverie" (1967, p. 116). I believe that the capacity for reverie is the ability to see an entire picture, even in states of fragmentation. It is the ability to daydream forward, to lose oneself in thought, to float about, to imagine a better future picture in unbearable situations. In fulfilling this function, the mother helps the baby, to name his anxieties, to calm down, and be contained in verbal thinking.

In one of his seminars, Bion stated that he had added nothing new to Melanie Klein's notion of "projective identification" (Bion, 1987). This, however, is not true. Bion's contribution was enormous. He linked projective identification to the capacity for thinking. The baby who escaped the frustration he could not face was also the baby who forfeited the opportunity to digest these unyielding materials and dissolve them within him. The baby had forfeited the opportunity to think. When the container was unavailable to him, he had immediately projected his distress any which way, learning to vomit any distress as soon as it arose. Bion describes this process as fragmented or splintered projective identification, it is a kind of projective identification that is splintered into tiny fragments (p. 46). This is a sort of pathological projective identification. Healthy projective identification has time to perform an entire process: the baby can wait for the mother to digest and return processed materials that are easily digestible. Splintered projective identification allows for no process of internalisation. We witness this in patients who respond all too quickly, voiding meaning, tossing out anything given to them, unable to allow the time needed for digestion and internalisation. This swift expulsion stems from a profound anxiety of words, which are not experienced as containing and curing, but as attacking and fragmenting (Bion, 1967, p. 93). As internal content had been voided, no transformation is possible. These states witness an attack on the link between analyst and patient, an attack on verbal thinking that renders the analysis concrete, unable to transcend toward metaphorical space.

The following short vignette illustrates my struggle to translate concrete thinking to metaphorical thinking: it is taken from a session taking place three months into analysis. The patient is a thirty-one-year-old woman, single, with a Master's degree in science. After three years of living on her own, she had come back to live with her parents.

Patient: Someone stole my bag, with my wallet and cell-phone in it. I was at a memorial service and I left the bag on the front seat. I didn't think people steal in cemeteries. I also lost my passport and all my documents. This always happen to me. I am constantly putting out fires. I'm paying for several cell-phones now, every month. This kind of thing happens to me all the time. I just keep losing and losing things.

Hanni: You're uncollected. Things fall off of you. This is an action which has failed to say something through words. Maybe what you want to say is that you're not being held.

P: I don't think so. I'm just not focused enough. I bought some bags of coffee at the super-market, I put them on the roof of my car. When I got home—no coffee . . . I just have to accept that this is who I am.

H: This absent-mindedness says something that needs to be translated into words. You're acting against yourself. Why are you accepting a state which is harmful to you?

P: What is there to talk about? I'm irresponsible and that's that.

Silence.

H: I don't feel like letting you get away with this. There's something here, and if we could figure it out, you'll be able to get yourself together.

Silence.

P: I suddenly remembered something from first grade. The teacher told my parents that I'm not there. I really wasn't there. But I translated the terms my teacher used into a kind of stupidity—I thought I was stupid. Every time she said I wasn't there—she was saying that I'm not focused, and I thought it was about being stupid.

H: You must have been wandering about in your own worlds, instead of being in the classroom. Actually, it was a cry for help. What's going on today is related to that. There is meaning behind your absent-mindedness and your losing things all the time. There is some wish, some demand, some fantasy. What is your association?

Silence.

P: Maybe what I'm saying is "I'm still small, please watch over me. I can't collect myself. Daddy, come watch over me." Maybe that's what I'm saying.

This was a turning point in our dialogue. At first, it was concrete, detached from meaning, later on, she was able to make room inside herself for thoughts she could hold on to.

Bion's theory of thinking teaches us that the space for thinking is unlimited. Every moment, a new preconception might arise, eventually turning into a verbal thought and a concept. The analyst should keep herself open to new preconceptions at all times and allow herself freedom of thought. The transition from preconception to thought occurs as long as we keep thinking. Every now and again, we must abandon worn and saturated concepts in favour of new preconceptions. The patient comes to analysis with the preconception that she would encounter a container. The analyst is equipped with the preconceptions derived from her knowledge. The transition from preconception to verbal thinking takes place only through the encounter with the particular patient. Only this actual, subjective patient can validate the analyst's preconceptions. The patient–analyst encounter is therefore crucial, because it is the platform on which thoughts can grow.

Preconceptions are necessary in all areas of life. They are the space from which enlivening thoughts are born. Thinking, in its Bionian sense, is no mere intellectual activity, it has a lot to do with intuition and emotion. For instance, one often discovers that patients who experience difficulties in establishing long-term relationships and building a family, lack the preconception for intimate relationships. At the encounter stage, that is, when the relationship is realised, they panic, as they are unconsciously certain that frustration, abandonment, and self-effacement lie ahead. Usually, these patients grew up without having witnessed any kind of healthy intimacy. Their preconception for intimate relationships has been erased, leaving only a sense of anxiety about relationships. From a Bionian perspective, one might say that the goal of analysis is to constitute, together with the patient, the preconception for intimate relationships, which could thereby occur naturally. The obstacle does not lie in reality, but in the missing inner link that had not registered an experience of benign intimacy.

According to Bion, for thoughts to be born, a coupling must take place. This linking of two elements generates a new thought. In order to think, we necessarily rely on such linking. Often, these links connect elements already internalised and existing within us, but they always include a joining of two. These two generate a motion, which engenders something new. The position of twoness is an important position, entailing the recognition of one's limitations, raising doubts and asking questions. It is a position of seeking and of the capacity to bear not-knowing (Bion, 1967, p. 113). Bion compares this position to the omnipotence of oneness. The omnipotent person does not seek out motion and does not ask questions, she already knows and therefore cannot think. She cannot learn from experience nor need another. She lives in a world that hinders growth and precludes learning. Behind omnipotence, says Bion, lies helplessness: omnipotence bars the question, and where there are no questions, there is no thinking.

Narcissus turned into a flower because he had lost his capacity for motion, being so riveted by his own reflection. In Bion's terms, what is missing is the link of love, which entails twoness and the growth-promoting motion inherent in it. Narcissus could see no one but himself; it is his fascination with himself that led to his demise. Thinking is a process that is constantly in motion: where there is no motion, there is no thinking. Bion states again and again that thinking is born from the coupling of two elements. Not being psychotic means acknowledging twoness. Non-psychotic thinking is a constant search for linking.

Bion believed that when one stops thinking, one ceases to be alive. I do not know if he was familiar with Hannah Arendt's book on Eichmann (Arendt, 1963), but he would surely have sympathised with her arguments. Arendt claims that Eichmann did not think, but acted like a robot. Had he thought, he would not have been able to do what he did. As she put it, "thinking is a form of moving in the world through freedom". It is this freedom that Eichmann lacked. According to Arendt: "Eichmann had no inner-dialogue, he lacked the act of thinking".

In his paper on the Grid, Bion (1989) relates that he borrowed from the BBC recordings of Hitler's speeches in his Nuremberg rallies. Bion mentioned that, fortunately, since he spoke no German, he could not be distracted by the contents of these speeches. Instead, he listened only to their phonetics, finding the pronunciation replete with β-elements. He sensed that Hitler, the speaker, was outside the scope of thinking. Bion's manner of listening to speeches in a foreign language allowed him to feel their raw elements bursting as-is from the unconscious. The words were only a screen, hiding the horrible truth, the unthinkable thoughts, the desire for murder and annihilation that were manifested as things in themselves, as objects unprocessed by and unrelated to thinking. This is an unnerving example of catastrophe originating in the absence of thinking, and of how omnipotent clinging to a single "truth", can breed genocide.

In his book, *Cogitations* (Bion, 1992, p. 220) develops, along several lines, his notion that thinking develops in the space created between two elements. The motion of a baby tilting his head in search of the breast is imprinted in us throughout our life. In this context, Bion (1992, p. 34) introduces a biological metaphor "tropism", which refers to the tilt of the sunflower's crest toward the sun. Ever since we turned our head toward the breast, we keep searching for figures toward which we can tilt our heads, figures we can admire and learn from. This is a form of growth and fulfilment. In the exact same manner, a baby that tilted her head toward the breast, and found no warmth and nourishment, will spend her life searching for figures to destroy, figures from which she can learn nothing. Her desire to kill them will preclude the formation of the link that enables thinking through the motion toward a beloved object.

The following vignette will try to illustrate the manner in which the child, who had been searching for the beloved object, has been left without a container. He was depressive, hanging in thin air with nothing to lean on. This twenty-four-year-old patient has been in analysis for six months.

> *Patient*: I always have this dark cloud hanging over my head. I just can't seem to ignore it. If I am by myself for twenty minutes, having some quality time with myself, the cloud is dominant. It's there. I know it. It sucks out the energy. It throws shadows. Even when I'm outside, getting a tan, there's this cloud above me, throwing its shadow on me. I love walking down the street, looking at people and dogs, but I'm in the shadows. The cloud turned me off, took away my meaning.
>
> *Hanni*: You often describe this cloud for me and I try to imagine it. I see it as made up of splinters. These splinters are your failed attempts to

communicate. You described your parents as contentious, always busy fighting each other. There was no one there to listen to you, to moderate your anxieties. Everything that was not understood, that was not translated from distress to words, gathered up into this cloud that hangs over your head.

P: I suddenly got this image from kindergarten. I am in my kindergarten, standing in front of the leaves, talking to them. I am asking them how come I'm alone, why am I not having fun, why am I not playing with the other kids? Leaves, why am I here talking to you?

H: This is a very moving image of loneliness and abandonment.

P: The leaves were the last resort. I remember them, myrtle leaves that made wind.

H: I wonder what happened before, before the last resort, when you tried to approach your parents.

P: I signalled my distress to them. I remember them fretting about me, unable to understand me. They didn't have the patience to find out. They wanted answers right away. "What did he do to you? What did the teacher say?" I was sad, and I didn't know why. And they wouldn't go beyond the surface. They wanted to solve it with another product they could buy me, thinking I just had a bad day, that's it was a one-time thing. They made me even more restless. They weren't strong and stable enough to listen to me and eventually I stopped turning to them for help. They did not know how to take in my pain, and I just didn't want to see their helplessness anymore, so I started saying everything is fine.

H: That's how the cloud gathered. Your distress found no words, your parents could not contain a sad, melancholy child.

P: They wanted a quick solution. I didn't know how to tell them I was different, I was lonely, I didn't even know it myself.

H: All that pain that was left uncontained built up into this cloud that is always floating over you, this cloud of sadness and rage that you have been bringing into our sessions. We are going to have to find words for this loneliness and his sadness, for everything that was left hanging in front of those leaves in kindergarten.

To sum up this part of the chapter, I will point out two things:

1. Without thinking, living is impossible. The potential for thinking is infinite: new preconceptions will always arise, becoming thoughts, which, in turn, will become concepts. As concepts

become saturated, they turn static, losing their vitality. When the analyst feels that she is going over the same interpretations and ideas again and again, her metaphors become cliché and her speech—jargon. The time has come for her to abandon her saturated concepts in favour of new preconceptions. This process is carried through a mutually enriching dialogue with the patient.

2.   Thinking is the coupling of two elements. It always poses questions. Questions evoke motion, curiosity, and vitality. The omnipotent person has no questions, so her space for thinking is blocked. Thinking grows through the willingness not to know. This willingness to defer knowing is central in Bion's theory. He borrows from Keats the term "negative capability" (Bion, 1970, p. 125). Joining two things that are utterly separate, this phrase constitutes an oxymoron, an impossible combination. Bion loved paradoxes and so negative capability, as a most vital capacity for inability, held great appeal for him. Not knowing is signified by a positive K, as it serves as the platform for all new knowledge and all motion. This capacity is especially pertinent to our therapeutic work as it entails the analyst's willingness to bear the patient's fragmentation anxieties and remain intact.

Bion's *Cogitations* was published in 1992, thirty years after his theory of thinking came out. This book, printed fourteen years after his death, is actually a collection of Bion's reflections gathered and published by his widow, Francesca Bion. Reading it gives one the sense of peeking into an artist's workshop while he works.

Several significant innovations to Bion's theory of thinking can be found in *Cogitations* (Bion, 1992). In fact, before I read it, I was troubled by the question of whether a patient who uses words could still transfer his β-elements to me; can the words being said be treated as lacking α-function. The patient is talking, seemingly possessed of verbal thinking, yet I feel that she is passing her β-elements on to me. They are not in her gestures or action, not in her body, and still, I am receiving uncommunicative, untransformed raw materials.

In *Cogitations*, Bion (1992, p. 222) discusses the patient's speech, which might, despite its verbal nature, be a raw β-element. Let us examine, for instance, the word "table". This word has a meaning we all share: we have all seen a table and know how to recognise one. However, beyond this shared meaning, each of us has another layer of meaning, one that is personal, particular, and uniquely our own. This layer contains our private chain of associations to the word "table". In the analytic session, the word "table" should appear alongside a stream of personal associations. If it appears by itself, without so much as a single association, it is like a musical note. If it appears alone, stripped of associations, it means that this word has been left untouched by the α-function. I will attempt to illustrate this point by the following vignette:

> *Patient*: I've been sleeping for hours on end. I slept for twenty straight hours this weekend. During the day, I keep my room dark. I don't want to see the daylight. I snuggle up in the dark and go to sleep. I want to stop sleeping so much, but I can't. Some weekends I spend thirty hours sleeping.
>
> *Hanni*: Your sleep is saying something we need to translate into an image. What is your association with this long sleep?
>
> *P*: [thinking for several minutes] I don't have any. It's just sleep.
>
> *H*: Can I share my association with you?
>
> *P*: Yes.
>
> *H*: I am trying to see an image. I see you in the womb. I feel that by sleeping you're trying to go back to the womb.
>
> Silence.
>
> *P*: Yes. That's interesting. I never thought about it that way. The image I'm getting now is that I was born as if from a glass of water that someone was pouring out on the floor. I was born on the floor. No one was there to hold me, define me, to give me borders.
>
> Silence.
>
> *H*: I suppose that is my job—to help you find another way to be born and to hold you.

This vignette shows my attempt to bring to life the thoughts that the patient had put to sleep. From here on, we slowly made our way through the various meanings of sleep, until we reached the place where she could remember her dreams, bringing life into our shared thinking in the analytic process.

Bion's distinction, between the words that evoke the analyst's associations and those tossed into space like useless objects, helps us discover the β-elements expressed on the verbal level as well. That is, the word before us is still a β-element waiting to be translated and worked through. When the table appears without any memories, it is actually an undigested fact. It is a table that has not been thought or dreamt and has therefore not been transformed into α. In such cases, the role of the analyst is to find ways to enliven the word "table". She does so by discovering the missing sense-impressions. If we want the word "table" to become alive, it must be linked to continuous sense-impressions that have been adding up in the store of memories. The α-function should link the table to the store of memories to which it belongs.

This has not occurred in the patient's life, as the word "table" is probably related to an unbearably painful experience. It had been so painful that the visual image simply vanished. According to Bion, the image and its context had vanished under the control of the pleasure principle, as the patient wished to void distressing stimuli. When the reality principle is in control, the image, painful as it may be, is inserted into the store of memories and will bring forth associations. Still, there is a third option, in which the image is inscribed in the psyche, but due to a failure of the α-function and an overwhelming emotional experience, remains isolated, severed, constrained, and lifeless.

Under the pleasure principle, pain is ejected, leaving no psychic trace, only physical discomfort. This is the familiar β-element. In contrast, when the reality principle is dominant, the experience is inscribed in the psyche as an ideogram, the visual notation of an idea. The inscription of the ideogram is felt by the analyst as an invitation for communication, for entering the place where an overwhelming emotional experience of pain or fear took place, where the α-function had failed. Both the voided raw β-elements and the isolated ideogram are waiting for the α-function to achieve the digestion of terrifying psychic material through the deciphering, containing power of words.

This teaches us that the verbal text of the patient may include primitive α-elements still unprocessed by the α-function. These isolated elements are scattered beyond any context, awaiting to be communicated and transformed. They became fixed wherever pain and anxiety were too overwhelming. While they were not voided, they are still lifeless and are spoken without any associative context. Just as β-elements exist in the psyche unlinked and unthought, so do these isolated α-elements exist unlinked, waiting to be deciphered.

Sleep, forgetfulness, and the cloud all depict unthinkable states that we, as analysts must try to link through our dialogue with the patient. These links are formed by the associations given by both patient and analyst. Both must activate their senses in the here and now in order for these elements to be infused with life and meaning.

Bion tries to approach each session with a patient as if it were the very first. This notion is drawn from his phrase, "without memory and desire". Today is not yesterday, so exact repetition is never the case; there is always something new. Bion sees analysis as a place of constant psychic growth. While he does not resort to the terms "sickness" and "cure", he believes that spontaneous development occurs through the therapeutic dialogue. His model has more to do with evolution than with medicine. The changes taking place in the patient's life are not the result of conscious decisions, but of the constant growth of the mind. A proper analysis will spontaneously evoke this growth through the therapeutic dialogue. This is why Bion refers to an ever present *becoming*: change is part and parcel of being. Experiences cannot be reproduced, we can only add new ones. Bion wants to enter the session with a fresh position, open to hear and see what is new, unburdened by the familiar and the known. Renewal will only emerge from the experience of here and now.

In: "Notes on memory and desire" (1992, p. 381), Bion writes:

> In any session, evolution takes place. Out of the darkness and form-lessness something evolves. That evolution can bear a superficial resemblance to memory, but once it has been experienced, it can never be confounded with memory. It shares with dreams the quality of being wholly present or unaccountably and suddenly absent.

We might wonder what Bion meant in saying "without memories". This notion has often been misconstrued. In order to get a better grasp of this idea, I turned to *Attention and Interpretation* (Bion, 1970, pp. 107–108), in which Bion mentions a container, filled with memories stemming from sensory experiences. Bion calls this type of memory "active memory". An analyst entering a session with an active memory is unable to assume the position suitable for observing psychic phenomena that are still unknown and are not sensually perceived. Bion cleverly distinguishes between memory and remembering: remembering is vital to analytic work and must be carefully differentiated from memory. Remembering a dream during the analytic session, the sudden appearance of a dream, constitutes a vital growth of emotional reality. This spontaneous remembering must be separated from active memory. The active memory, with which the analyst enters the session, disrupts the operation of the containing function, which relies on unsaturated elements. Remembering is not memory and we must not confuse the two. In memory, the essence is time. Time if often considered a cardinal aspect of psychoanalysis, but this is a mistake: time plays no part in the growth process. Mental growth is both timeless and catastrophic. I believe Bion is here referring to the catastrophic change that engenders the disjunction and confusion that lead to growth. Perhaps Bion is trying to say that, just like catastrophes and traumas that occur suddenly and unexpectedly, change can also take place suddenly within the analytic process, undirected and unforeseen by us. Remembering is a process that happens as part of experience and cannot be predicted. In order to be able to feel what belongs to the growth that is occurring now, I believe we should observe the places that have evoked our feelings. Feelings trigger our intuition, without which no analytic dialogue can take place. Bion refers to intuition as the sum of all our senses. Rereading his paper about the Grid, I only recently realised that he is not talking about sight, smell, hearing, etc. Rather, he believes that bodily senses have a psychic counterpart in the form of intuition. The psyche can perceive other psyches. Naturally, sight, smell, and hearing also function within the session, providing valuable information, but the psychic sense entails much more. In other words, remembering drops in uninvited, and is of great importance in analytic work, both for the patient and for the analyst. For example, according to Bion, members of the same family cannot analyse each other, as their containers are loaded with memories that preclude any neutral observation.

From this we learn that should the analyst suddenly recall, during her dialogue with the patient, a story the patient once told her, she is not supposed to block it out. This would be to misread Bion. On the contrary, she should link the story to what is going on here and now. Such spontaneous material is, in fact, the inception of a new thought. Perhaps active memory is another oxymoron, because memory is constraining, static, and blocking, hindering the birth of new thoughts. We may, therefore, say that in analytic work, memory resembles lifeless α-elements, which cannot engender new links. In contrast, remembering is the process that gives life to the elements in the store of memories, letting them out into the light of day and providing them with new meaning. Remembering creates a new link and actually operates as an α-function, deciphering material arising in the here and now.

I will conclude with a short case presentation. I will try to depict a state in which my own thinking was under attack by an isolated α-element that was born inside me. As long as it remained isolated, it haunted me, blocking my ability to think together with the patient. As soon as it entered the therapeutic dialogue, it came to life through the links formed by the patient's associations during the sessions.

This patient started her analysis with me at the age of thirty. She was an intelligent, attractive, and very sexy woman. She came to see me several years after the termination of her previous therapy with another therapist, which she described as a success. For a year before the beginning of her analysis with me, she had no intimate or sexual relationships with men, and throughout the first eight months of analysis she reported an utter lack of interest in men, including sexual interest. In answer to my question, she related that she masturbated, but I felt uncomfortable about asking her to describe her masturbatory fantasies. I suddenly became very preoccupied with the question of whether or not she was a lesbian. The question pestered me. It did not arise from my experience in my sessions with her, but from a highly problematic area: I started thinking that I might fail this analysis and that after she was done with me she would see another analyst who would find out soon enough that she was a lesbian. Then, he would think I am a lousy analyst, sharing my blindness with others. I was preoccupied and restless; this thought became stuck in my mind, completely isolated, until I found myself asking her, with no relation whatever to our current therapeutic dialogue, if she was ever attracted to women. This question caused a deep crisis in our relationship whose traces are still visible today, in the middle of our second year together. Her reaction was fierce. She said the analysis was worthless and that she wanted to quit. If, during the past eight months, I could not even get to know her, she had nothing more to do here. She accused me of working by the book and not by the feelings I had been getting from her. She said I did not know her at all and that talking to me was a complete waste of time. Her anger was immense, and I admitted my mistake. During the following sessions she was still angry, attacking me repeatedly. I told her that she felt lonely, just as she did when she was a child, when she felt that her parents could not see her or perceive her distress. This difficult situation slowly began to build a new kind of link between us. The opportunity to vent such anger and have it acknowledged has brought us closer together.

I knew my question was unfortunate and utterly unrelated to the therapeutic dialogue. Nevertheless, it brought about a turning point in analysis. Up until that question, we never mentioned sex. Afterwards, much sexual material began to surface. She told me that once, during puberty, she had sexual relations with her sister, who was about her age. This was a one-time event. Another memory from her adolescence came up: she remembered having trouble falling asleep, being wide awake at night and sleeping during the day. She would see her father watching porn tapes in the living room. He used to leave the tapes in a place where she could find them, and she would watch them by herself. She felt that he knew she was taking them and that they shared a kind of unspoken, implicit bond. The intense sexual arousal she had felt then, at a very young age, after watching those tapes, has only recently resurfaced. Grown men have been taking advantage of her since she was eleven years old, and she thought there was nothing wrong with that because she also enjoyed herself. There were many men that she actively seduced. She never spoke of this at home and her parents were oblivious to the deep depression she was in.

At nineteen, she had her first boyfriend, who was fourteen years older than her. After more than a year of beautiful, intense companionship, she felt her sexual excitement diminishing. She demanded that he fantasise about all kinds of girls while sleeping with her. In bed, she wanted him to treat her as no more than a sexual object. He could not bear it and they had a very painful breakup. This was how we started to discover the arousal her father had created with the tapes only he and she knew about, which expressed their quasi-incestuous relationship.

Today, she is seeing men again. She wants them to love her, but in bed, she demands to be treated as no more than a sexual object. She wants to feel passive and humiliated. If the man is not being alienated and mean to her, she has to close her eyes and fantasise painful and humiliating situations in order to be sexually satisfied. Only that one unfortunate occasion managed to bring about her anger at me and the stream of associations that followed, unearthing her sexual bind.

Today, we are starting to make sense of this bind of her sexuality, real-ising the extent of her internal splitting—between being a beautiful, intelligent, and talented woman and a mere sex object. This uncovered a latent element of sadomasochism, which, in Bion's terms, is a kind of attack on the link of love. Positive love will turn into negative love whenever the proper link between love and sexuality fails to develop.

My fear of being blind allowed an isolated α-element burst out of my mind. Had it stayed inside, and remained unverbalised, it would have become a thing in itself, a question with no context. In this case, the patient was the one who performed the α-function, finding the links to enliven a thought that was stuck inside me, untransformed.

This closes the circle we have opened by asking how thoughts are born. We have seen thoughts come to life through emotional linking as patient and therapist share the creation of a new thought. The link is the space between the two people: dynamic, alive, and changing. As Bion might have said, emotions expressed directly and spontaneously in the session, even anger and disappointment, breathe life into this link, strengthening the life instinct, reinforcing the relationship with reality and tempering the death-instinct.

CHAPTER FIVE

Looking at the myth of Oedipus following Bion

This chapter focuses on Sophocles' *Oedipus Rex* (Sophocles, 2007), in light of Bion's thought. It attempts to trace the links between the myth and unconscious processes—personal as well as social—that are illustrated by the myth. Bion had great respect for Freud's discovery of the Oedipus myth as a foundational human narrative. Many elements of the myth are universal, but people and societies vary in the degree of complexity and intensity of many of these elements. Bion believed that the Oedipus myth was the paradigm that made the birth of psychoanalysis possible. In his book *Cogitations* (1992) Bion writes about intuitive psychoanalytic thinking. In *Attention and Interpretation* (p. 7) Bion uses a verb "intuit" for emphasising "that intuition opens the door to the unconscious". The Oedipus complex, Bion believed, was Freud's greatest achievement—a discovery that was made possible by Freud's unique intuitive ability. And Bion adds that we always stand in awe and wonderment when facing great discoveries.

This immediately brings us to Bion's paradoxical thinking. In fact, he was disturbed by the awe and wonder that most people feel in the face of great paradigms. A brilliant idea, he thought, was like a cut, a caesura. Bion (1989) developed this metaphor of the caesura in unexpected directions: much like the birth of an infant, so too, the birth of an idea. And much like the way we are entranced at the moment of birth, we turn our heads when a great idea or paradigm emerges. Paradox enters because the very idea that gave rise to a new theory and way of thinking can also give rise to the danger of a stasis in growth and paralysis. Bion was concerned about our tendency to be captured by ideas, to turn them into religions, or ultimate truths, leading to a loss in our freedom of thought. As psychoanalysts, he wanted us simultaneously to know the theory and forget about it, so that we would not find ourselves bound and trapped by concepts like the Oedipus complex or transference. He wanted us to be able to look at a concept and turn it upside down, to look at the potential of as yet unborn thoughts—in short: to be free to keep moving conceptually and to keep looking for new perspectives. When, by contrast, we stand to attention before an idea, we lose freedom of thought. When we become too awed by an idea, it turns into a cliché, or maybe even a fetish.

Bion had the courage to approach the Oedipus myth from an angle that was different from Freud's. Bion introduced his metaphor of binocular vision (Bion, 1961), a point of view that allows movement between margins and centre. So, when we put sexuality at the centre, Oedipus will form the focus, and the sphinx will be in the margins. But when we put the desire to know at the centre, the sphinx will form the focus, and Oedipus will be in the margins. What is beautiful and creative in this approach is that one way of seeing does not cancel out the other. The two perspectives are in dialogue. Thus, Bion's contribution offers a new way of looking at an apparently familiar and well-worn idea.

For Bion, the myth of Oedipus Rex presents us with a metaphor for each person's search for meaning and individuality. The mythological narrative shows us the suffering and destruction a person has to endure before he or she can find his or her humanity. The wish to reach one's inner truth, and to investigate the mystery of one's life, is never ending, but it is accompanied by pain and suffering. Every human is fated to a certain degree of blindness. Each of us is an actor in his own life, unaware of what it is that drives the narrative. There is a tragic aspect in this blindness of ours, which is associated with the understanding that we are.

The position of a person who comes for psychoanalysis or for psychoanalytic psychotherapy is ideally that of a person who sets out to explore. This position is emotionally identical to that of Oedipus when he sets out on a journey with the aim of discovering truths about his life, even if they are painful. The position of the patient in psychoanalysis is that of the one who comes to find answers to the sphinx's riddle, ready to try and reconstitute a picture from the unconscious fragments that are interwoven with the narrative of her or his coming into being and existence. Oedipus is an investigator first and foremost. He continues his search for truth relentlessly, even in the face of great anxiety.

The sphinx, in the story of Oedipus, is a horrifying monster, its body composed of both female and animal parts. As such, the sphinx represents the enigma, the undeciphered riddle: what creature has four legs, then two, and then again three? The answer takes us back to humankind. Human beings are those who walk on all fours when they are infants, on two legs when they are adults, and then use a stick in old age. Although the riddle is simple to the point of banality, it is, at the same time, elusive and hard to crack. The backdrop to it is formed by a society in distress, perhaps social catastrophe.

In the myth, the sphinx is located in the public space, strategically at a spot from which it can commit horrible acts on a helpless city whose king has died. As such, the sphinx represents the unconscious processes of what Bion would call the collective mentality of the society. When society is flooded by disasters, this indicates that something is amiss in the leadership's ability to protect the people. This monstrous sphinx, this patchwork of body parts, is an unintegrated creature, it does not feel, a horrifying composite, who does not have the ability to feel. The sphinx is the offspring of Echidne, a monster herself, who was not acquainted with human feelings. Thus, the sphinx herself is the victim of bad parenting, who never received containment, who failed to reach wholeness, and who remained unintegrated. Bion's theory of thinking allows us to say that the sphinx's riddle is asked from the fragmented schizo–paranoid position (Bion, 1967). The question, which refers to one part of the human body, is asked by a creature composed of partial objects. When schizo–paranoid thinking threatens to become dominant, a solver-of-the-riddle is required to pull in an integrative direction and, thus, to reveal the human being as a whole object. This is by no means simple, and solving the riddle is not all there is to it. If we want to discover the human being within us we must set out on a painful journey of personal change, learning from experience (Bion, 1962a).

I would now like to address the question of how Oedipus solves the sphinx's riddle, and why this solution is actually one more illusion. Oedipus suffered infantile trauma: Laius, his father, wanted to prevent his fated death by his son's hand. Just a few days after he is born, Laius hands over Oedipus to a shepherd with the order to abandon the infant on mount Kithairon. In order to ensure that no one takes the child from there, King Laius binds the infant's feet and pierces them with a pin. As a result, the infant's feet swell, hence his name Oedipus: swollen feet. When he is grown up, Oedipus solves a riddle about feet: it would seem that his infantile trauma provided him with a barely conscious preconception of the solution to the riddle of the sphinx (Bion, 1967). Oedipus' feet were scarred, marking his body with the terrible vulnerability and helplessness to which he was exposed as an infant left to its own devices. This was an unthinkable thought, because it was terrifying. In the language of Bion and Bollas (1987), it was "unthought known". Oedipus knew something that he could not think, and could not think something that he knew.

I would like to mention here Bion's paper "On arrogance" (Bion, 1967, p. 86) in which he makes the connection between infantile trauma and the development of arrogant and omnipotent thinking. So difficult is the trauma that its bearer has to protect him or herself by a carapace of all-knowingness. Oedipus had intuitive access to the sphinx's riddle about the feet. He solved the riddle by reference to his own marked body—but he made the transition from a preconception to a thought, and from there to solving the riddle in one gigantic leap but failing, as he went along, to solve the riddle of his own life. The trauma, when not approached with emotional knowledge, hurls him into a trap that will lead to a chain of tragic disasters. The fast and brilliant solution represents a barren knowledge that will be proven deluded.

In his *Cogitations* Bion mourns the limitations of language. He argues that the word *omnipotence* also implies its opposite, impotence. He thought that it was a great shame that our vocabulary does not include a word that conveys both these meanings at once. Indeed, when he solves the sphinx's riddle, Oedipus acts from an omniscient position. What he presents is the arrogant knowledge of the person who knows it all, who is sure he has a claim on all knowledge. This type of knowledge is associated with a leader who is blinded and drunk with his or her victory. Oedipus, until the city of Thebes falls prey to the plague, is caught in hubris, convinced that he has managed to avoid his fate as decreed by the gods. He is sure he has everything: a queen, a kingdom, a family, unaware of the fact that he is actually on the brink of an ever-closer catastrophe. He oscillates between being totally oblivious to whatever it is that drives the events of his life, and being omniscient, challenging, and provoking the wisdom of the gods. According to Bion, these two extremes are really one: the person who pretends to know everything is also the one who suffers total blindness.

Moreover, the sphinx, in abstaining from dialogue, represents an extreme state of social violence. Whoever cannot come up with the answer, she devours—and when she is defeated, she ends her own life. The social condition into which this translates is a state of terror and it asks for omnipotent leadership. Intimidated and scared, the people respond with fantasies of redemption. The leader who is chosen on the basis of such feelings will provide an illusion of power and security, and will promise peace and quiet. The city of Thebes tempts Oedipus to take the role of the omnipotent leader. And Oedipus lets himself be tempted and comes up with an immediate solution. He performs a miracle and becomes the redeemer. Where everyone else has failed, Oedipus comes, sees, and triumphs.

So, Oedipus defeats the sphinx euphorically, followed by the grandiose gestures of receiving the queen and the kingdom. Though he brings peace to the city of Thebes, this does not last for even one generation. What initially appeared as redemption and triumph, with the passing of time is revealed as the worst of disasters. Oedipus, who managed to solve the riddle so easily and without effort or suffering, turns out to have been a young man, lacking the real maturity leadership requires. His leadership, which is built on total blindness to himself, unleashes a string of catastrophes to himself, his family, and society as a whole, which, because of him, receives punishment in the form of sickness. And, thus, we see how close the pole of omniscience is to that of blindness.

This can be seen even in the very first episode of *Oedipus Rex*: how near to the height of achievement is the pit of defeat. Here we are presented with Oedipus as he boasts contemptuously to Tiresias, the blind prophet:

> Come on, tell me how you have ever given evidence
> of your wise prophecy. When the Sphinx,

that singing bitch, was here, you said nothing
to set the people free. Why not? Her riddle
was not something the first man to stroll along
could solve—a prophet was required. And there
the people saw your knowledge was no use—
nothing from birds or picked up from the gods.
But then I came, Oedipus, who knew nothing.
Yet I finished her off, using my wits
rather than relying on birds. (pp. 467–478)

Tiresias answers Oedipus:

You have your eyesight, and you do not see
how miserable you are, or where you live,
or who it is who shares your household.
Do you know the family you come from?
Without your knowledge you've become the enemy of your own kindred,
those in the world below and those up here. (pp. 496–502)

The sphinx's question is asked from an inhuman, cynical view-point—it is linear and lacks depth: as though the essence of humankind is in its body parts and the chronology of a lifetime. Correspondingly, the solution is trivial and fails to do justice to the greatness of humanity. Oedipus' euphoric triumph reminds me of Israel's military victories, because they represent shallow solutions to very complex problems, bringing calamities for which two nations are paying with human sacrifices.

In addition, one might say that Oedipus was able to solve the Sphinx's riddle so quickly because it was a general, universal question. In contrast, unravelling the enigma of his life and discovering his own identity demanded that he undergo a life-long ordeal. This is parallel to the process that takes place in therapy, as the patient seeks the kernel of truth that is her own. According to Bion, the solution to the riddle of the Sphinx lies in the realm of knowledge, and Oedipus effortlessly answers it using logic and common sense. However, the answer to the riddle of his life, has to do with psychic agony, and is an arduous journey through the realm of experience. Toward the end of the play, Oedipus is no longer asking "who is the killer?" but "who am I?", "who are my parents?" Having solved the universal riddle, he now faces the enigma of his own life and his own identity: the answer leads him to inevitable catastrophe (Halperin, 1979).

When Thebes is threatened with the plague, this chapter of Oedipus' successes draws to a conclusion. Oedipus starts to undergo a transformation. He abandons the omniscient position and faces the question. Doubt sets in and he starts on a persistent search. This is when Oedipus turns into a tragic hero. Here is a man who faced destruction from birth and wreaked much destruction himself without being aware of doing so. Oedipus touches and moves us. He stands exposed in his vulnerability and weakness, in his inexhaustible search after the truth. Oedipus gains a human dimension. He represents the tragedy of the person who comes face to face with the truth of her or his life. This process of looking for the truth, while enduring uncertainty and pain, is parallel to the one Bion calls *becoming O* (Bion, 1970a, p. 22).

The story of Oedipus suggests the difficult transformations a person has to undergo in order to discover her or his self. Oedipus' triumphal progress changes direction into a journey into himself. It is a solitary journey: he stands alone and exposed facing the terror that the words of the oracle instil. The revenge of the sphinx attacks him with all its cruel might. Oedipus feels that in order to heal the illnesses of society he will have to take responsibility for his actions. The solution to his life's riddle causes him much suffering but touching this pain in himself enables him to become empathic to the suffering of the other. Choosing this difficult road of suffering and searching, Oedipus leaves behind the false position of the omniscient man and becomes more and more humane. When he finally reveals his true identity to himself, he is freed from the perverse act of intercourse with his mother, acknowledges his murder of his father, and thus liberates society from its sickness. As a king, victories and temptations prevented him from perceiving social suffering. He puts his own eyes out in order to start seeing the truth. When blindness strikes, truth stands revealed. Oedipus experiences meaningful change through suffering. The pain of experience turns him into a different person. But as soon as the truth comes out, it is also clear that Oedipus will not be able to undo his past actions. Instead he can change himself, and what changes is his attitude to himself and his own actions. His transformation is from relying on the external powers of a mighty king to turning to his own internal strength. As he relinquishes his kingly power, he accedes to his human power. The human ability to recognise one's own limitations is what eventually heals society. While solving the sphinx's riddle brought Oedipus power and wealth, it is when he solves the mystery of his own life that he gains what it takes to face the tragic truth. And so the journey into himself emerges as his greatest victory.

The myth instructs us that even in the most difficult and tragic of times, changes can be made. Such change must be internal, and occurs when a person faces her or his inner truth. And so, Oedipus learns that the fate of which the oracle informed him, is actually matched by another fate, namely that of humankind. Oedipus' own fate has changed by means of a renewed and different knowing, namely, his refusal to deny. This type of knowledge is emotional and symbolic. While facts cannot be changed, a person can change her or himself. As he exiles himself, Oedipus becomes increasingly human. By leaving and taking his fate into his own hands, Oedipus removes himself from Apollo's cruel control.

At this point, Oedipus changes his life story and replaces a conclusion foretold with a new dynamic of becoming whose end has not been set out in advance. This is a metaphor for psychoanalytic therapy: the psychoanalytic journey requires the courage to face life events that are not amenable to change. We can, however, change our understanding and attitude to them, thus creating a new beginning that holds the joys of discovery and creativity.

Oedipus, then, is a leader who chooses to become empathic to the suffering of society—that is: to become acquainted, emotionally, with the nature of human suffering. What he needs to do is to go through a process of transformation from action to reflection. He puts himself at the disposal of a process of emotional thinking and a readiness for dialogue with reality—however painful this may turn out to be. There is a greater chance, when a leader shows willingness to bear pain without resorting to immediate action, for social transformation. When a leader is in touch with pain and processes mourning, chances for a reduction in the loss of human lives grow. Oedipus takes off his royal gown, blinds his own eyes, and starts looking inward. His ability to take insufferable pain and to admit his error and flaw, liberates the truth, which is the life stuff of society. From this point on, Oedipus becomes renowned for his deep knowledge, his teachings of hidden truths.

It is those leaders who have learned to process mourning who are most likely to heal their distressed societies. Leaders like Anwar Sadat and Yitzhak Rabin underwent transformations: they displayed human sensitivity, a deep recognition of social suffering, tiredness of war, and along with this, a determination to bring about change. That they were both assassinated bears witness to their visionary capacity, to the way they were ahead of their times.

The Bible, too, includes several instances of leaders who succeeded in abating the distress of their societies once they truly encountered suffering. Like Oedipus, Joseph and Moses suffered childhood trauma. Both, like Oedipus, were abandoned. Both had the ability to contain social trauma. Joseph, like Oedipus, sins through arrogance and superiority—towards his siblings. He then experiences a steep fall as a result of his excess of confidence. His first, youthful dream inter-pretations are egocentric and insensitive, with catastrophic results. Only after being thrown into the pit, suffering exile, slavery, humilia-tion, and incarceration, does he learn to understand and empathise with social suffering. His ability to contain and survive distress is reflected in his dream-thought that is intuitive and allows him to uncover what is occult and unanticipated.

Another perspective on the myth can be found in Bion's chapter on the theory of thinking (Bion, 1967). Here he elaborates on the connec-tion between the development of thinking, on one hand, and affective conditions in early childhood, on the other. The more containing these affective conditions are, the more is independent thinking likely to flourish. What Bion has in mind is not intellectual thought. This type of thinking can also be found among intelligent people who never received emotional containment. He means emotional thinking, which allows a person to be in touch with reality in all its painfulness and with all its attendant frustrations, without falling to pieces. Such thinking does not unfold in a vacuum, but through a fertile dialogue with reality and through the constant learning from experience. This leads Bion to conclude that all thinking is born from the "mating" between two elements. He believes that during the analytic hour a birth takes place: the analyst merges with/immerses in his or her own thought in order to give birth to an analytic intervention. The analysand, on her or his part, immerses in her or his thought. Thus, each undergoes inner processing, but the eventual encounter between their reflections will give birth to a new idea. This process is an infi-nite chain. The ability to immerse in thought is an emotional process. Thinking, for Bion, is a "mating" between two elements. He believes that in order to avoid psychosis, the individual must recognise the existence of both these elements. Non-psychotic thinking acknowledges the need for two that search for *links*. These links occur in the space between the two, a space that is in constant motion and development. Omnipotent thinking, by contrast, is founded on unity. As it knows of no duality it does not feature a dynamic. The omnipotent person knows everything and is singular. He does not look for links. Questions create motion, but the omnipotent person has no motion. Many layers unfold once Oedipus starts asking questions. He asks until he reaches the truth. It is this ability to ask questions that brought redemption for the city of Thebes. Hence, emotional thinking always poses questions. Omnipotence, on the other hand, blocks the space of questioning.

The notion of *links* is central to Bion's theory. To paraphrase somewhat freely: the link is the creative space in which an encounter between two gives birth to a new development. Bion seems to have been extremely preoccupied with this space between the two. When analysing one particular element, its link to another element will always appear in close vicinity. These two elements are in motion and their interrelations are dynamic. Paradoxically, they complement each other, attract each other, and simultaneously maintain a certain tension. We could even say that they are, at the same time, each other's opposites. And as such, therefore, each cannot be without the other. Some focal pairs in Bion's theory are, for instance: container and contained; establishment and genius; concept and intuition; past and future; infant and mother; patient and therapist; Oedipus and the sphinx; psychic vision and psychic blindness.

As he analyses these narratives of the Oedipus myth, Bion touches on the ethical position of the leader vis-à-vis her or his constituency: it would seem that the role of the psychoanalyst vis-à-vis her or his client, as he elaborates it, is parallel to that of the leader. This role, we could say, is that of the questioner, the observer, and researcher, who asks and waits, who contains and feels the distress. Our own society is in dire need of a leader with the capacity to contain and the courage to solve the riddle of the sphinx. A leader who will set our society free from the monster whose grip keeps two peoples caught in an interminable chain of catastrophes.

PART III

GROUP

"The point that I wish to make is that the group is essential to the fulfillment of a man's mental life."

Bion, *Experiences in Groups*, p. 53

"The individual is a group animal at war, not simply with the group, but with himself for being a group animal and with those aspects of his personality that constitute his 'groupishness'."

Bion, *Experiences in Groups*, p. 131

CHAPTER SIX

An introduction to Bion's contribution to group dynamics

Biography

I will start with some important biographical events in Bion's life affecting his thinking about groups.

1. Bion was born in 1897 in Victorian Imperial India. He was raised mainly by a maid and a governess, both Indian, who often told him tales from the Mahabharata, whose language he could not decipher, but whose impact he was never to forget. Bion was sent off on his own to England at the age of eight. He was educated at Bishops Stratford College. This was a very difficult period for the young Bion, away from his family. During that period Bion learned to make good use of his imagination, but still suffered from nightmares.

2. In 1916, Bion joined the armed forces, and served in the Royal Tank Regiment on the Western Front. He took part in a terrible battle, in which thousands of soldiers were killed. At one point no officers were left, and Bion, a twenty-year-old junior officer, was required to take command. Bion remained profoundly affected by this terrifying and cruel ordeal for the rest of his life.

3. While he was training as an analyst at the British Institute of Psychoanalysis, the Second World War broke out. During the war Bion was an officer in charge of the Military Training Wing at Northfield Military Hospital for a brief period of six weeks. Following this experience Bion wrote his first paper on groups, entitled "Intra-group tensions in therapy: their study as a task of the group".

4. The last event in Bion's biography that I wish to indicate here, is his move from London to Los Angeles in 1968. This took place when he was about seventy, and while he was holding central positions in London's psychoanalytic establishment. While in Los Angeles, he was engaged in much writing, psychoanalysis, painting, and lecturing. According to him, he fled London because of his important positions, since he "Didn't wish to be drowned in honour", and lose his capacity for individual and independent thinking. The quotation has double meaning and a flavour of bitterness since until then people used to praise his *Experiences in Groups* (Bion, 1961) but had not read his later books.

To sum up the biographical section: Bion had lived on three continents, was involved in two World Wars, underwent one trauma as an eight-year-old child, and another, terrible, trauma as a young officer in the war. His manifold experiences, his transferring between countries and cultures, his many professional identities as an army officer, football player, mathematician, painter, philosopher, classics' scholar, physician, psychoanalyst—all these aspects contributed to his distinct way of writing, as well as to his ability to observe and analyse group processes in an exceptional way. His contribution is due to his unique thinking and life experiences.

The object-relations theory interlaced with Bion's theory of thinking

Melanie Klein's theory of object-relations (Klein, 1975a) had a profound influence on Bion. Bion had undergone analysis with Melanie Klein, and although he was ambivalent towards her, he absorbed the main principles of her theory. However, Bion renewed Klein's concepts and charged that traditional theory with paradoxical and avant-garde spirit. I will first indicate the main Kleinian terms relevant to the topic, while indicating Bion's elaboration or translation of each term.

Melanie Klein had placed great emphasis on the individual's internal world from the moment of birth. The mother is an object (Object) for the infant, who is itself a subject (Subject). The little subject is filled with desires, phantasies and anxieties, and it experiences its mother as an omnipotent object. For the infant that object is supposed to simultaneously fulfil his needs and to constitute a container into which it is possible to project all that is unbearable or difficult to contain. The most important term here is "phantasy", meaning the way the infant experiences both the internal and external realities. Bion adopted this observation, which emphasises mental experience. His great contribution concerning this point was in the transfer from the mother–infant dyadic world to the conductor–group world. Bion opened a new world for us, through his discovery that a group behaves like a regressive infantile subject, and regards its conductor as an object of omnipotent forces, for better or for worse. Bion's discovery is the most important paradigm in the theory of group behaviour. It means that the group is not only the sum of its participants, but it is also an entity existing beyond the individuals. The group has an unconscious, which is regressive by nature. This group unconscious is controlled by irrational forces and it uses no reality testing.

When a participant in the group is speaking in the group, he speaks in his individual voice, but is simultaneously the mouthpiece for the group unconscious. Each participant in the group has a role, which the group delegates him to fulfil. This process, in which an individual is delegated as a representative for one or another aspect of the group, is an unconscious one. It can be identified in the group behaviour, but less so on the declarative level. The individual chosen by the group for a certain role is the one with the valency, that is to say, the individual with the tendency towards that role. For example, if the group feels the need to attack the conductor, it will encourage the person who finds it most difficult to accept authority to perform the attack, while the group itself remains innocent. The individual, including his valency, is weaker than the group as a whole. The group pushes the individual and may take control of him.

Every group has a group mentality, which equals the sum of its needs, wishes, desires, and phantasies, which are hidden in the group and are not expressed in words. This idea is of the greatest importance for the understanding of the complex relationships between the individual and the group. Understanding that the group mentality is stronger than the individual's, allows us an insight into the individual's tragic position as a victim of the group. The group has a strong magnetic power, which it exerts on the individual. However, just as it may help him grow, it might also stop his development, harm him, and bring out of him some psychotic aspects. The group causes a conflict within every individual, between the wish to belong to the group and the fear of being absorbed by it and losing individuality. A person in a group is capable of doing things that he would not do on his own. Once we understand that the group is the subject and the conductor is the object, we become aware, as conductors, of the unconscious behaviours and processes we must decipher. We become aware of the space and tension between Subject and Object.

Klein (1975c) puts strong emphasis on the occurrences inside the room during therapy. Because of the focus on what is taking place in the room, many interpretations are connected with transference, with the therapist as an Object and the patient as a Subject. The therapist–patient relations are at the focus of the exploration. Every act is symbolic, referring to the unconscious phantasies of the patient in regard to the therapist.

In his *Experiences in Groups* (1961), we can see how Bion discovered one of the main tools in understanding group dynamics: the use of the here and now. Through the position of the explorer viewing every verbal and non-verbal occurrence in the room, through the glasses examining emotions, thoughts, sensations as all of these are manifested in the room, a whole world is discovered. At any given moment the dynamic group is a micro-cosmos. Once we relate to the group as a micro-cosmos we may reveal different behaviours re-enacting life outside the room. The importance of working in the here and now is mainly the proximity to the experience. Looking at things as they happen allows the group to work on the emotional level. For example:

> I conducted a group of professionals under the title: Gender and Generations. A young male colleague conducted the group with me. Soon enough middle-aged women started expressing different phantasies concerning the relations between my younger colleague and myself. One of the recurring phantasies was that I was tense while he

was speaking, that I kept an eye on him, that I tested him every time he intervened, that he was like a child whom I was supposed to educate and so on. These reactions seemed to me to be a defence against the sexual attraction he aroused in these women, and against the envy of him being so young and unavailable to them. They had turned him into my son, a child who constitutes no threat to them. In the here and now it was possible to gather the different reactions and to show the kind of hierarchy they created in the room, without their phantasies having any concrete expression in reality. The possibility of viewing matters as they are occurring caused excitement in the group, leading to insights concerning the way in which the older generation belittles the younger one, also in our professional relationships outside the room and outside the here and now.

Melanie Klein's theory focuses on defence mechanisms. The most important defence mechanism discovered by Melanie Klein is the projective identification (PI). Bion deals with PI in a unique way of his own, which contributed greatly to the understanding of group dynamics. Melanie Klein discovered this mechanism through her clinical work, and she attributes its roots to the early relations between infant (Subject) and mother (Object). The infant may suffer an unbearable emotion, for example, a strong aggression accompanied by phantasies of destroying the mother, because he envies her for being competent and for the milk she is able to produce. This aggression is so frightening and threatening, that in order to get rid of it, the infant projects the aggression on the mother. The mother, as Object, is supposed to contain this aggression for the infant in a moderate and non-destructive way. In the PI, contrary to the projection, the infant identifies with the aspect that was projected. That is to say, the infant does not wish to give up his aggression. The infant wishes to know that the aggression exists there for him. The infant had only deposited the aggression with the mother for holding and maintaining this aspect. He does not wish to give up the aggression as an aspect in his repertoire, but for the time being the infant wishes to know that the mother is holding the aggression for him, until the infant himself grows stronger, or until the aggression becomes moderate.

Bion regarded PI as having a very important role in group dynamics. The PI creates a fascinating mosaic of tensions inside the group. First, the conductor is the Object on which the group projects all its anxieties and unbearable emotions. Bion explains: "The analyst feels he is being manipulated so as to be playing a part, no matter how difficult to recognize, in somebody else's phantasy" (Bion, 1961, p. 149). The important point about the PI is that as a conductor one indeed falls into the phantasy and feels the distress, and only after one has been there, is it possible to decipher the dynamics, which have taken place.

> During one session of group dynamics for professionals, I had the feeling that the discussion in the group was trivial, ritualistic, and constituted intellectual slogans, without anyone being in touch with themselves or their feelings. As the session was progressing I was feeling more and more distressed. I began to feel a kind of paranoid anxiety. My thoughts were: I am not a good conductor, they do not trust me, they just want to pass the time without letting anything happen here. They are all indifferent and it is only I who carry the anxiety. Apparently I am not good enough for them. As my anxiety was mounting, I became even more paralysed. Finally I intervened, saying: "I would like to share with you what is bothering me. The discussion today seems to me to be shallow. I have begun to feel that you don't trust me enough to bring up true emotions, and that I'm the only one here feeling anxiety and that time is being wasted. Perhaps I am holding for you the feeling of lack of trust and lack of security which you have towards each other and towards the group." This intervention had opened a new dialogue in which people agreed with what I said. An emotional shift took place. People were saying openly that they had no trust in the group and therefore they refrained from bringing up emotional or substantial materials. People said that earlier they were afraid to say openly that they had no trust for one another. Talking about it allowed the group to begin establishing trust.

Projective identification also takes place intensively among the participants. This mechanism is the base for creating roles in the group. The classical role is that of the one who goes on the attack on behalf of all the rest. The "bad" guy, who helps everyone else to remain innocent. Another role is the clown, who is pushed into making everyone else laugh at difficult moments, thus preventing him from being in touch with his grief and pain, which the group is afraid to face. Another role is that of the one who says unintelligent things or does not speak to the point, which tires everyone. He is kept in this role out of the fear of everyone else assuming this role, in case that person starts speaking to the point.

Bion's theory of thinking

So far, I have been describing terms stemming from the Kleinian theory, indicating how Bion developed and implemented them into the world of the groups. However, it should be added now that Bion developed a theory, which is above and beyond the theory of object-relations. The implementation of ideas from the object-relations theory is but the first layer in Bion's theoretical contribution.

Bion developed an original theory of thinking. He considered that the thinking process is a function of the personality. In his *Learning from Experience* (1962a), Bion refers to two principal and different elements of thinking. The first, called "alpha" elements, refers to elements that can be thought. The second, called "beta" elements, refers to elements that are impossible to use for thinking. It is the alpha function that translates what is absorbed by the infant through the senses in a pre-verbal form into words, dreams, expressions of feeling, and dialogue. It affects the transformation from thoughts that cannot be thought to thoughts that can be thought. At first, the mother performs this function for the infant. She translates the infant's distress for him, gives names to his hardships and anxieties, and thus calms and contains him.

These concepts are important for shading light on the unconscious processes taking place in the group. The group is a regressive place, in which people experience uncertainty, struggle with finding their place, and live on a high level of anxiety concerning their presence in the group. They are occupied by the questions of how to find their place in the group and how the conductor relates to them. It therefore seems that the group is speaking in beta code. Because of the level of anxiety and the degree of regression, thoughts that cannot be thought are filling the room. The group expresses those thoughts through different patterns of behaviour that do not undergo a transformation to thinking. People say concrete things that occur to them, but they are unable to express what goes on inside them. The function of the conductor here is to execute the alpha function, which is the mother's function. The conductor is supposed to collect the different behaviours and the words said, and give them meaning. Thus the conductor makes it possible for the group to move from code to code, and to learn the language of the unconscious.

A participant in the group says, "The bus on the way here was so packed. Everybody pushed and shoved, I thought I'd suffocate. The conductor should translate this saying to the metaphorical level, one that can be thought. For example: you're saying that this group, too, is packed and suffocating. You need to push in order to find your place here." The conductor is the one who does not relate to the concrete contents, but to what lies behind them, and who observes the process in order to transfer it to the level of thinking. The conductor will pay attention to tone of speech, its speed, who speaks after whom, who keeps silent, do people leave the room, do cellular phones ring. Also, what is the arrangement of sitting—who sits next to whom, do men sit opposite women, what happens after the conductor speaks, and so on.

Bion coined the term "container". The container is essential for the transformations of the kind I have described to take place. The conductor should be the container who collects behaviours, which seem meaningless, deciphers them, and gives them meaning. Thus he creates calmness and facilitates the work in the group. The conductor is supposed to contain the group's PI, which appears in the form of elements that cannot be thought. The conductor contains these elements, moderates them and hands them to the group.

Material, which has not been transformed, will remain in the group's space without containment. Bion calls this kind of material "nameless dread". The more such material exists, the more the group becomes psychotic, and busies itself with acting out. On the other hand, the more transformation is taking place, the more dialogue and work in the group are made possible. The containment function is a central function in the conductor's work. It is connected with his ability to decipher, find meaning and discover connections between seemingly unconnected elements. This theory of thinking evolves from the emphasis Bion put on learning from experience. This is not logical thinking, but rather thinking evolving from the epistemophilic instinct, the instinct to investigate and to know. This is a kind of a drive evolving from the emotional experience. The group is learning through the experiences it undergoes. The conductor learns through being tuned with his emotions and sensations. Bion placed emphasis on the senses. The conductor is supposed to use his senses and pre-verbal experiences in order to reach new thoughts. Bion argued that the therapist needs not only concepts but intuition as well, and must use them both simultaneously.

In *Second Thoughts* (1967), written some nineteen years after *Experiences in Groups* (1961), Bion develops the concept of the "container", on which I elaborate in another chapter of this book. Regarding observation in the group, it is important to note that the work of containing and deciphering is gradually being performed by the members of the group, and not only by the conductor of it. When group members grow through the group process, their capacity for metaphorical thinking is augmented and their ability to contain each other develops. Bion described situations in which the container and the contained switch roles: the members may contain the conductor's difficulty, attaining further growth through this experience.

It seems that this part of his theory evolved from Bion's experiences as a child, when he heard stories told in a foreign language and learned to use all his senses, as well as his experience as a lonely child away from his family and his terrible experiences in the war. He had to make much use of intuition and to invent the concept of the container in order to survive, and to learn a great deal from his difficult experiences. While exploring the group process, Bion is not afraid of unconventional ideas that are bothersome and that disturb everyday peacefulness.

The phases and how they are expressed in the group

I will now try to integrate several theories and concepts:

1. Melanie Klein's phases
2. Bion's basic assumptions
3. My own learning from experience.

Bion was very interested in the phases of development postulated in Kleinian theory. Melanie Klein described two main phases: the schizo–paranoid phase and the depressive phase. Bion regarded human life as a constant oscillation between the two phases: SP and D (He writes PS instead of SP).

This is a developmental model, although in fact Bion did not regard the group as developing along phases. Based on my experience, however, it seems to me that group dynamics do undergo such a development.

First, phobia. Groups usually begin their lives on some level of phobic anxiety. The anxiety paralyses, and there is still no initiative, neither for approximation nor for distancing. Bion (1965, p. 124) showed how claustrophobia and agoraphobia may exist in the same form, and may interchange between each other. It seems that what causes the paralysis in the group is the feeling of the individual member that if he walks out he will lose his way in the open spaces, remain lonely, and miss an important group experience, while simultaneously feeling that if he stays the group will swallow him up and erase his uniqueness. In most cases there is a member who takes the risk and decides to speak, assisting the group to move to the next phase.

Second, paranoia. In this phase the type of anxiety changes to paranoid anxiety. This is the anxiety in which the individual feels that the conductor and/or the group threaten, accuse, or persecute him. According to Melanie Klein, the paranoid anxiety evolves from the destructive instincts inside the subject's internal world, of which he wishes to rid himself. In order not to see himself as bad or dangerous, he projects these instincts on to the objects, then fears that the bad object will destroy him. In the group the paranoid phase will be expressed in the perception of the conductor as omnipotent and the group itself as weak, helpless, ignorant, infantile, and innocent. Bion regards this phenomenon as a phantasy growing in the group without any reality testing. The group members regard the conductor as an omniscient authority. According to their phantasy, the conductor must supply them with solutions to all their problems, while they come only to suckle. They disregard their life experience and their ability to think. Since the conductor is regarded as omnipotent and omniscient, his failure to supply the required answers makes him seem a bad person. The group is in a religious state of mind, looking for a god. Bion revealed here an unconscious behaviour, stemming from the group's need to rely on an omniscient external authority. This points to the dangers inherent in charismatic leaders who can lead people like a herd, because of the human need for relying on the one who knows. When the conductor does not fulfil the phantasy, the paranoid experience is strengthened. The group assumes that the conductor is hiding knowledge and ability from the group members. It often happens that a member of the group is willing to fulfil its dependency need and fill in the vacuum. Bion explained that it is impossible to fulfil dependency needs in the long run, and that the leader who supplies the dependency will eventually cause a disappointment, and then will be deserted. Also, in the long run, this pattern becomes boring, and people would discover that there are capabilities inside themselves, and they no longer need a dependency leader. In this phase, the paranoid experience, stemming from insufficient satisfaction of the dependency needs, is a strong one, and the group continues to regard the conductor as judgmental and aggressive. Typical behavioural patterns we may view in the group in this phase include: attempting to behave as good children, attempting to seduce the conductor into supplying answers and solutions, pleasing the conductor and the group, hiding angers and disappointments, being considerate, proposing to the others that they work in the group, and the fear of taking a position and depositing of all the aggressive aspects with the conductor through PI. There will also appear many patterns of suspicion and avoidance.

Bion spoke of a basic assumption: fight–flight. He found that when facing difficulties it cannot handle, the group closes ranks against a common enemy. In the case of the dynamic group, the common enemy may be the conductor who did not meet the needs for dependency. It may also be the work group itself, when the group feels it is too dangerous to work as a group. The common enemy may also be an external element, on which the group projects all its evil, for example: the directorate of the institute in which the group sessions are taking place. When the basic assumption: fight–flight is active, there appears a phantasy that all that is evil is outside, and the group forgets its internal conflicts and sub-divisions, uniting together as one body against the external enemy. In the paranoid phase the group is mostly occupied with flight. There is still no confidence and trust in the conductor and in the group as a work group. The group prefers to flee, because the danger of personal exposure and the vulnerability are still felt strongly. The move into the next phase occurs once the anger, disappointment, and aggression that have been accumulated in the group require a form of expression, and the members of the group feel secure enough in the group to move from a concealed to an overt expression of frustration, pain, and aggression.

Third, schizo (Split). In this phase the type of anxiety is changed to a confusional anxiety. The group is in a state of confusion. At some point it is no longer clear who is bad and who is good, what is right and what is wrong. The group has the ability to give and to love, but in it there is also anger and destructiveness looking for means of expression. Perhaps the conductor, who has not given easy solutions, is not totally bad, but is here in order to allow the group to grow and find answers within itself. The confused group is not ready yet to handle a situation, that contains both good and bad. Therefore, the main defence mechanism at this phase is the split. The split allows orientation in the group's world. It divides the world into black and white, good and bad, thus there is certainty and calmness. In its emotional position the group is like a child watching a Western, and immediately wishing to know who are the good guys and who are the bad guys. The human need for total good and total evil exists throughout life. People who are addicted to soap operas also love them because it is clear who is the bad, depraved man, and who is the beautiful, clean, innocent woman who also happens to be the victim. In such films everything is clear, and everyone knows whom to hate and whom to love.

Fight behaviours could appear in the group in this phase. They could be directed outwardly towards the conductor, while hoping he will survive the attacks rather than collapse or abandon the group. In this phase there could also appear subdivisions in the group, including sub-groups, ranks, respected people, and unwanted people. Here we might see the phenomenon of the scapegoat, that is to say, a participant in the group who draws the fire, who is pushed into playing the victim. This would be the participant against whom the group is united in its attack. Thus the group finds an easy channel for releasing aggression.

When the split mechanism becomes stronger, it may become so extreme that people can no longer handle the threatening instincts; we might see in the group a kind of freezing of the instinct and stopping of life. The split will be expressed through a kind of a renewed avoidance. People will bring to the room nothing but intellectual aspects. There will be much using of the head and avoidance of expressing emotions. All this constitutes defence against losing control and destructiveness. People will think in categories and stereotypes. There might be created an atmosphere of alienation and indifference that might make the participants anonymous.

Fourth, mania. The manic phase is a kind of burst of energy and enthusiasm. It is in fact a kind of pause before the encounter with the depressive phase. The unconscious anxiety is replaced by depressive anxiety. It is the fear of falling into depression and despair. The manic phase is the one of false optimism, of groundless joy, of the illusion, of feeling grandiose. It includes the feelings of megalomania, of omnipotent feelings, of feeling drunk with power. This is a defence against disillusionment, against the encounter with the grey and integrated reality, in which black is mixed with white, in which a person who is good to me can also be bad to me. The group is denying dependency and need.

The main behaviours appearing in the group would be: telling jokes, bringing up solved and closed dilemmas, a state in which no questions are asked, everything is fine, the group may be broken up already, there is nothing more to work on, and so on. There could appear a kind of disregard for the conductor, accompanied with the feeling of victory and superiority. Devaluation of the conductor can even be expressed by sadistic behaviour towards him, ignoring totally his interventions, harming him and his abilities with no show of guilt or regret. The group idealises itself and denies any dependency on the conductor. The manic aspect in the group constitutes an extreme portrayal of what Bion calls basic assumption: pairing. Bion found that the pairing phenomenon would appear in the group when its members do not wish to work in the group and explore themselves. They do not wish to make an effort to attain revelation or insight. In a situation like that they create false optimism, which is not based on any evidence. The group members are using slogans and clichés, in order to avoid confronting the real problems. Sometimes pairing may appear as personification: two members are elected by the group to hold a dialogue among themselves. The group sits back as in a theatre, waiting for the pair to give birth to the redeemer. They wish for salvation without any effort on their part. It can also be viewed as copulating with an idea, with some salvation-bringing ideology, such as in: if we all hold hands and love each other the world will be redeemed. This copulation creates a phantom pregnancy, because no real solution can be born out of passively expecting salvation. In a group dynamic the copulation with an idea, which would redeem the world, is always a kind of alternative to the work of the conductor who worked through questions, exploration, dialogue, and touching the painful and missing. At such a stage the atmosphere in the group may be one of sexuality and eroticism. If there is a couple acting it out for the group, such a couple does not demonstrate the ability to love, but is rather a demonstration of exhibitionism and flirt, while the group occupies itself with pleasant voyeurism.

Finally, depression (Klein, 1975b). This phase appears after the group has tried everything in order to make its life easier, but no solution, neither magical nor schizoid, really helped. The group is now ready to confront the everyday reality, in which the group's members discover they have needs and dependency, not the kind of the infantile absolute dependency, but the kind of interdependence. The group members recognise that they are not perfect, that there is in them both good and evil, strength and weakness. The group is ready to accept the conductor as an experienced, valuable person, forsaking the wish that he be omnipotent or else be regarded as impotent. The realisation that the conductor is a human being helps the group members to accept themselves as human beings, flesh and blood, people who have suffered losses and pain, who have made mistakes, but may bring their stories to the group. This is the phase when people are capable of feeling guilt for what they have done wrong without falling apart, but rather reconciling with the facts and finding ways for reparation.

Bion calls this phase work-group. It means that the group members are joining together in order to work and in order to confront reality. Melanie Klein called this state constructive depression. Usually there are forces in the group that allow this development to occur. If not, the group might get stuck in one of the earlier phases, or fall into despair and melancholia, which would be the negative solution for the depression.

Bion believed that it is necessary to confront the depression. In order for growth to take place, the pain must be touched. Bion emphasises that the human being who is searching for truth, who explores the riddle of his life, is constantly in a state of development. What sometimes seems to be a dead-end, and endless repetition, also contains growth. Searching for truth, learning from experience, but simultaneously living every experience in a fresh and virgin-like way—all this is called by Bion "becoming O". This concept symbolises the endlessness of searching and growth, and the human being's ability to be in touch with his original experience and the truth of his life.

I live in an area of conflict where two peoples, the Israeli and the Palestinian, have failed to achieve peace. The relations between the two peoples have existed for a very long time on two, totally, different levels. One level represents the alpha function and is expressed by peace talks, the attempted dialogue, efforts for co-existence, and the intention of dividing the territory. The other level is the one of terror and violence, which represents the beta elements. Whenever there is progress in the peace process, there is also an escalation in violence and in terror attacks. I hope, for the sake of our future, that it will be possible to translate the language of violence to the language of dialogue.

Bion aspired to bring down separating walls and to look at things from unconventional points of view. This chapter constitutes my own interpretation of Bion, which is influenced by my own environment and culture. I believe that the opportunity to discuss a theory, from some different points of view, would expose the reader to further exploration, which is infinite.

CHAPTER SEVEN

Myths, memories, and roles: how they live again in the group process

Often, when Bion mentions the Oedipus myth, he also refers to the Biblical narratives of the Tree of Knowledge and the Tower of Babel (Bion, 1970a). He believes that these are three different narratives with the same key components. Each of them features the desire for knowledge and punishment for aspiring to divine wisdom. These three myths are interwoven in the life story of each human being. In one way or another we are all bound to encounter related dilemmas, though each of us experiences them in her or his unique way. It is interesting to observe that in each of these three narratives, knowledge is acquired through the senses: *taste* in the case of Genesis, *hearing* in that of Babel, and *vision* in Oedipus. An incisive developmental change happens, in each of these stories, through a sensory experience.

Looking at group analysis from a sensory perspective, we can find interesting parallels in thinking. Foulkes and Anthony (1957, pp. 198–199) use the metaphor of "mirroring" as a main element in the work of the group. Looking through the mirror in group analysis means the ability of a member to look inside himself through the observation of other members: "The group situation has been likened to a 'hall of mirrors' where an individual is confronted with various aspects of his social, psychological, or body image". The process that Foulkes calls "mirror reactions" resembles the journey of King Oedipus in search of his lost identity. Only when Oedipus had lost his sense of sight could he then look inside himself. Another metaphor employed by Foulkes and Anthony (p. 30) depicts the group process as constantly changing in "kaleidoscopic" fashion.

In coining the term "resonance", Foulkes and Anthony (1957, p. 200) use an auditory metaphor to indicate a very important way of communicating in the group. This concept is immensely useful for understanding the "Babel language" of group members, as each of them reacts to the same event from a different stage of development.

Here are some parallels between the Genesis episode and Oedipus: life in the Garden of Eden is based on a prohibition issued by an all-knowing God: "Thou shalt not eat from the Tree of Knowledge of Good and Evil". It is this very statement, and the way it attracts Adam and Eve's attention to the existence of the tree, that forms the essence of temptation. The prohibition articulates the option to eat the fruit of the tree. According to Fromm (1966), Adam and Eve's act of dis-obedience symbolises the inception of humans' freedom of choice. The first couple's act is, of course, predictable. Fromm draws attention to the inner contradiction at the centre of the book of Genesis: though God is omnipotent, the two humans, whom he created in his like-ness, aspire to his knowledge and threaten his uniqueness. God then appears as jealous of humankind's daringness and responds by exil-ing the couple from Paradise.

Oedipus, exiled from his paradise and in search of his fate, also defies authority and is punished. In both cases, the omniscient author-ity comes under threat from humans' ability to undo the clear lines separating between those in possession of all knowledge and the total ignoramus. When Adam is chased out of Paradise, like Oedipus, he chooses his fate. Adam and Eve are sent out into a world that contains pain, loss, and death. Consciousness, like in the case of Oedipus, leads them to recognise their limitations and to understand that they will never be omniscient. They are doomed to struggle for their existence and they must take responsibility for their lives. Much as in the Oedipus narrative, here, too, the Fall leads to growth, flourishing, and self-discovery.

Bion is preoccupied with the profound conflict between the desire to know and the fear of knowing. Each human being must experience a crisis of disillusion, each of us is exiled from Paradise—a process that starts when we leave the womb and includes all the difficult separations and losses we encounter. Bion, referring to these myths, argues that our ability to endure a painful truth and stay whole, and, simultaneously, the ability to know that we shall never know it all, are cornerstones of psychoanalysis. They are needed by both patient and therapist as together they try to decode the mystery some of whose parts will never be solved.

The Tower of Babel narrative, which he mentions in various contexts, arouses Bion's curiosity. He believes that the group, essentially, is fated to stay unsaturated. The myth of Babel is, so far as I know, the only one of its kind that lacks a hero or heroine. Instead, it is the group that takes centre stage. The word *group* is attractive and off-putting at one and the same time. Every one of us fears to be swallowed by the group yet equally worries lest she or he be expelled by it and remain alone. The Tower of Babel represents the difficulty each individual experiences in finding her or his place vis-à-vis the group. Each of us faces difficult, or even traumatic, moments in this context. In the Babel episode the group moves between being whole and unified, and being disintegrated. Wholeness is represented by the entire Tower as it reaches into heaven—a powerful phallic symbol. As such it represents the group's ambition to compete with divine knowledge: "Let us build a city and a tower that reaches the sky".

The group's bid for omnipotence and to penetrate into the realm of God is penalised by total disintegration, a linguistic chaos that makes communication impossible.

This is also the point of inception of the paradox this episode shares with the other two narratives. Punishment, once more, is also the start of growth and flourishing. If we want to find the difference, or reach differentiation, the existent structure must be taken apart. This falling apart and disbanding brings in its wake renewal, the emergence of a variety of languages and cultures. The initial apparent catastrophe eventually brings growth. Each of these myths deals with the desire to know, each of them involves an attack on the senses. Each of them, moreover, recounts the concession of a wish for omnipotence and the consequent gains.

The Human Soul was expelled from Paradise and was condemned to search, wonder, and ache. It is a soul torn between the wish to be inquisitive and know more, and the fear of discovering painful truths. Our desire to broaden our consciousness is therefore always in conflict with its opposite: the wish to leave things lying in the depths of the unconscious abyss. The saying "let sleeping dogs lie" reflects our anxiety when faced with the danger of waking those drives that are better left dormant and of which we would rather not be aware.

Freud (1916–1917) argues that babies are born with "the episte-mophilic instinct". This term combines the Greek words for knowl-edge—episteme—and for love—philia.

Klein (1975b) sees this concept as crucial to the various develop-mental phases of life. She posits an inseparable connection between the wish to investigate and gain knowledge, and the drive to love and to hate. In each phase, there is a conflict between the wish to know and the fear of knowing. One may therefore say that knowledge and emotion come into being hand in hand.

Freud supplied the foundation for this theoretical way of thinking. According to him, the ability to think, as well as the ability to tolerate frustration, develop when the reality principle takes control, substi-tuting for the exclusive control of the pleasure principle. When a person is able to tolerate frustration, the process of search and growth will begin as an alternative to the immediate satisfaction of the drives (Freud, 1911b).

Bion used the theoretical background laid down by Freud and Klein to develop a far-reaching and original theory of thinking. He contributed three terms for explaining the development of thinking: "alpha function", "alpha-type elements", and "beta-type elements". As I have developed at greater length elsewhere in this volume, Bion explains these terms as follows:

> The alpha-function operates on the sense impressions, whatever they are, and the emotions, whatever they are, of which the patient is aware. In so far as the alpha function is successful, alpha elements are produced, and these elements are suited to storage and the require-ments of dream thoughts. If the alpha-function is disturbed, and there-fore inoperative, the sense impressions of which the patient is aware and the emotions which he is experiencing remain unchanged, I shall call them beta-elements. In contrast to the alpha-elements, the beta-elements are not felt to be phenomena, but things in themselves. [. . .] Beta elements are undigested facts and therefore they are not available for thought. (Bion, 1962a)

This means that a whole universe of strong emotions is stored within us, even though we are unable to think them. Bion's theory enables us to grasp the excruciating conflict that human beings face when searching for the truth of their lives. Formidable obstacles are bound to lie in the path of this search, as acute emotional elements obstruct the process. In effect, there exist things that are too frightening or too difficult to contemplate.

The psychoanalytical function of the personality is another contribution of Bion's to understanding the connection between knowledge and emotion. This function is imprinted in all human beings from the day of their birth. That is to say, the ability to explore the unknown, the aptitude to look into the riddle and mystery of humanity, is imprinted within us. This function, expressed by Bion's "K function", should assist the participants in group therapy in studying not only themselves but also their relationship to the world that surrounds them. K stands for the pursuit of Knowledge. The less this function comes under assault of unbearable emotional elements—such as envy—the more successful it is (Bion, 1962a).

A person who takes part in the group process may be likened to an explorer who makes a pledge together with a group of people who have all agreed on a joint mission: to explore a hidden world long gone and forgotten. This world has nevertheless left behind some traces and signs, which are in fact powerful enough to compel us to inquire into the meaning of our lives.

Foulkes and Anthony (1957, p. 58) explain this exploration as a group discussion aimed at revealing hidden content. They interpret the group process as the individual analyst interprets the dream.

Bion argues that the exploration that people conduct into their own lives is represented—in a general cultural context—by the mythological story of the sphinx. The sphinx represents the enigma, the as yet unsolved riddle. In the myth, the sphinx is portrayed as a female—in fact, as a monstrous combination of female features with those of different animals. It is a startling combination, simultaneously evoking curiosity and horror. In common language, "sphinx" also signifies a blank face on which no expression can be seen. A person with such a face is both menacing and alluring, constituting an unsolved riddle as well as a symbol for hidden knowledge.

According to the myth, Oedipus was the only one who successfully solved the sphinx's riddle, which is so banal but at the same time so difficult, so close but so distant: "What is it that goes on four feet, three feet and two feet, and is most feeble when it walks on four?" Oedipus' answer was: "Man—on all fours as a baby, on two feet at maturity, on three as an old man with a stick." This answer is, simultaneously, surprising and trivial, but it implies a new riddle, since it reviews a whole sequence of life in one short sentence. While describing the development of a human being from the primeval beastly state of walking on all fours to the human stance on two feet, it also implies that this state is temporary and short lived. In his play *Antigone* (which was in fact written before *Oedipus the King* although the events depicted in it occur later), Sophocles celebrates the wonder of human life: "Numberless wonders, terrible wonders walk the world, but none the match of man—the great wonder . . ." (Sophocles, 1982).

The concept of the connection between knowledge and emotion is found in the Bible in the concise expression "to know a woman," such as in "the man knew his wife Eve" (*Genesis* 4:1). This expression, which establishes a connection between love and knowledge, also implies the connection between knowledge and life, and the creation of life.

Exploration, learning, and the acquiring of knowledge constitute an experiential process that lasts throughout human life. Knowledge that results from experience evokes a range of emotions, from happiness and love to fear and pain. These experiences constitute what Bion calls "becoming O", by which he means: becoming in order to find, again and again, as if for the first time, the internal reality, the essence of the self and the experience of learning (Bion, 1965).

The above considerations serve as an introduction to the understanding of three myths, which Bion saw as representing human culture. He mentioned these myths several times as paradigms of the human psyche, thus supplying the initial line of thought for this article (Bion, 1963a). I have tried to develop this idea further, and to analyse these myths according to the viewpoints suggested by Bion. The myths in questions are:

1. The eating of the fruit of the Tree of Knowledge.
2. The Tower of Babel.
3. The story of Oedipus.

These three myths recur in different variations within the private myth of every human being. Each one of us relives the main elements that constitute these myths through his or her own experience. These mythical elements, as I shall later show, come to life most vividly through the process of group analysis. However, before entering the realm of the group, I will recount the process that led me to look for the integration of the ideas presented by Bion and Klein, with those of some other theoreticians.

Only after being preoccupied with these three myths for a long time have I realised that they each involve one of the basic senses through which a baby communicates with the world surrounding it. The fact that these specific myths were singled out by Bion to represent human culture becomes even more meaningful once we discover their sensual elements, that parallel human development.

A baby's first connection with the world is an oral one: it first uses the senses situated in the mouth; thus also the myth of the Tree of Knowledge is connected with tasting, the sensual experience that occurs through the mouth. The Tower of Babel is associated with the mixture of sounds; it is an experience of assault on the sense of hearing, an assault that causes chaos. Hearing is the second sense that develops in the first month of life. Anzieu calls the normal connection of the baby to the world of sounds surrounding it "the Sound Envelope" (1989). Finally, in the story of Oedipus we find the assault on the sense of sight. Chronologically, the sense of sight is the last of these three to be developed.

One might argue that the development of culture parallels the development of the baby. In each one of these myths there is a crucial narrative development that occurs through sensual experience. The recording of these experiences in some of the major myths of human culture points to the vital importance of these experiences in the development of culture as a whole, as well as in the development of the individual.

It is interesting to place this in the context of the work of Elias Canetti, whose three volumes of autobiography, portraying his early life, are chronologically arranged. The first volume, portraying his early childhood, is called *The Tongue Set Free* (1979), the second is *The Torch in My Ear* (1982), while the third is titled *The Play of the Eyes* (1986). The titles symbolise an eventful biography, in which meaningful occurrences and changes take place through acute sensual experiences, and their sequence reflects the same pattern of development mentioned above. During my practice with group analysis, I have found that many childhood memories that surface in the group are connected with concrete sensual memories, which have left a distinct mark on the person involved.

Sandler (1960) has discussed the "Background of safety" in the life of the baby. This is the normal condition, in which the baby learns how to perform perceptual actions, and so organise for itself the amorphous sensual material that engulfs it. The baby is thus protected from the danger of being traumatically overwhelmed. But the baby that comes under an overflow of stimulation, or under stimulation of extreme intensity, cannot organise the inflow and will try to defend itself against being overwhelmed. Every time the senses come under an assault that is too severe to tolerate, the baby will withdraw into numbness, and in the worst cases, into a psychosis. Generally speaking, a deficiency in the "background of safety" can be imagined as a state in which the muscular tone is continuously tensed, even during rest.

In the psychoanalytical literature it is often argued that concrete sensual memories exist that cannot be transformed into dreams or thoughts, because they are connected to an unbearable fear, for example. These memories are therefore stored away in their unchanged form. Gampel argues that through an incidental sensual experience that occurs at a certain moment in the life of the adult, the memory returns and is lived again, as if a sealed drawer has been opened. Gampel calls such memory "the concrete metaphor of horror" (1999). And indeed, the experience of horror occurs also in the three myths that I have mentioned above.

In order to integrate the work of the different theoreticians I have mentioned so far, it is necessary to offer two hypotheses that should be studied and checked further in the context of group analysis.

First hypothesis

Just as the myths of culture evolve out of sensual occurrences that develop into metaphorical and symbolic occurrences in the life of humanity, the individual's life story is also transformed through an intense sensual experience that attacks the senses, creates horror, and bores a hole in the protective mental envelope. Such a hole may be likened to the crack that became the gate through which Adam and Eve left their protective and harmonious paradise.

When a child endures a strong sensual experience, which is bound to influence the child's development, a turning-point takes place. This experience can lead to a response of contraction and the retreat behind a protective shell, or to a breakthrough and a discovery of new worlds.

Second hypothesis

Anzieu's terminology concerning the "psychic envelope" leads me to form the second hypothesis. The psychic envelope enables the baby to feel internal responses to touch, sound, smell, and light in such a way that makes him feel protected and taken care of. The absence of this enveloping function creates anxiety and a sense of disintegration.

My assumption is that when a hole is bored into the psychic envelope, the experience of such a hole will resurface through some occurrence in the group that will cause the person to relive the old experience. When a participant is exposed to an experience that causes horror, he or she may grow a hard shell to cover and hide the vulnerable and alarming spot. This shell is expressed through the role this person then assumes in the group. Once individuals assume a role within the group, they lose their flexibility and contact with their true needs. They actually provide for some of the group's needs. They unconsciously hide themselves from what might be a new assault on the weak and frightened parts of the self.

In order to verify these hypotheses I shall return to the myths as recorded in our mutual cultural history. For each of the three myths I shall describe a case that contains an element that points to a parallel between the history of culture and the history of the individual. Each private story includes elements that have sunk deep within the psyche and are now forgotten, and the individual's ability to relive them is made possible only through the processes opened up by the group.

The eating of the fruit of the Tree of Knowledge

Life in Paradise revolved around the prohibition dictated by the authority of the omniscient God who decreed: "As for the tree of knowledge of good and bad, you must not eat of it" (*Genesis*, 2:17). But in the very act of drawing Adam's and Eve's attention to the existence of such a tree, the temptation was introduced. The phrase "must not eat" implies the possibility of eating.

Fromm (1966) argues that this act of defying authority marks the starting-point of human history. According to Fromm, this first act of disobedience is the beginning of human history, because it is the beginning of human freedom. In psychoanalytic terms, it is the beginning of individuation.

This act of disobedience was, in fact, predictable, since, according to Fromm, a fundamental contradiction is inherent in the *Book of Genesis*; God is an absolute ruler, but He has created a creature in His own image, who becomes His own potential rival. God is depicted here as if He were envious of man for his daring, and feeling threatened by him, reacted by banishing him.

One might say that this complicated relationship towards authority lies at the basis of human culture. The omniscient authority is threatened by the human capabilities to break and erase the clearly defined borders between the holder of all knowledge and the ignorant. Fromm argues that the exile from Paradise, just as the exit from the womb, means being transferred from a whole, harmonious world into a world of disharmony and tensions. And, indeed, here is a man who shapes his own destiny. From this moment on he must give up the harmonious existence of Paradise. With his acquisition of knowledge, man is expelled from Paradise. This knowledge brings with it painful disillusionment, but at the same time it brings about the possibility of growth. New life can only evolve through pain, and therefore "in pain shall you bear children" (*Genesis*, 3:16). Growth occurs through the knowledge that resources are not given for free, and therefore "by the sweat of your brow shall you get bread to eat" (*Genesis*, 3:19). Man must fight for his existence and accept responsibility for his life and the life of his family.

Man is expelled into a world of pain, suffering, need, and death, but had he not encountered these elements, he could not have grown and developed. The phrase "fool's paradise" reflects the state of living under the illusion of harmony and refers to people who refuse to view reality's limitations and to be introspective and discover their own weaknesses and mistakes. Such people, having chosen not to eat the fruit of the Tree of Knowledge, live in ignorance that blocks their growth. In fact, they are living in a fictitious world, in a bubble that might burst at any minute.

In a group session one participant, who was born and raised in a kibbutz, shared the following childhood memory. At the time when she was in kindergarten she was once fascinated by the beautiful growth of red chilli pepper bushes growing next to the children's house. The red chilli peppers were a delight to the eyes and so she picked a few and put them in her mouth. They were extremely hot and brought tears to her eyes. She tried to wipe her eyes with her fingers but that only caused the pain to spread to the eyes as well. The children's house garden, that familiar and safe place, suddenly became alien, threatening, and painful.

This childhood memory was recounted to the group in the context of exposing this woman's roles in life and her place within the group. It turned out that she was feeling lonely in the group just as she had felt that day next to the chilli pepper bush. She experienced her isolation in the group—on the metaphorical level—as an assault on her senses.

All this brings to mind a question that often preoccupies people in the mental health profession, and that is as often avoided and left unanswered: how did the group process cause the emergence of such material? And what is the "added value" of the group therapy experience when compared with the individual one.

Some important answers are given by Foulkes and Anthony (1957, p. 83):

> The group analytic situation brings to light unconscious meaning, unconscious motivation, and interpersonal reactions which are unknown. During this work of discovery, the patient experiences and understands in a way that touches deep emotional feelings and not merely his intellect . . . The group analytic process releases a host of factors which operate to increase the patient's insight and forms a sort of training ground where his relationships with other people can be tested.

It should be pointed out that within the "here and now" of the group there lies a hidden wisdom. It contains a kind of emotional pressure that makes the reconstruction of early experiences possible. It is not sufficient to know about something; the group process acts on the level of experiential knowledge, and it resurrects long-forgotten experiences. When this woman felt that she had been abandoned by the group or was under its assault, it was our task as group analysts to explore into what caused her to feel this way. With what picture in her internal, private repertoire did the "here and now" feeling of loneliness cross? What was it in her own world that caused her to experience the group in such a way?

We must consider the "here and now" as a concrete metaphor of the life outside the group. An entire world might be represented in a single moment of the group's life. The estrangement and loneliness that the woman felt within the well-known group revived the estrangement she experiences in her life outside the group. Our ability to treat her feelings with respect and explore here and now the development of the estrangement and alienation, will lead us to the childhood memory that is a concretisation of a metaphor as well. From the childhood memory we then return to the group, and from there to the woman's life outside it, and thus the full circle of exploration is completed.

In order for such an exploration to take place, the willingness to partake of the hot chilli peppers of the personal Tree of Knowledge must exist. All human beings have their own personal version of that tree. Tasting its fruit is a painful experience of disillusionment and of coming of age.

In the case of this participant, it was this experience that led her to realise that the role of an omnipotent woman who needs no one else in her life is a role that creates loneliness. It also functions to conceal her needs and her vulnerability that live in dread of an assault. This role was recreated in the group; it is the shell of the little girl who stood bewildered under an unexpected assault.

The recreation of a role such as this makes the step onto a new road possible. It is a less safe road, but one that leads to a new life.

The Tower of Babel

"Come, let us build us a city, and a tower with its top in the sky" (*Genesis*, 11:4). The tower they intend to build will penetrate the heavens, trespassing God's kingdom. The tower is a phallic symbol, representing an infinite size. This myth reveals the wish to acquire limitless knowledge. The attempt to rival God by attaining His level of knowledge brings about punishment. The group is punished with the loss of coherence and with confusion. The people, initially united as a group, were scattered over the face of the whole earth. They had had a common language but their speech became confused, and they thus lost the ability to communicate with each other.

Here, just as in the story of the Garden of Eden, curiosity and the desire for knowledge go hand in hand with punishment. In the story of Babel the punishment is delivered in the form of confusion, fragmentation, and eventually alienation. Man will never attain the status of an omnipotent and omniscient being. The structure of the myth, which concludes with painful separation and punishment, indicates again that the inquisitive human soul faces a perilous path, and that the desire for knowledge both evokes and is contradicted by the fear of knowledge.

This deep-rooted human fear of knowledge manifests itself in the way that the creators of the myths saw fit to punish man for his curiosity and his desire to challenge God. In every human being there exists that hidden part that wishes not to know, not to be enlightened, not to see.

The people of Babel, due to their ambitious and pretentious enterprise, were punished by collapse. They leave the story in a worse condition than when they entered it. This mythical construction leads us back to the paradox we discovered in the story of the Garden of Eden, namely that in order for there to be a growth, something must break down; for the sake of advancement there must be a retreat, back to zero if need be. In the retreat there is also strength, not just weakness. The story of Babel indicates that in order to build, there is a need to dismantle the original wrongly built structure. The destruction of the flawed structure leads to the rediscovery of the primary molecules that facilitate a remodelling, since without the dismantling of the existing structure there would be no void that would enable new construction to take place.

Once again, as in the story of the Garden of Eden, the punishment that causes the lowering of human status is, paradoxically, an incentive for growth. In place of the stifling uniformity that they desired, human beings are delivered into differentiation and individuation. The scattering all over the face of the earth is an opportunity to acquire variety and enrich themselves instead of sticking to the tower that represents one-dimensional existence, rigidity, and absorption in the anonymous collectivity.

Through the following case of a participant in a group we shall now be able to look into the second sensual manifestation—the sound envelope.

This woman is pretty and elegant, has a pair of beautiful, very expressive eyes, but her mouth is tightly clenched. In the group she speaks intelligently, but her tone is even and neutral. Every time she concludes what she has to say it seems that her words are leading nowhere, and they are largely ignored. The feeling is that when she speaks, she says much, but one cannot really absorb what she says. She says general and non-personal things out of which nothing new can grow. The group does not enter a dialogue with her; once she stops talking there is a short silence and then someone raises a different issue.

In contrast to her dry tone of speech, her eyes are full of expression, whenever she speaks and nobody responds, her eyes reveal pain and distress. It seems as if she is the prisoner of her own words.

On one occasion, when we were dealing with roles outside and inside the group, she relived and shared a childhood memory in which a severe assault on the sound envelope had occurred:

> I am about two-and-half years old, sitting in my crib which had an iron railing. It is during war-time and suddenly a very noisy alarm goes off. The family lives on the fifth floor and everyone has to go down to the shelter. When my mother comes to pick me up and carry me down to the shelter I stand up and hang onto the crib's railing with both hands. My fingers tighten around the bars and my hands cannot be prised loose. I don't utter a scream or any other sound. I am terrified. Mother tries forcefully to loosen my hands from the railing, but it is difficult and takes a long time. Mother is angry with me.

This story has been retold over and over to me many times throughout the years. The connotation was always "You were a bad girl, you put the whole family in danger".

The well-known, everyday sounds enveloping the girl's world were suddenly changed into a hair-raising alarm that brought terror and shock and caused the acute contraction of the muscles in the hands.

Contrasted with the words she had been using until then, which affected the group like a kind of sedative, this memory was so sharp that it pierced the group's atmosphere like an unexpected alarm. It seems that the utterance of even words, recited in a monotonous sequence, can have the same effect as the confused language of Babel: sounds with no meaning, sounds creating a shell that proclaims:

"don't touch me!", while all along an internal alarm is raging and shrieking, crying soundlessly: "hold me!"

This concrete sensual memory opens up an entire metaphorical world for exploration. With this example I wish to look further not into the state of the individual, but rather into that of the group. We must bear in mind that the individual holds an important aspect for all the members of the group. The group process sheds light not only on the life of the individual but on the trans-personal dimension as well. This is the dimension within which we find ourselves as members of the same culture.

When the participants in the group—as a group—became numb and were unable to listen, it did not reflect only the woman's difficulties in communicating. One can also find here the unwillingness of the group to make the effort required in order to listen and discern her pain. The group has an aspect that prefers to stay neutral, prefers not to touch. On the metaphorical level, the group also spreads out clenched hands that will not hug. On its unconscious level, the group manoeuvres the individual into a constant role because it needs a participant who will maintain the monotonic tone and put the group to sleep. This is required so that the participants will not have to listen to their own internal alarms and will not have to feel anxiety or pain.

The myth of Oedipus

The main events of the myth of Oedipus according to its best known version—the play *Oedipus the King* by Sophocles—are as follows.

Laius, king of Thebes, has learned through the oracle of Apollo that he is destined to be killed by his own son. Therefore, three days after the son is born, an attempt to divert the prophecy is made. Jocasta, the child's mother, hands the baby to a shepherd slave who is to abandon it on the Cithaeron Mountains.

King Laius has the baby pierced and pinned through the ankles, so that no one will wish to pick it up. The baby's legs swell, hence his name Oedipus ("swell-foot"). But the shepherd feels sorry for the baby, and, instead of abandoning it, gives it to another shepherd who serves the king of Corinth. That shepherd unties Oedipus' legs and brings him to his town, where he is adopted by King Polybus, who has no children of his own.

Oedipus is raised as a prince, but once, at a banquet, a drunken guest tells him he is not Polybus' son. Polybus and his wife Merope try to reassure him, but Oedipus goes to Delphi to find out the truth through Apollo's oracle. He does not receive a direct response to his inquiry about his origin, but is told that he is fated to kill his own father, sleep with his own mother, and have children by her. Still believing that Polybus and Merope are his real parents and that the accusation he heard at the banquet was motivated by envy, Oedipus decides not to return to Corinth. He believes that by keeping a distance between himself and his parents he can avert fate.

At the same time, King Laius is travelling incognito from Thebes to Delphi, and Oedipus meets him at a place where three roads meet. A quarrel starts and Oedipus kills Laius and his attendants, not realising, of course, that he has killed the king of Thebes who is his own father. Only one person escapes the fight: Laius' servant, the shepherd who was ordered to abandon Oedipus on the Cithaeron Mountains, returns to the town and announces that the king was killed by highwaymen.

Meanwhile, the Sphinx oppresses Thebes and devours all the young men who fail to answer her riddle. Only Oedipus succeeds where all others have failed; the Sphinx dies and the city is saved. Oedipus' reward is the throne of Thebes as well as the queen, and thus he unknowingly sleeps with his own mother who bears him two daughters and two sons.

Following a peaceful period, a devastating plague strikes the city. Oedipus sends his wife's brother Creon to Delphi and the oracle replies that in order to stop the plague, Laius' killer must be found, and then executed or exiled. Oedipus decides to find the killer by any means. The only person who knows the truth is the blind prophet Tiresias, who has guessed the killer's identity but will not reveal it. Paradoxically, the blind man is the only person in town who can see clearly.

But Oedipus, after pronouncing a curse on the unknown killer, does not rest, and stubbornly pursues the investigation in his effort to expose the killer who defiles the town.

Gradually, Oedipus is filled with anxiety, sensing that it may be that he was the killer, and that the murdered person was his own father. Eventually, Oedipus calls for the old shepherd, and in a long investigative scene the terrible truth—that Oedipus was the son of

Laius and Jocasta—is exposed. Jocasta takes her own life, while Oedipus blinds himself and goes into exile.

In the story of Oedipus we again find the motif of a human being who believes he can challenge the divine. Oedipus sinned—just as the protagonists of the former myths have sinned—by trying to avoid his fate and thereby knowingly challenging divine knowledge and power. He, too, thought that he could evade the all-seeing eyes of the gods, and, like Adam in the Garden of Eden, leads himself into the trap. Among the Greeks this sin was known as "hubris", namely the sin of pride and arrogance of a human being who challenges the gods and believes he can defeat their schemes.

Throughout his dramatic life story, Oedipus commits grave misdeeds without realising the meaning of his actions, and thus lives in a fool's paradise. He has everything he could wish for: wife and children, kingdom, wealth, and respect, but in fact he has nothing at all. The catastrophes befall him one after the other, but he has no idea of their cause, living in blindness, unaware.

However, the very moment a doubt is raised, a crack is opened into the unknown. Oedipus becomes the paragon of inquisitiveness. He will not give up in his effort to uncover the truth. Now he symbolises the victory of curiosity over fear. His quest for knowledge continues through anxiety, pain, and suffering.

The more he enquires, the weaker and more vulnerable and exposed he becomes. But he will not give up his right to know the truth, and he will not allow it to be disfigured. While becoming weaker, he gains strength. Through his inquisitive and creative stance towards reality, Oedipus becomes increasingly the master of his own fate.

The myth of Oedipus brings us face to face with the necessity of accepting our limitations and feebleness as human beings as well. We can never control all the consequences of our lives.

The human being will always be a complex creature, torn between knowledge and ignorance. According to the myths, only God is omniscient. In all three myths the divine power is depicted as hostile to humanity's search for knowledge; the excess of inquisitiveness is considered sinful and the attempt to know too much ends with punishment. Human beings must accept their limitations.

As Oedipus' catastrophe unfolds, the chorus sings: "O the generations of men, the dying generations—adding the total of all lives I find they come to nothing ... You are my great example, you, your life, your destiny, Oedipus, man of misery ..." (Sophocles, 1982).

However, we must remember again the great paradox: the recognition of our limitations grants us power; disharmony, pain, and disaster may also be the inception of growth, and that in two ways:

a) The blind Tiresias can see, and Oedipus, in order to see, blinds himself. When Oedipus is blinded he turns his gaze inwards and for the first time can see for himself what he did and how he sinned. Until then, the external events have blinded him, and when he stopped looking at the distorted reality and looked inside himself he could see correctly. Previously hidden worlds were now exposed to him as he gained insight. This experience is parallel to what Bion describes when he speaks of "becoming zero" or when he speaks of the need for finding "a ray of darkness in the light".

b) Oedipus learns of the possibility of feeling guilty and is thus able to accept responsibility and save the town from the plague. As therapists, we know that the ability to feel guilt is a high level of development that contributes to the maturing of the self. Only when Oedipus realises his guilt and accepts his responsibility is he able to do right. Oedipus is an example of the hero who courageously faces the naked truth.

To sum up the oedipal drama, we can say that the story of Oedipus will forever remain ambiguous. It is a story that simultaneously contains blindness and the ability to see. Human beings will never be able to see and know everything, and Oedipus is a paradigm for all human beings and their mental disability.

We have experienced taste and sound, now we will follow Oedipus to the light. This can be illustrated by clinical data.

A participant in the group, a man who had an impressive academic career, caused conflicting feelings among the other participants. Some aspects of his behaviour were exasperating while others were endearing. Especially offensive to the group was his intellectual and rational side: for any dilemma that was raised in the group, he supplied an instant rational solution. In spite of his high intellectual ability he analysed emotional events that were told in the group in a simplistically trite way. And he would give advice that no one found of use.

We discovered that this was all caused by this man's inability to tolerate any open question that might leave somebody in a state of uncertainty. His lifestyle indicated conformity with the establishment, an adamant defence of stability and an aversion to any revolutionary act. As such, he contributed greatly to different establishments and to the preservation of the existing order.

But on the other hand, when he was not required to accomplish a task, he was found to be creative, intuitive, and humorous, and to possess freedom of thought, all of which were obscured when he was called on to perform a task. These two parts—the creative and mischievous person on the one hand and the rational lecturer on the other—were leading separate lives. Only when he was "off duty" could he let his feelings and creativity surface. But the tasks, the roles he had to fill, were placing a grave burden on him. He described himself as a person who was looking for something he had lost, but who did not know what was it that had been lost.

His searching, creativity, wisdom, and willingness to help both individuals and the group as a whole led some people to grow fond of him and to wish to pull him out of his well-structured shell of rationalism and predictability.

A childhood memory he brought to the group shed a new light on much of his behaviour and helped us see it from a different perspective. In this memory he was a kindergarten child. His family imposed some very strict rules on their children, one of which was that a child must be in bed by 8 p.m. and must never get out of bed after that hour.

I lay in my bed. The time was after 8 p.m. It was during the Feast of Tabernacles. Suddenly I felt as if my parents had left home and I was filled with fear. I knew I must not get out of bed, but nevertheless I went to check where my parents were. I walked quietly from one room to the next until I finally located them, sitting inside the Tabernacle, under the light of a lamp. I ran back to bed but could not fall asleep, thinking of the punishment I was certain to receive. I actually didn't know whether my parents had seen me or not. Only years later, when I studied the laws of physics, did I gather that one can see from darkness into light but not the other way around. Therefore, my parents could not have seen me that night.

The question whether he was seen or not had bothered him for many years. He was greatly disturbed by the ambiguity. In the group he was always struggling to prevent the ambiguity that he could not tolerate. In his professional life he is occupied mainly with research and the cataloguing of knowledge. Metaphorically speaking, the dark rooms in his childhood memory represent the unconscious part of which he was afraid. When he is lecturing or explaining something he feels he is in control and that he is expanding the illuminated areas. But this is a fictitious light that obscures the sight of the darkness and of the dim parts. In the group he took upon himself the role of preventing himself as well as the group from remaining in the sphere of the unconscious.

His behaviour inside the group as well as out of it recreates his childhood memory, where he was attracted by the light but also frightened by it. The light inside the tabernacle became the symbol of a search, but at the same time, of the fear of seeing his parents in intimacy, lest some life-riddles that he was too afraid to explore might be revealed to him.

Once he told us: "I am like a moth which is attracted to a source of light not knowing whether the light will warm it or burn it." When he said that, he was unaware that he was talking of the small, frightened child in the darkness, the child who, seeing his parents sitting together with the light shining upon them, wishes to come closer, but retreats, because he is afraid he will be punished.

This story includes, although in a sublimated version, the story of Oedipus who is inquisitive and is punished for it.

On a metaphorical level, the story includes the eternal conflict of therapeutic work: how far should we strive to reach the light and to what extent should we avoid it. The fear of being punished sometimes causes things to remain in the dark. At the same time, if the self allows itself to stay in the dark without feeling guilty, new insights will begin to spring out of the unconscious.

Conclusion

Every person has his or her way of reliving the fate of human history, and every group has its own way of reliving the fate of history of the individuals of whom it is combined. The collective and personal histories re-emerge time and again within the group in innumerable ways. This is the wisdom of the group process, and that is the strength of the group.

The group operates in trans-personal dimensions. If we, together with the group, allow ourselves to lose our way, we will be able to come in contact with worlds that cannot be re-experienced or understood outside the potential space of the group. Through this space we may return to ancient places and at the same time study the possibility of re-emerging into the world, this time through a different door, one door out of the many doors that will remain unknown forever.

CHAPTER EIGHT

Bion's links: how they are manifested in the Foulkesian matrix

Introduction

B ion defines three types of basic links, and designates them: *K* for the link of Knowledge and the desire to know; *L* for the link of Love; and *H* for the link of Hate. Much has been written about K function, and the link it designates is considered complex, challenging, and more highly developed than love and hate. In this chapter I will focus mainly on love and hate.

It seems to me that one challenging question is that of deciphering the plus and minus signs assigned to the links. What is meant by Love plus (+L)? And Love minus (–L)? What is Hate with a plus sign (+H), and when shall we give Hate a minus sign (–H)? These are issues Bion does not clarify. He keeps his thoughts on an abstract level, invites the reader to go on thinking, and leaves a great deal of room for interpretation and elaboration.

What is the meaning of the term *link*? It first appeared in *Learning From Experience* (Bion 1962a, p. 42). We can say that, according to Bion, the link is the space where an emotional experience occurs. Such an experience is only possible within a relationship. The link is the space in which the meeting of two entities causes something new to be born.

These two entities can be two ideas, or two people, or a person and a group, or two sub-groups.

When Bion first wrote about links, he said that he chose to include all the different types of links under three categories: L, H, and K, because these comprise all existing possibilities. They include envy and gratitude, depression and guilt, anxiety, and sexuality.

Later (1963a, p. 13) Bion added passion, which he defined as "an emotion experienced with intensity and warmth though without any suggestion of violence".

Bion also used these links in his study of cultural myths (Bion & Bion, 1992), and he found them interwoven into the central myths that interested him, which were: eating from the Tree of Knowledge, the Tower of Babylon, the myth of Narcissus, and Oedipus the King. Bion claimed that these four myths represented civilisation, and that they were re-enacted in countless variations in every person's life.

The myth of the Tower of Babylon introduces the dynamic of the group, which oscillates between the desire for unity and cohesion and the desire to disperse, differentiate, and create variety. These two poles, or extremes, exist in every group. The tall and unified building is a claustrophobic symbol, while the mixture of languages and the scattering of the group in all directions are agoraphobic symbols. This tension is imminent in the life of every group.

It is interesting to note that the myths of the Tree of Knowledge, Narcissus, and Oedipus are all connected to love and sexuality. The myth of the Tower of Babylon stands out as different from the rest. I believe that the difference lies in the fact that in this story the group is the focus of attention, the hero of the story, and that there is no single, prominent, identifiable leading character.

It appears to me that the group is not a natural breeding ground for love. In a group, the group member is not an only child. Neither is he one of a couple. In the group, members face the limitations of love. They receive partial empathy. Part of the empathy is given to another member of the group, sometimes to a rival.

A group working together for a long time acts according to the reality principle, forcing its members to face life's limitations. Even if the group has some stars among its members, their light dims with time. The group phantasies are constantly in conflict with the life of the group, which is mundane and sometimes dull. Narcissistic injury constantly repeats itself in the group.

Members of the group can love and be loved in the group; however, this experience is fragile and never total. The ancient myth concerned with the group speaks of breakdown. It contains the tension between assembling and dismantling. This is why the group is a fascinating place to study the tension between love in the plus sign and love in the minus sign.

I have chosen to interpret the minus signs of both love and hate as signifying various states of non-living, of absence of libido. These are states of stagnation or sterility in relationships. The minus sign indicates emotional coldness, absence of passion, absence of growth. Perversion is a good example of –L. In perversion, the subject becomes an object for use. Obsessive love is an example of –L. It is a love that leaves no link, and is destructive both to the lover and to the beloved. Minus L is found in any space between two that does not create something new. It is not fertile and does not generate growth. Due to elements of exploitation, obsession, sadism, or parasitism, –L always involves an injured party, or both parties destroying each other. Minus L claims victims, and therefore is destructive.

It is important to recognise when hate is +H. It seems that +H means hatred towards negative and destructive people and states that are indeed hateful. Winnicott (1949) writes about objective hate. Even parents can feel understandable hate towards the intolerable behaviour of their child. In other words, hatred towards something bad, which is expressed and released directly, can bring about change and growth in stagnant or destructive situations. Many different emotions belonging to the Hate cluster can be a constructive force. Expressing direct anger, rising up against injustice, criticising corruption, attacking a person abusing a child—all of these are expressions of hatred containing passion. Hating with passion is a link that can repair and engender life.

Minus H is concealed hatred, which builds up throughout the years. It is a hatred mixed with bitterness, envy, and resentment. This kind of hate sucks and drains away life, and does not lead to growth. There is no passion in –H. Minus H can be found in the individual; for instance, a person who feels unfulfilled and feels growing resentment and envy towards someone who seems to be self-fulfilled. This person is bitter and sour. Minus H can appear in the group, directed at the scapegoat. Minus H appears in the inter-group space as a hidden and denied racism.

Minus H occurs between nations. It is painful, indeed unbearable, to watch documentary films of Hungarian Jews marching in masses down a busy central street, arms raised, at the end of 1944. Eight hundred thousand Jews were cremated in Auschwitz in three months. This happened when the Nazis were already weak, when they could have easily been overthrown. The Hungarian public remained silent. The Jews were led away while the Hungarians turned a blind eye, and business went on as usual. This is the ultimate example of –H: passivity, turning a blind eye on a horrendous evil occurring on one's doorstep. A small uprising, the refusal to abandon the Jews, would have rescued them.

It seems that the closer we get to plus, in both hate and love, the stronger the life instinct. Whenever we move towards minus, in love as well as hate, the death instinct intensifies. A good example is Bion's (1967) "On arrogance". In it Bion shows that the arrogant person with a cynical attitude does not generate life, and in fact is dominated by the death instinct. By contrast, the person with self-esteem has no need for arrogance, and maintains a fruitful link with the world around him.

We can say that the creation of fertile links in the analytic group will promote the growth of its members. At the opposite pole to linking and creativity, Bion (1967) identifies the reverse phenomenon, which he calls *attacks on linking*. In this state, there are no links. The members of the group will feel detached, indifferent, and lose the capacity for metaphoric and symbolic thought.

It seems to me that the attacks on linking increase in states of uncontained anxiety. This is unavoidable in the life of the group. The process should be seen as a spiral. The links achieved are sometimes attacked, but then regained in a different manner and with new meaning. Reassembly does not always follow an attack. In the clinical examples, I will try to consider states of growth, but also states in which the group fails to help a member of the group create new links.

In this respect it is important to mention the difference between psychological catastrophe and catastrophic change. Bion defines catastrophic change as a change that seems to be catastrophic, but leads to new growth and development. This development would have been impossible without the catastrophic change. In other words, it is a crisis that engenders something new. Sometimes the present state of things must be rocked and shaken up for growth to occur.

The myth of the Tower of Babylon illustrates this idea. It became necessary to destroy the unified and limited tower in order to expose the variety, the wealth of languages, and the diversity of cultures. What at first seemed to be calamitous and disastrous was in fact growth-enhancing.

In the lives of the group members as well, changes, which at first seem catastrophic, can, in time, be growth-enhancing. Many changes in a person's life are experienced as a catastrophe: disease, immigration, divorce, losing a job; yet sometimes these crises generate growth.

Billow (2002) argues that the human experience is one of aloneness. Every person experiences aloneness, which means being alone in a positive way. This is solitude and not loneliness, and has to do with the ability to live and to enjoy a rich inner life. Yet although the experience of aloneness can be pleasant, it can, in a person's dynamic life, move towards the experience of emptiness and loneliness. Hence, human beings are creatures who require both their individual space and a social space. There is a longing to live among other people in order to feel emotional vitality and to be filled through interactions with other human beings.

The analytic group is the place where the internal conflict between individuation and the need to belong is most strongly manifested. The individual has the need to be part of the group, while at the same time to be him- or herself.

This is a complex situation. The pull to be with people, to give and to receive, arouses tensions originating in the unconscious. These tensions in turn arouse painful and anxious emotions once they reach consciousness. Being in a group with other people for a long time reveals to the group member that he is not always nice and pleasant. The group excites hidden emotions such as neediness, aggression, envy, sexuality, competitiveness, and hate.

Billow claims that there is no such thing as a group that only excites experiences of love, joy, sympathy, and empathy. These relations, if studied authentically and without falseness, always retain an ambiguity and a sense of tension and danger. For example, the need to love often appears alongside the fear of abandonment, so that within a group, it is hard for love to blossom free of fears and inhibitions. When anxiety is aroused, self-esteem sustains a blow, the attempt to be a good and benevolent person fails, and development is arrested. It is impossible to grow without undergoing these painful experiences.

While Bion was developing his work on links, Foulkes developed the concept of the group matrix. Pines and colleagues (1968) review Foulkes' work, showing that the basic concepts of his theory are surprisingly similar to those of Bion. The matrix, which includes the notions of the *nodal point*, the *mirror reaction*, and *resonance*, is based on principles closely resembling Bion's thoughts on linking. Foulkes' basic assumption is that human beings are primarily social creatures. The group precedes the individual, because the individual is born into the group. Foulkes believes that the infant is born into a network of communication, which determines his identity from the start. According to him, the group is the basic psychological unit. A person in isolation is like a fish out of water.

If we try to integrate Foulkes' and Bion's thinking, we find that Foulkes' network of communication is indeed made up of links. The matrix develops gradually, and enables us to map the patient's difficulties as they become re-enacted in the context of the group. The relationships formed by the patient with his family and social environment are repeated in the communication created by the group. The patient brings his symptom to the group. The symptom is an expression of a conflict that has not been expressed emotionally in words. The group process enables a shift from symptomatic expression to verbal and emotional expression. We can say that the development of communication between the members of the group is identical to the therapeutic process. The opening, closing, and attacking of links are the dynamics that create a matrix. It is within this dynamic that changes in the ability to understand and to be understood, and to contain material arising from the unconscious, take place.

Foulkes, was interested in changes and how they come about. He wrote (1971) that the purpose of group therapy is to lead to insight and adjustment. By using the term adjustment he emphasised internal psychological change and rebuilding the inner world. Adjustment, according to Foulkes, is not submission to authority or compliance with group norms, but rather a matter of self-discovery through the processes of communication taking place in the group. In this Foulkes resembles Bion. However, unlike Bion, Foulkes does not emphasise the pain entailed in growth, at least not in his theoretical work. He does concentrate on traumatogenic processes in his clinical work. Nor does he focus on psychotic anxieties. Nor does he stress the disintegration that precedes integration. Foulkes focuses on linkings rather than attacks on it.

Foulkes had a deep faith in the healing power of the group, and for this reason he appears to be more optimistic than Bion. Nonetheless, both of them stress the mutual dependency that is so important for the creation of links and for creating a working group. Bion believed that the group culture is often disturbed by the hidden group mentality. By contrast, Foulkes (1975a, p. 96) believed in the healing power of the group culture:

> The knowledge that each group member is interdependent with the others sets the group on a very reasonable level of tolerance in these matters. Confidence in the group, mutual respect and confidence in the conductor are naturally of the greatest importance for the whole procedure.

One could say that both Bion and Foulkes lay emphasis on the interpersonal space and on the unconscious processes taking place in this space. If we consider Foulkes in Bionian terms, we can say that Foulkes believes more in +L and +H, and seldom analyses –L and –H.

We can look at Bion's links and Foulkes' matrix as seeds of the intersubjective theories that have been developed later, especially as understood in France by Kaes. Kaes' ideas resonate with Foulkes and Bion since they emphasise the unconscious levels that exit within the relationship among persons. "Each subject is separately governed by an unconscious process" Levin (2008, p. 264).

"The French model prevents the concept from becoming saturated, keeping it open for thinking the negative, absence, and alienation as fundamental unconscious relationships" (p. 266).

This perception corresponds with the concepts of Scharff & Scharff: "The self is a dynamic organization of purposes and commitments whose behavior is governed by conscious and unconscious motives, and whose developments and functioning are inseparably linked to the social environment" (2005, p. 21).

Clinical examples

A shift from –H and –L to +H and +L

I will now present vignettes from two consecutive group sessions.

Yehuda, fifty-four, was abused as a child. His father would beat him brutally for no reason. He has memories from the age of six or seven of his father's outbursts of blind rage. He remembers terrible beatings, and his mother passively present and turning a blind eye. His mother never defended him or tried to stop his father.

In the group, Yehuda talks about feelings of neglect, humiliation, and rejection. These feelings continue to overwhelm him. If I do not address him and his feelings in the right way or at the right moment he desires, he feels once again like a humiliated and abandoned child.

In this meeting, both David and Israel told Yehuda he meant a lot to them. Each of them expressed affection towards him in different ways. David told Yehuda that he was the most significant person in the group to him. Because he too was an abused child, he feels that Yehuda holds the key to his own problem.

In response to these expressions of affection, Yehuda froze. His body language became tense and rigid. He ignored the comments directed at him.

> *Therapist*: What's happening to you? What do you feel when people in the group tell you that you mean so much to them?

> *Yehuda*: I'm not interested. It's a burden. I can't be the centre. I can't stand it when people expect something from me.

> *T*: Your body language showed you were scared. You were offered affection, and affection does not necessarily entail expectations. It can be affection for the sake of affection. Maybe it's hard for you to let go of the child who runs away and hides, who doesn't want to be seen.

> *Israel*: I hate seeing you like this. I do feel you are signalling a sort of closeness to me.

> *Na'ama*: You show so much understanding towards the things other people in the group say.

> *David*: To me you convey coldness. But I still feel that inside you are warm.

> *T*: Maybe what scares you is the closeness, the intimacy. What will you do if that happens?

> *Y*: I think that's true. In the group, I discover that emotional closeness and intimacy scare me. If I go on with my associations, I think intimacy entails terrible disappointment, and that's very dangerous. In fact, it is a mortal danger. To expect something from someone and to be disappointed.

That's mortal danger for me. Mortal danger. I'm afraid of treachery, of being abandoned. I can't believe or trust.

T: It works the other way around, too. You're afraid to disappoint when someone trusts you.

I: So how is it that you've been married to the same woman for twenty-something years?

Y: With my wife it's not so dangerous anymore, but even to her I don't give myself completely.

T: You said "mortal danger" three times. When you were a child, you were helpless and terrified when facing your father. Mother betrayed you, she didn't defend you. It was like a psychological death. You were little, and unprotected.

Y: You're touching my worst memories. Sometimes I ask myself, why didn't I rebel? I remember that once I ran away and he ran after me and caught me and beat me so hard, I never ran away again. [Yehuda turns to Israel] So if you say you like me, it's scary. It's dangerous for me.

T: Because injury will follow?

Y: For sure. Absolutely no doubt. I'll either be hurt, or else I'll hurt others. Best not to start the cycle. Never expect anything. Never fantasise. This goddamn kid keeps popping up. He's my prison guard.

N: Were you ever violent?

Y: Yes. I beat my son. It was tragic for me. Horrible. The end of the world. But this time I had help, my wife watched over me. She understood, and kept watch. My son doesn't remember it as something so terrible. After my wife helped me, I managed to watch over myself. Later, I got close to my son. I talked to him about what happened and I felt relieved. But even today, I don't trust myself completely. I'm afraid I might have an uncontrollable outburst.

D: Yehuda, I've got to tell you something. You broke the chain of violence. You should be the proudest person in the world. What you did is huge. Huge.

Yehuda sits quietly, looking embarrassed, blushing. The group is silent.

Vignettes from the following session:

Shimon: I used to stutter until I was nineteen. I was terribly ashamed. I went to a doctor and he told me, you leave this room right now and start stuttering everywhere. Talk and stutter. Fail, and fall, and keep going. Don't stop talking, and do it everywhere. I did exactly what he told me, and slowly, the stuttering went away. I stuttered, and was ashamed. I remembered the doctor standing behind me and telling me, go out into the world and talk.

Yehuda: That's very moving. Nobody ever said anything like that to me. Nobody ever said, fail, and fall, and in the end you'll triumph.

T: The story of the doctor awakens a longing for a parent figure to lean on. One who tells the child, go out into the world standing up straight. Shimon received the doctor's blessing, but he also dared. Maybe you too, Yehuda, should take risks. Express emotions in real-time and see what happens to you.

Y [addresses me assertively]: Okay. So let me tell you something. Twice in the last session, you got mixed up and called me by a different name. I was terribly hurt. I felt like that neglected old kid, and I crumbled up and sat in the corner. Now I want to be angry with you. Why do you get confused and call me by a different name? If you care so much about me, why can't you remember my name?

The group was silent. I could hear my heart beating. I was taken by surprise, and now I was the one who was scared. I told myself I should speak truthfully.

T: When you rebuke me like that, I feel very bad but at the same time I'm happy to see you expressing your anger directly for the first time. That's a good question, why I called you by a different name. I don't want to cover it up. Maybe it has something to do with some unexplored feelings I have towards you. I've sometimes felt helpless with regard to you, especially when you asked again and again—"so what do we do now?" "What can I do?" Your repeated question restricted my thinking, and maybe forgetting your name was an expression of anger.

Y: Your answer makes me feel good. I feel good when you say what's going on inside you.

T: We can talk, too, the way you talked with your son. There was something on my part that wasn't holding. To forget your name is like injuring your identity. It's good that we can clear up anger and try to fix things.

Following this session, Yehuda felt he was becoming stronger. He was able to confront his boss at work. He stopped reacting fearfully and submissively to every authority figure. But in the midst of this movement, he began to regress.

The following is an excerpt from a session that took place two months later.

Na'ama always aroused the group's aggression. People in the group said she lacked tactfulness, was inattentive, talked too much, that her tone was monotonous, that she spoke unintelligently, and so on. Na'ama grew up on a kibbutz. Her parents were different and stood out in the kibbutz's social milieu. They were uneducated and had very marginal jobs on the kibbutz. Na'ama was strongly rejected by the kibbutz children. Her memories of feeling different and that she did not belong re-emerged now, when the group rejected her.

In this session, the group members once again attacked Na'ama, rejected her, and abused her. I always felt she was trapped in a childhood scene and did not know how to make the group like her. She became a scapegoat, and was used for discharging anger. She always drew fire and always behaved as if the attacks did not hurt her. But it was obvious she was suffering. Suddenly it occurred to me that whenever the group attacked Na'ama, Yehuda remained silent, his gaze distant and detached. He seemed indifferent, and he showed no emotion. I decided to address him and talk about his attitude.

> *Therapist*: Yehuda, you're sitting here in silence, indifferent to Na'ama's pain. In this way, you relive the role of your neglectful mother who ignored you. You return to the mother you hate. The indifferent mother who didn't try to stop your father's violence against you. Here and now, Na'ama is the abused child and you the passive mother.

Interpreting the silence as conveying a message from the unconscious shook the group. Yehuda began to move uncomfortably in his chair. He blushed and said that my interpretation touched him very deeply. He felt that something new had been broken through and opened up in him. Later in the session, the group came to the conclusion that in order to save himself, he would have to identify experientially with the humiliated child within him. He would have to get close to this child, to love him and accept him. Instead of identifying with the neglectful mother, he would have to resist her and save the child. His apathy towards Na'ama brought to light his apathy towards the abused child within him.

In the middle of the group discussion, Na'ama burst into tears for the first time. She said she suddenly understood that the rejected child in her wanted to be loved by her. She said she wanted to make up with this child and stop putting a frozen mask on its face. So far in the group, she never changed the expression on her face, always appearing like a statue. Her frozen and monotonous behaviour always provoked even more aggression. Weeping softened her, and for the first time, she received empathy from all the members of the group.

We all left this session deeply moved. It marked the beginning of loving the humiliated children inside—the children that made us feel ashamed, that made us want to run away from them, erase them and all the painful memories they held. The rejected and humiliated children in the inner world prevent the development of self-esteem and self-love. Na'ama and Yehuda held these scenes for the rest of the group members, each of whom had a rejected and hurt child within. This session broke through barriers and enabled us to do deeper work later on. Yehuda had a series of dreams, which he brought to the group almost every week. Na'ama gradually freed herself of the role of the scapegoat.

In describing this group process, I have tried to demonstrate the transformation from repressed hatred that settles like sediment over the years, to open hatred expressed as direct anger, which can dissolve hard, blocking elements. I have also tried to illustrate a process in which hatred is replaced by love through renewed contact with the rejected, shameful child inside, who we would rather run away from because he is a stain on our self-esteem. This child emerged in the group in need of compassion and a loving mother. The group process enabled such mothering to materialise.

So far I have addressed love and hate as the fundamental materials studied in the analytic group. I will now turn to variations on this theme. I will demonstrate transformations from a minus link to a plus link through changes in the emotional positions of the group members. I will also try to demonstrate situations in which such a transformation does not take place, leaving the group with minus-type links.

Self-gratification as an escape from love

So far I have demonstrated situations in which a transformation took place. However, there are frustrating situations in which the group or a member of the group remain locked in a minus-type link. I will now describe such a group situation.

patient uses the analytic language as a defence against real contact.

I believe that sterile use of language is a kind of minus link, because it prevents a creative relationship between the analyst and the group. It can be called –L. The jargon becomes a metaphor for cliché, and nothing new ever happens.

Pseudo-intellectual talk in the group leads to a loss of the group's vitality and creativity.

CHAPTER NINE

The "untouchable": racism and prejudice in the analytic group

T o investigate the "untouchable", it behoves us to take a closer look at what is "touchable" in an analytic therapy group. What is mean by "emotional touch"? We are not going to look at physical contact but with emotional contact that occurs between people, among the inner worlds of members of an analytic group. In down-to-earth language, we are looking at heart-to-heart contact. The heart expands when it comes into contact with the heart of an Other. Emotional contact occurs among group members and between them and the group conductor.

Derrida (2012), writing in a psychoanalytic framework, speaks of "Tact" (as in "tact-ile") and sees this kind of con*tact* as one that ignites our imagination and our fantasy life. He speaks of a meeting point of gazes, a moment of eye-to-eye contact. The ability of two people to look into each other's eyes at the same time enables a crossing of boundaries but paradoxically at the same time preserves a proper distance. According to him, this kind of touching bumps up against a boundary. There will always be part of the Other that remains impenetrable—what he calls "a respectful distance".

Bion defines this kind of touch as "Caesura" (Bion, 1989). He is certain that the caesura is the most important and sensitive place in which emotional contact between two people takes place. It is here that the boundary between them is clarified. That is, the notion of caesura has a double, paradoxical meaning, both a separation and a joining simultaneously. Towards the end of his life Bion (1989, p. 56) speculated that this is the most important area to investigate in order to understand inter- and intra-psychic processes. This is the conclusion he draws at the end of his article, "Caesura":

> Investigate the caesura; not the analyst; not the analysand; not the unconscious; not the conscious; not sanity; not insanity. But the caesura, the link, the synapse, the transitive-intransitive mood.

Derrida's definition is parallel to that of Bion. The two agree that the moment of this touching contains mysterious elements that are hard to define. Both attribute to this kind of touch a point of contact with the world beyond, an exalted and transcendental world, one with no end. It is also a reminder of death and transcendence. Touch implies impermanence, a coming and going. It also involves touching the boundary of the Other, which can arouse desire for more contact and hope to be loved.

It takes a certain skill to create this kind of contact. Implied here is the potential for power and expansion. Speech comes after eye contact. Now there is more contact, but through language. In the analytic therapy group, speech is the main channel of communication This is how members communicate their desire, their fantasies, and even the magic of being able to touch the Other's inner world.

In order, however, for the "magic touch" to occur between two people, there is a prior condition that must be met, namely, the ability to be in contact with one's Self. If there is gap between some aspects of a person and other parts of his Self, it is reasonable to assume that in a group, he or she will feel cut off or threatened when these parts appear in the reports and stories of other members.

Case study

I will now describe a meeting of my analytic group that took place on 2 September 2012. It was the first gathering after a long summer vacation. At first there seemed to be little emotional contact among group members. This became more clear in retrospect after an outburst that took place in the second part of the meeting.

Of the nine members, two were absent from the meeting, one because she was near the end of her pregnancy and approaching birth, the other because of a trip abroad. A third member was late by about ten minutes. In the group there are three men and six women.

At the beginning, discussion was quite shallow. Some members said they were happy to be back and that they had been waiting for the group to start up again. No one brought up anything particularly emotional or significant. One member said he felt like a pupil again, on the first day of school, when everyone tells what he or she did over the summer. Another said he felt bored, like at a slide show evening. The atmosphere was flat, and there was little emotional expression.

The member who arrived late had been in the group for three months. She is a lesbian. I'll call her Ayia. She is a good looking woman, dark skinned with an Eastern, oriental look. She is the adopted daughter of reserved and self-controlled parents of German origin. She describes her parents as generous but people who gave her a strict upbringing, which made her up-tight and always careful to use proper language. She spoke in a quiet tone and had a rather tight and careful look about her. After some point in the session she said that the superficial atmosphere in the group was, unfortunately, very familiar to her. It simply reflected real life outside the group, in which people are alienated from one another, each in his own world. There is no authentic conversation. That is the way it is. She supposed there is no reason for things to be otherwise in the group.

She went on to tell how she would get excited and keyed up from articles written by a certain journalist (a woman). She waits the whole week to read her articles. This particular journalist speaks the truth and says what she has to say in a totally straight-forward way. The journalist really voices Ayia herself. In addition, she watches the TV series called "Mehubarim", a reality programme about men. There she discovered that men are in fact able to speak about their emotions. She was always so certain that men are boring robots. Then she told the group about a moment she had had in the group three months prior, on the day she had joined the group. A member, David, had talked about himself in a very emotional way. It had been a very strong and unexpected experience for her. But even so, she would be happy if there were no men in the group. When she concluded, she said that again, as on every Thursday, she was excited waiting for the article written by the journalist she liked so much. Thursday is the day she loves the most. (I should point out that our group meets on Monday nights.)

At this point, I said that there seemed to be an atmosphere of alienation in the group and that people were not really touching each other. I also pointed out that the men were not reacting to what had been said. And finally, I thought but did not say that the truly desired object appears on Thursday not Monday. It seemed to me that Ayia was expressing a thought for the whole group, namely, that at that particular moment they did not feel the group was very desirable. However, for some reason I could not say this thought out loud. I felt some anxiety because of the flat atmosphere, and feared that if I said that the group did not appear desirable, I would destroy any hope for contact.

There were some moments of silence. People moved restlessly in their chairs. Following the silence, Avraham, the oldest member, began to tell in great detail about a trip abroad he had taken in August with his eldest grandson. He talked about his difficulty in getting close to his grandson, who had been very quiet during their whole trip. He told how he was very preoccupied with what his grandson thought of him, how he wants to invite the boy for a talk and ask him what he had learned on the trip about the kind of grandfather he had.

Avraham is an educated man of Eastern, Oriental origin, divorced, who for a long time has been doing a kind of self-examination, in which he has concluded that in his youth he was a rigid, distanced, and aggressive father. He lacked all emotional closeness to his children and had even been a kind of dictator with a heart of stone. Two of his children cut off connections with him. Every time he thinks about this, he feels he has missed out on something, becomes regretful, and begins to cry. He experiences an intense, overwhelming pain. Now, however, he did not touch his pain but focused mainly on the fact that through his grandson he is trying to repair for the fatherhood he missed out on.

People reacted with an empathy that had a false ring to it. It seemed to be covering over a lack of interest and a kind of emotional shut-down. Members tried to support him, compliment him on the trip he took with his grandson. But for some reason there seemed to be no real contact among people.

It seemed that until now nothing genuine had happened. There was a sense of things being underneath the surface that we were not getting at. I felt a kind of quiet before the storm, and I was more and more tense. I tried to say something about the long vacation that had interfered with the work of the group, but no one picked up from there.

Suddenly there was an unexpected change. Ayia turned to Avraham and told him he was boring her. He was taking valuable time in the group to tell his long story. He was only concerned with himself. The only thing that interested him was what his grandson thinks of him. He was just going on and on and whining like a slut. The word "slut" was a surprise (the word in Hebrew is *cusit*). The way she used it was street slang and not part of the group vocabulary. The word itself is one that men use when talking about a woman they see as a sexual object. It is also a word that in Hebrew, "*cusit*", is a play on words for "vagina". It is insulting when said by a man. What she might have been trying to do by using the word herself was to attract attention, behaving like a seductive woman, and she was furious that he was preoccupied with himself and waiting for compliments from the group.

The talk went on and no one related to the word "slut" that had been said in the room. Avraham did not react either and continued to behave as if it had not bothered him, as if it had nothing to do with him. The group's avoidance of responding to the word seemed to me significant, and so I repeated it and asked Ayia what she had wanted to say exactly by using that word. She said that she did not know. It had just slipped out. Then Avraham turned to her and said in a patronising tone, with barely disguised anger, "How you use words without realising what you are saying!" I tried to show Avraham that though he had not overtly reacted to her attack, he was then trying to educate her. This was his way of expressing his anger.

I told Ayia that Avaham was taking the role of the father whose sons had left him. And she was taking the role of the daughter whose biological parents abandoned her. Perhaps she was angry at Avraham because he is from an Eastern, Oriental background just as she is. She might also be angry because for her he has taken on the role of the father that abandoned her. She was quick to respond that he does not have the role of her biological father because when she opened her adoption file, she discovered that her biological father did not even know of her existence. Nonetheless, she continued, it was important for her to point out that Avraham represents the kind of Eastern,

Oriental man she cannot stand. All the negative characteristics she sees in kinds of men, she sees in him, a kind of combination of an Eastern man and a slut.

Avraham continued sitting quietly and did not respond. To my question regarding how he felt, he answered that he did not care what Ayia thinks. For him, she was invisible and had been for the last three months, from the moment that she entered the group. He feels disdain for all lesbians and homosexuals. They are people with whom he would not sit in the same room. He is absolutely repulsed by them. Ayia was shocked and said she had never been so insulted in her life. She demanded I throw Avraham out of the group.

One of the members began to shout at Avraham and asked him how dare he speak like that. Others also expressed anger. He responded by saying that he would not change, that is the way he is. He hates lesbians and homosexuals. I told him that the way he spoke shows that he had been hurt by Ayia, and that perhaps she touches some of his own fears that his son who lives abroad might be a homosexual. Perhaps he does not return to Israel and try to reconnect with his father because of the father's prejudice. To my surprise, Avraham said that there was something in what I said, that relatives had hinted as much. He said that if it turns out that his son is gay, he would accept him despite his great hatred for gays and lesbians.

The group was very upset. Everyone shouted together, mostly at Avraham. Only one female member said that if he felt this way, it was his right to express himself. This member pointed out that Ayia's using the expression "an Eastern, Oriental man" and "slut" was not less insulting than what Avraham had said to Ayia.

But the group was mostly angry at Avraham, and showed much empathy towards Ayia. She declared that this was the first time in her life that she had heard things like that. If I did not tell Avraham to leave the group, she would leave.

I tried to summarise, and said that we had entered an area that was very difficult to touch, that of racial and gender prejudice. When this topic is spoken about, it usually leads to an explosion. This is what happened when Avraham expressed prejudice towards gays and lesbians and Ayia, towards Eastern, Oriental people. She is denying her own oriental origin (the origin of her biological parents), and she sees in him something negative. He is denying unfinished business within himself regarding homosexuality. Each one of them had touched prejudice in its rawest form. And we had actually seen that there was no calm way of dealing with it. There was just an explosion. People responded by shouting all together. It was impossible to think. It was an attack on thinking. The feeling was that after the superficial silence of the first part of the meeting, dynamite had been brought into the group. There would be no chance that Ayia and Avraham could be together in the same group.

That night, after the meeting, I thought that Avraham and Ayia had been "holding" prejudice for the whole group, and that it was difficult to treat this component because it is so difficult to acknowledge. The moment it is touched, there is an explosion. Like dynamite thrown into the air. These topics are usually denied, but when they do surface, there is no touching them, just an explosion.

That very evening I got an SMS from Ayia in which she wrote to tell me that she had decided definitely to leave the group. She wrote that she was doing so because I had not protected her and had not thrown Avraham out of the group. Neither would she come to say goodbye but would send me payment by mail for that evening's meeting. Her announcement depressed me and made me quite anxious and doubtful about my ability to contain all the group members in the middle of such a difficult conflict.

During the week, I found myself telephoning and sending e-mails to three group members, something I had never done before. My rationalisations had to do with various technical matters, but the truth is I wanted to tell them about Ayia's sudden departure. Happily, each of them read my thoughts and contacted her to request that she not leave the group. I rationalised to myself that the illegal action I had taken was more than justified by the therapeutic capacity of group members. I had just given them a little push in this direction. The result would be beneficial to them as well as to Ayia. Ayia in fact was very moved by what they had done and decided not to leave the group.

In the next meeting, Ayia told everyone that she had noticed that from the moment she entered the group, and during the subsequent three months, Avraham had ignored whatever she said. He never addressed her and related to her as if she were invisible.

The following months in the group were very stormy. People were hurtful to each other and also were hurt. There were no expressions of interest about a new baby that had been born to one of the members, and no one related to the death of the mother of another. However, slowly and gradually people took responsibility for the evil within themselves. This seemed to facilitate a growing closeness between Avraham and Ayia and between other "pairs" who had hurt each other.

Afterthoughts

From this process one can learn about certain aspects of group life that are difficult for members to come in contact with. However, it is apparently necessary for them to do so in order for true touch to take place:

1. Acknowledgement of the evil inherent in prejudice and racism. It is very difficult to take responsibility for these traits within us but their violent appearance in the group room paradoxically brought about greater closeness and contact that was not possible beforehand.
2. Acknowledgement of parts of oneself which are projected on to a member of the group. For example, only towards the end of January 2013 did I begin to realise that Ayia really wanted to be a slut that begs, seduces, and does not protect herself so well . She was not in contact with that part of herself.
3. Denial of the life cycle. Difficulty in seeing and acknowledging the birth and death that had occurred in the lives of the members was because of the difficulty and fear of touching changes in their lives and changes in the group.

These three points intertwine with each other and represent unconscious processes which block the touch with the untouchable. It is not easy to acknowledge the badness in myself and sometimes even the evil. But, denying it is dangerous and prevents change. Only by touching these aspects, can we undergo a transformation that in turn can help turn malignancy into generosity. Contact with the evil within me is necessary for change. It is not easy to make deep, inner connections like these in an analytic group.

Such a storm in the group's life is also not easy for the group analyst. I am aware of the fact that by my acts during that week, I exposed my countertransference toward Ayia, which was strong. I looked at her as a wanted daughter that I would like to adopt. Also, I felt that her leaving the group would be a painful loss for the group and for me. I felt anger towards Avraham, and was afraid that because of his aggression the group would fall apart. But, eventually, I succeeded in releasing the negative pairing: Avraham–Aiya. I said that they expressed anger for the other group members and some of the anger was with me, but had been displaced onto each other. I realised that they were angry because of the long summer vacation and because of the group's composition that forced them to live in the same room with people they hate. I had to be in touch with many kinds of emotions for finding again my balanced voice that could contain the group as a whole.

Hopper (2003b) helped me to explore my countertransference. By his metaphor of the wounded bird he explores profoundly the rich levels that interact among the group's members including the group analyst. He depicts an intersection of transferences and countertransference in a creative and curative way.

Group analysis is often identified with a soft, humanistic perspective that emphasises empathy as a curative element. However, many group analysts have reported their work with aggression in groups. One must also remember that Freud (1921c) speaks of the death instinct as well as the life instinct. Klein (1975a) sees aggression as a positive element in emotional development, and Bion (1962a) is certain that destruction and hatred are inherent within us and in therapy. It is possible to convert these feelings into something constructive and beneficial.

In the group event I described, transgressing acceptable language was a transgression of unwritten law. The word "slut" went beyond acceptable language in the group. Also, humiliating a group member about a quality that is central to his or her self-definition or identity, in fact such as "Eastern, Oriental man" or "lesbian" only created alienation and prevented intersubjective contact. Of course in the case that I have presented these words were intended to be insulting labels, and the group analyst is obliged to find a way of speaking that is truthful but not hurtful.

The dynamics around this event were surprising and similar to Bion's notion of "the catastrophic change". The dynamics that he describes are like those described by Kristeya (2005), that is, the larger the hurt inflicted by ridiculing or dismissing someone, the greater the need to re-emphasise law and order. When there is an abjection (Kristeva, 2005), accompanied by contempt and rejection, there is a strong need for law and order until stated and unstated rules are once again followed. Being cast out is connected to questions of boundaries. The outcast phenomenon challenges the existence of boundaries but also brings about unity. Paradoxically he/she also guards the limits of the group culture. He/she clarifies just what the group boundaries are. The moment the word "slut" is used, not only are the boundaries of language challenged, but the boundaries between men and women are as well. Calling a man a "slut" is to cancel out his manhood. It also mixes up the sexual identities. Paradoxically, bringing a tone of scorn to the room brought an end to alienation. The ensuing explosion brought chaos and creativity, which opened the door to the start of contact. "Slut" is a word that sprung from the unconsciousness, because one can imagine that Ayia carries within her the baby that was scorned and abandoned by her mother. According to both Kristeva and Bion the rehabilitation that follows hurt restores authentic contact. In my group, real contact could only begin after the group could contain the expression of raw aggression.

The word "slut", though denigrating, led at the end to the creation of real contact, whereas the more clear categories "lesbian" and "Eastern, Oriental man" only led to distancing and alienation.

Douglas (1966) shows that in the many oppositional pairs found in society there is an inherent hierarchy. Therefore, one should not see the oppositional forces within them as horizontal but, rather, vertical. For example, the pair East/West or man/woman are not on the same level with regards to the division of social and political power. The East is an inferior political category to the West, just as the woman is with regards to man. In Judaism, the definition of the woman as impure during her monthly period stands in opposition to man, who is not impure. So these expressions, which are related to ethnic background or to gender, are not innocent and their covert purpose is to humiliate and devalue.

Sontag (2003) speaks of our exposure to war photos that we see regularly on TV, the Internet, and in the newspapers. We see pictures of destruction and devastation, corpses, torn limbs, and collapsed buildings, and all this does not stir us to action. We, the educated class, are not monsters, but we have failed in the sense that we lack imagination, empathy, and the capacity to contain this awful reality in our thinking. We, who deal in group analysis, have a hard time acknowledging the fact that empathy is limited and the ability to imagine the suffering of the Other is also limited. In the group we convert alienation, distancing, and emotional coolness into human warmth and contact. But there will always remain areas that are frozen and untouchable.

Another aspect of being human, a worse one, is looking into people who are rejected because of our uncontrolled attraction to cruelty. This is the pornographic aspect of looking. The emotion that causes drivers to slow down when they drive by an accident is not just curiosity. For many people, it is also the desire to see something shocking. This attraction is not rare and there comes with it a degree of relief, that the person suffering is someone that was driving in my lane and what happened to him did not happen to me.

Sontag (2003) suggests that such phenomena are an inborn desire to be cruel. People like to look at pictures of suffering. People draw pleasure from the pain of others. According to this point of view, which is beyond the ken of group analysis, we learn that liking cruelty is natural to human beings no less than empathy. This is the opposite pole from empathy.

In her book *Regarding the Pain of Others* Sontag reaches a conclusion that is relevant to our work as group analysts. She speaks of the fact that we must be aware of the scope of suffering that results from human evil. A person who is regularly surprised by the evil and corruption in the world has not reached moral and psychological maturity. Each person reaches an age at which he/she loses their right to be innocent, shallow, and ignorant. Clearly Ayia, who says that "she has never heard anyone talk about lesbians and homosexuals as she did in the group", has chosen a stance of innocence that ignores the reality in which she is living.

On a deeper level, that of the group unconscious, ignoring the birth and death that happened during the life of the group is actually ignoring life. The difficulty in touching the subject of death is clearly described in the book *Spirit* by Ben-Naftali (2012a), which describes the figure of her grandmother, who, when she was young, left her family in Eastern Europe and emigrated to Palestine to begin a new life. Her mother and brothers died in the Holocaust while she was living in Tel Aviv. She married and raised a family and did not know that they had died and how they died. News of them only arrived much later. Her guilt and shock were so severe that she could not mourn. Because of her inability to mourn, she could not tolerate real contact with her children and grandchildren and the life around her.

The inability to deal with death was also wordlessly present in the group. While one of the members was in mourning, the group acted like the figure of the alienated grandmother in the book *Spirit*. Some weeks had passed like this until a dramatic event occurred. The member whose mother had died brought her grief out into the open and told of her great disappointment with the members, who had totally ignored her. This confession that directly expressed the insult she felt enabled a group transformation from indifference to generosity. The member finally came into contact with her own feelings when she stopped denying her pain. Contact with herself led to contact with group members, who were finally able, for the first time, to feel her grief. From then on there was a new warmth in the group.

In summary, the areas that are hardest to touch are those areas of human evil, aggression, racism, and prejudice. These are areas that are hidden from our awareness, and therefore it is hard to take responsibility for them. From the most difficult group events we learn about the unconscious. At first, these painful areas appear in the form of acting out, in the desire to throw someone out of the group, in hatred and massive projections that members put on each other. As the process continues, however, a dialogue is created and the emotional dynamite is transformed owing to the group container. Also we learn that empathy and compassion are more authentic and significant after conflict and hurtfulness. The group that succeeds in dealing with evil within it will become able to reach a heightened degree of empathy. We also learn that on the level of the group unconscious, it is difficult to acknowledge temporariness, change, and death. The price of ignoring these is that vital life, too, is missed.

PART IV

SOCIETY

"Beta-elements are especially dangerous to society in times of threat, tension, and uncertainty, when they will burst out in the form of social violence with no transformation. They cannot be transformed to the level of dialogue, and they appear as concrete acts. They represent a situation of a loss of faith and a great deficiency in the capacity for reverie. They appear in the most primitive and cruel forms. They do not respond to any discourse, to any human language."

Biran, *Bion's Legacy to Groups*, p. 96

CHAPTER TEN

The difficulty of channelling rage into dialogue

I n this chapter I wish to focus on the relationship between the
Israeli society and the Palestinian society from a psychoanalytical
and group analytical point of view, emphasising the processes
taking place in the social domain.

Introduction

I try to build on Bion's theory of thinking by applying his main
concepts to the domain of the social unconscious. I will draw on some
of the main ideas of Foulkes regarding the foundation matrix. Bion's
concepts about group mentality, group culture, and anonymous pool,
are all relevant to this project.

Foulkes defines the foundation matrix as follows:

> I have accepted from the very beginning that even a group of total
> strangers, being of the same species and more narrowly of the same
> culture, share a fundamental mental matrix. To this their closer
> acquaintance and their intimate exchanges add consistently so that
> they form a current, ever moving and ever developing dynamic
> matrix. (Foulkes, 1990, p. 228)

Foulkes' idea of "the fundamental mental matrix" is crucial. We often forget the powerful influence of society at large on our small groups. We share an illusion that our analytic room exists in a kind of an empty space. Foulkes reminds us that the foundation matrix of the wider society always envelopes the dynamic matrix of each and any group.

Bion's concept of group mentality, resonates with the foundation matrix:

> I shall postulate a group mentality as the pool to which the anonymous contributions are made, and through which the impulses and desires implicit in these contributions are gratified. Any contribution to this group mentality must enlist the support of, or be in conformity with, the other anonymous contributions of the group. I should expect the group mentality to be distinguished by a uniformity that contrasted with the diversity of thought in the mentality of the individuals who have contributed to its formation. (Bion, 1961, p. 50)

Also important is Bion's concept of group culture: "A group culture is a term I used to describe those aspects of the behavior of the group which seemed to be born of the conflict between group mentality and the desires of the individual" (Bion, 1961, p. 59). I think that "the anonymous contributions", "the uniformity", "the anonymous pool", and "the group culture" all are connected to the concept of the foundation matrix; they build the common infrastructure of society. They tell us about the social environment, the values, the beliefs of group members. We can conclude that all these concepts of Foulkes and Bion are referring to aspects of the "social unconscious", which has been developed more recently by several group analysts such as Hopper (2003b).

The Israeli–Palestinian conflict

Both Israelis and Palestinians are currently experiencing a traumatic reality, saturated with violence. Both are the victims of an accumulative and incessant terror. Even those persons not directly or physically harmed experience anxiety and agitation. Everyone is exposed to ongoing violence and terror. The constantly decreasing intervals between the repeated acts of revenge on both sides cause the society to be in a fragile and unstable mental state. The repetitiveness of hostility and revenge cause a feeling of helplessness and of life lived inside a trap. The reality is one of escalation. What yesterday seemed to be an unlikely nightmare, today becomes constant reality. The lines between reality and imagination are blurred. When anything is possible, anxiety mounts high.

Rage is a central phenomenon of this traumatic reality. Rage can be defined as a primeval, archaic element that cannot be verbally expressed. It appears in a raw form through actions releasing an accumulated destructive energy. The aim of such actions is to cause the other side a final, irreversible catastrophe, accompanied sometimes by the total sacrifice of the self, such as in the suicide attacks. Thus rage is a primeval substance that knows only one language—the language of violence. Its victims are anonymous and accidental, its one and only aim is to shed blood. The expressions of violence have predetermined scenarios. The next act of violence is very similar to the previous one. The question that arises is: why is it impossible to translate the language of violence into a language of dialogue, in spite of so many victims of terror and such unbearable pain suffered constantly by both peoples?

If we borrow some major concepts from Bion's theory of thinking (Biran, 1998), we will find that these societies suffer a deep-rooted thinking disturbance. As a psychoanalyst, Bion bases his theory on the primary relations between mother and baby, but it is possible to apply his concepts in our attempt to understand various processes within the socio-cultural domain.

By this I do not mean to suggest that social systems and persons organisms are the same. Hopper (2003b, p. 159) says that "the essence of the social is that it is human and the essence of the human is that it is social".

Bion (1967c) refers to two principle but different elements of thinking. The first is called "alpha type elements". These are elements that can be thought. The other are the "beta type elements" of which it is not possible to think.

"Alpha function" is the element that translates what is absorbed by the baby through the senses in a pre-verbal form into words, dreams, expression of feeling, and dialogue. Alpha function makes the transformation from elements that cannot be thought to those that can be thought. Initially the mother provides this function for the baby. She translates the baby's distress for him, gives names to his hardships and anxieties and thus calms and contains him. Through this process she introduces the baby to a kind of container. Through the contact with the containing mother, the baby gradually learns to translate his experiences, to moderate the sensory impressions, and bodily sensations, for itself, and, through the mother's mediation, he learns to create thoughts by himself and consequently to build concepts. Through the verbal expression that he will later learn, and through developing the ability to think and sublimate, he will be able to moderate his distresses and frustrations, and learn to contain the raw materials through transformation to the level of emotional expression, dream, imagination, dialogue, and sublimation.

In contrast to this important developmental process, which is responsible for the ability to transform and therefore for the development of thinking, there are sensory impressions that have not undergone transformation, received a name, translated to a communicative word, or appeared as a thought. These sensory impressions just remain as they were in their raw state. Bion calls them "beta type elements". These are raw materials that have not undergone any processing. They are like undigested particles that cannot be thought or sublimated. The less successfully the alpha function is executed by the mother, the more the baby is exposed to confusion and frustration, so that more numerous beta elements remain, emerging mainly at times of distress in the forms of acting out, psychosomatic disturbances, thinking disturbances, violent outbursts, and so on.

The quality of the beta elements is a concrete one, which does not change or transform into a metaphor or an idea. When the baby is overwhelmed by such elements he experiences what Bion calls "nameless dread", finding himself in great distress. This description demonstrates that we are not dealing here with a rational or logical thinking theory, but looking at a thinking created through experiencing and learning from experience. It is an emotional thinking, creating in us the abilities of intuition, common sense, and creativity.

If we apply this set of concepts to the socio–cultural domain, we will be able to identify in society, especially in times of distress, a regression to some type of "pockets" of undigested elements that do not undergo a transformation but rather break out as beta type elements. These elements emerge from storage just as they are. They are repetitive by nature, and learn nothing from experience. Time and life experience have no impact upon them. A prominent and painful example of these social beta type elements is expressed in the incessant repetitiveness of social violence that has been constant in the Middle East for many years, and except for technological upgrading has undergone no transformation.

These elements are not channelled towards dialogue. They appear as concrete acts. Their expressions are cruel and primitive, and they understand no human language. This is a situation in which society is regressive, and the mother–leader who may cause the transformation is missing. It is a kind of social sickness. The relations between the two peoples, the Israeli and the Palestinian, are in two different realms. One level represents the alpha functions and is expressed by the peace talks, the attempted dialogue, the efforts for coexistence, and the intention of dividing the territory. The other level is that of terror, which represents the beta elements. Both peoples live in a pathological reality, in which it is impossible to learn from experience, and so, simultaneously, those who talk continue to try talking, and those who kill continue to try killing. They live in a paradox—as the language of dialogue gains force, so does the language of terror. These are two languages that are alien to each other, but respond to each other without communicating. The language of dialogue is one of faith and of looking forward. The language of violence knows no future tense and dreams no dreams; it is constructed on the wish to kill and the thirst for blood. A dialogue will never end at the same point it begins— something must occur along the way. Terror will always begin and end according to a predetermined scenario.

The nature of the two types of elements are summed up in Table 1.

Table 1:   Beta and alpha elements

Beta type elements	Alpha type elements
Elements that cannot be thought	Elements that can be thought
Are not channelled to imagination	Expressed by the ability to imagine
Concrete. Recognise no past or future	Expressed by the ability to dream forward
Are not channelled into words and dialogue	Expressed by the ability to hold a dialogue
Expressed through violent actions	Undergo transformation and moderation
Emerge impulsively during frustration	Tolerance of frustration
Repetitive and circular	Change and develop

I wish to deal with the dilemma: what are the differences between the two qualities appearing in the above table, and what will allow the violence, which is not channelled and remains in its raw state, to undergo a transformation and be available to the alpha function? What will make it possible to dissolve the terror and turn it into dialogue? What are the differences between the primitive quality of terror and the mature quality of dialogue?

As the mother translates for the baby, the leadership must execute a successful translation from beta to alpha for the people.

Omnipotence vs. the acknowledgment of limits and limitations

The willingness to kill, to go all the way with the destruction wish, emerges from an omnipotent position. This is the position of the omnipotent and omniscient, who does not recognise the limits of reality or the existence of the other and the different. The need to conquer, to achieve, to rule, derives from this omnipotent position. The leading motivation is to possess. It is a concrete level, similar to that of a little child, who wants a certain toy just because a friend wants it. The need for possessiveness can reach the level of "it shall be neither mine nor yours; divide it" (1 Kings, 3:26). A person under the influence of the omnipotent fantasy would feel he deserves all his heart's desires, and would not have the ability to share or to recognise the existence of the other. Cain killed Abel because he had something Cain did not have (Genesis, 4). Cain could not bear Abel's advantages or his different identity. Possessiveness is characterised by a total and concrete nature. In our case, it is the wish that the land will belong to me, and me alone.

The willingness for dialogue derives from a much higher level of maturity. A transfer will occur from "possessing" to "belonging". "To belong" indicates a metaphorical level of relating to space. War emerges from the position of possessiveness, while dialogue is born from the position of belonging. When one is willing to belong to a space without being its possessor, it can lead to a situation in which each of the two peoples can project their identity, uniqueness, and wishes on to the same space. The same Jerusalem could belong, on the emotional level, to two different peoples. Each one could deposit its own meaning in the same concrete space. Belonging has no concrete limits. Both peoples can dream of Jerusalem, and one dream does not interfere with the other since dreams have an unlimited space.

Both peoples find it difficult to move from the level of possessiveness to that of belonging. It is difficult to move in the space of metaphorical thinking when both existential and paranoid anxieties are at their highest. The fear that the other wishes to annihilate me makes it impossible to reach above the level of concretisation. Only once there is development and a movement from possession to belonging will coexistence in the metaphorical space be possible. In the metaphorical space each people can deposit its own history, identity, and truth without harming those of the other. What the two peoples are in need of is a transformation from possessiveness to belonging (see Table 2).

Extreme social narcissism vs. the ability to love the other

Eissler (1975) defines the term "cultural narcissism". This is the internal force, which pushes us to overestimate our religion, our nation, our political camp, and so on. We are impressed by those who resemble and think like us. This force is one of the causes of conflicts and wars.

Green (1981) says that every culture is structured on inherent paranoid processes. The distinctive character of a certain culture is affirmed through the devaluation and rejection of another culture. Often it is the culture of the neighbouring people. Minority groups that are different from us are a good object for projection. We project anything that is unbearable within ourselves onto these groups, such as evil, aggression, weaknesses, inferiority, and so on.

Social or cultural narcissism is a dangerous force that can become powerful and extreme. Bollas (1992) wrote about the danger that such narcissism can create a "fascist state of mind". Hidden in such a mentality is the fear of the other, the one different from ourselves. In its extremity, this fear is defined as xenophobia.

Table 2:   Possession vs. belonging

Possession	Belonging
Omnipotence	Acknowledging the limitations of power
The need to conquer and rule	The ability to share
To possess	To belong
A concrete space	A metaphorical space

In its extreme form social narcissism includes the blind infatuation with a leader, being overwhelmed by his force and losing the individual faculty of judgment. Indeed, Freud (1921c) had already analysed this phenomenon. The phenomenon grew to monstrous proportions with the rise of Nazism and the blind worship of Hitler as a symbol of nationalistic and racial narcissism. This type of extreme narcissism turns others into non-humans and thus objects of violence. The violence of Auschwitz was a statistical, bureaucratic, and industrial violence. Terms like man, human being, or individual were annihilated.

The narcissist tendency in society is primitive, defensive, and eventually leads to solutions of hatred, rejection, and violence. A narcissist position evolves (Freud, 1914c) from superiority, and therefore prevents a dialogue. Dialogue is born out of the willingness for reciprocity, from recognising the other, touching him, being close to him, knowing him without fear. Dialogue is a search for companionship and the willingness to make concessions. It is important that both parties be able to know, respect, and then to love each other. In order to facilitate such a dialogue, a distinct national identity should be created. Differentiation between two cultures, between two peoples, would allow for a discourse that would be less threatening and contain a recognition of mutual existence. Such a dialogue can only take place from the level of recognising and feeling secure in one's own identity, while recognising the different and distinct identity of the other.

On an individual level much has been achieved. Together with reports on the terrible terror attacks directed at anonymous individuals, we read and hear stories of friendship, good neighbourliness, trust, and sometimes good relations between employee and employer among Israelis and Palestinians. On the human level and among small groups, the grace that seems impossible on the social level sometimes becomes possible. This is the grace that evolves from individual contact on the human level, and the ability to see the other as a person in distress (see Table 3).

Living in a perverse world vs. *living in a world that recognises laws and boundaries*

Werbart (2000) says that a perverse society is characterised by the ease with which it is possible to break any taboo created by human

Table 3:   Social narcissism vs. ability to love the other

Social narcissism	Ability to love the other
Impressed by the similar	Accepting the different
Projection on the other	Ability to contain weaknesses and urges
Dehumanising the other	The ability to defend human dignity
Superiority	Reciprocity

civilisation. The overflow of images saturated with violence that can be witnessed constantly on the television screen turns death into a daily guest in every family's living room. Anything can be shown and no filters are applied. Violent scenes, which would be hidden or blurred in the past, now appear as pornography, as raw material. The exposed and damaged human limbs appear as they are, and in immediate prox-imity to the violent occurrence. The line between fictional films and the bloodstained reality is blurred. Human beings have the perverse wish to peep at sexual abuse, violence, suffering, torture, and death, to satisfy the archaic, primitive part that is buried inside civilised man and that is normally restrained by taboo. Once the taboo is violated, a primitive quality is released, fuelling acts of violence and sexual abuse in the family and on the street. Seeing the atrocities on television, it seems that anything goes, nothing is forbidden. The taboo's important function is to create frameworks, to draw lines between right and wrong, good and evil, between generations, between that which may be touched and that which may not, between the living and dead, the human and non-human, between that which is publicly permissible and that which is private. The taboo has an important role in develop-ment. It represents the father, the law and the boundaries of reality. The line, which may not be crossed in reality, allows for the develop-ment of imagination, creativity, and art. When once and again we are being exposed to images, which leave no room for imagination, reality becomes chaotic and undifferentiated. Violence becomes banal and mundane, a constant stimulation to human evil.

Life with no boundaries, distinctions, or frameworks is a life in a world that encourages expressions of rage, violence, and the breaking of all limits. In order to be able to transform these materials into a civilised level of dialogue, boundaries must be restored. It is necessary to, once again, identify clearly what we are allowed in our imagination only, but are forbidden in reality, in order to restore human life as a sacred value. A regressive condition of the loss of boundaries could dangerously damage the mental health of the next generation.

So far I have referred to changes in the state of mind of the two peoples, changes required in order to reach a dialogue that strives for peace. These changes are not happening, and even seem to get further away from us. On the Israeli side, the elements rejecting a dialogue have gained force. The social atmosphere in Israel is saturated with militaristic notions. Alarming phenomena of cultural narcissism are taking place. The feeling is that everyone must identify with the mainstream, and those who think differently feel condemned. It means that the freedom of thought is gradually being lost. Soldiers who refuse to serve in the Territories are regarded as the enemies of the people. The invasion of the Palestinian towns, especially Jenin, by the Israeli army, and the terrible suffering inflicted upon the Palestinian population, indicate the existence of nationalistic forces constantly striving for war. Luxurious settlements are being constructed for Israelis in the midst of a people experiencing constant economic hardships.

We experience a vicious circle of Palestinian terror leading to an Israeli military retaliation, leading again to terror, endlessly. The wish for revenge leads to the death of civilians and soldiers on both sides time and again. This is a war without a victor.

Also on the Palestinian side, those beta-elements that make no dialogue possible became more manifest. The most extreme and disturbing phenomenon is that of the suicide bombers, constituting the most extreme form of the unwillingness to hold a dialogue.

When analysing this phenomenon of the suicide bombers, I wish to emphasise that behind them stand the terror organisations. These organisations constitute the psychological infrastructure for the emerging of terror. In order to understand this painful phenomenon we must analyse the psychodynamics of the terror organisations.

A terror organisation is a kind of totalitarian organisation. Totalitarianism can be defined as a state in which people are told what it means for them to be happy. Individuals lose the right to decide on the course of their own lives. The autonomy of the person is lost. Such is the case in terror organisations, where human beings are alienated from themselves, and the control over their consciousness is in the hands of others. The person's awareness is alienated from his identity, and he becomes an actor in a drama written by others, in which he performs a pre-subscribed role. Accordingly, the suicide bomber, as we regard him, or the martyr (*shahid*), as regarded by the other side is, by both views, a person robbed of identity as an individual who is the master of his own will.

Hopper (2003c) defines such extreme social processes as massification, which means being a part of a mass and losing personal identity. Massification (Hopper, 2005) is a defence against the fear of annihilation.

The terror organisation supplies its members with a narcissistic value. They deny being mere mortals. Their death is not experienced as a loss, but as an ideological mission, which will bring redemption.

Freud called such a situation, in which we create a representation of such a good world, a situation of ego-ideal. It is a world where vulnerability or mortality do not exist. The ego-ideal rejects and represses the real self. In terror organisations the ego-ideal is realised by the suicide bombers, who are no longer in touch with their natural and spontaneous will to live. The suicide bomber is changed from being a subject to being an object. This process of taking a role for an entire organisation is described by Hopper (2012) as personification. The suicide bomber personifies aggregation by turning himself into an object, and at the same time personifies massification by becoming a missioner of the holy and idealised missions of the terror organisation. The members of the organisation who operate behind the scenes, and send these young bombers, are usually older by a generation, representing the figure of the ideal, omnipotent father, who receives his legitimation from God, and fulfils a divine mission. The ideal fathers heading the organisation create an image of purity and holiness for the acts of terror and murder.

The suicide bomber becomes an object carrying out a mission. In order to exist as such an object, he must lose contact with his real ego. We can assume that in his normal state he has the will for life like any other human being. An acute example of the loss of contact with the will to live, and for the continuity of life, is the woman, a potential suicide bomber, who after being apprehended spoke without emotion of the possibility that her only daughter would be orphaned. "My daughter will be proud of me for the mission I fulfilled," she said. It means that in this system of values the mission stands much higher than the motherhood instinct that was crushed and repressed.

The shocking, recurring terror incidents demonstrate that the suicide bomber loses himself before the attack to the point of losing contact with his own body. Our body is the closest thing to us, but, inspired by the leaders of terror, the suicide bomber's body is alienated from him. It is no longer his, becoming a mechanical, lifeless object. He is no longer human. He turns into a bomb, with the sole purpose of destroying the evil outside. Anything outside the organisation is considered the enemy, without differentiation. It makes no difference whether it is a baby, a pregnant woman, a sixteen-year-old girl, or an eighty-year-old man. The suicide bomber sees no human beings. He sees an undifferentiated human mass. Just as his own individuality is totally erased, so is the individuality of the other erased. This is a state of depersonalisation.

Following one of the terror attacks, an eye-witness reported that the suicide bomber smiled before activating his explosive belt. This smile is in great contrast with the horrific scene that followed it. I assume that at this stage the suicide bomber is not in touch with reality, but rather experiences a fantasy, in which he becomes one with the ideology of those who sent him. One cannot smile at such a reality, therefore it seems that his body is here, but his mind is somewhere else, experiencing an acute and ecstatic fusion with the ideology.

An escalation of violence has occurred among each of these peoples, and they have each distanced themselves from the language of dialogue. Instead of dialogue we witness a destructive culture of "let me die with the philistines" (*Judges*, 16:30). Still, it is our duty to look ahead with some optimism. The current situation cannot go on. My hope is that the recent deterioration will lead to the beginning of the channelling of horror and anger into dialogue.

When society is overwhelmed by such painful processes, we are in need of a working group, combined of representatives of both peoples, willing to think together. We need a group, which possesses creative thinking, which will free their peoples of their paranoia, their redemption fantasies and their delusions of unilateral and omnipotent solutions. Each of these two peoples must build a team that will conduct negotiations in a state of sanity, making its mark on the insane social context in which we find ourselves.

Emptiness and apathy vs. the ability to hurt and mourn

Freud describes trauma as caused by great quantities of stimulations that break the crust protecting the ego, leaving a hole in the mental space. It is like an internal bleeding that empties the ego. Anzieu (1989) developed the term "skin-ego" to describe the crust protecting the ego. He showed that any violent attack, either physical or mental, is directed against the mental shell protecting the human being. Violent and perverse attacks cross the boundaries, which protect the mental hygiene. Self-defence against such an unbearable pain is often through disengagement and encapsulation or, in other words, putting on a shield. But disconnection and fortification also block the enrichment, growth and nourishing that the psyche gains through its contacts with the outside world. Adopting such a position of disengagement and erecting walls of apathy makes it possible to continue sustaining blows, while simultaneously continue to hurt and destroy, without being able to dissolve or ease the traumatic experiences.

Change will occur only when depression sets in, or with recognition of the damage, victims, and suffering caused by the violence. Only with the ability to mourn that which was lost and will never return, can there be movement in the direction of dialogue. This should be mourning on the national and social levels. The omnipotent and narcissist positions mentioned earlier do not recognise the possibility of "there isn't any" or "there never will be". In these positions, when the world does not give one what one wants, one attacks it. Only through the recognition of want, loss, victims who cannot return, will emotional learning from experience become possible, and a strong will to stop the suffering and pain arise. From an apathetic position, the vicious circle can go on forever. Only from a position of recognising concession, of touching the suffering, will transformations begin. The wounded nation will create for itself a rehabilitated identity, recognising want, separateness, and the right of the other to mourn. Both peoples need to recognise on the emotional level the collective meaning of loss. They need to start a new chapter of both the self and the other.

These thoughts about the possible and the impossible, about the oscillation between hope and despair, lead me to reconsider the human part within ourselves. I believe that the majority of people from both nations want peace and quiet. It is therefore necessary to look once again for answers in the human sphere. We must try to listen to Primo Levi's cry, who, after experiencing the Holocaust, asked "Is this a Man?" In order to re-examine human fate we may return to the myth of Oedipus Rex, which is in fact a metaphor for every man's search for meaning and separateness. The Oedipus story is a metaphor encapsulating the suffering and destruction through which man must pass in order to discover his human side.

In the Oedipus story the Sphinx appears as a kind of terrifying monster, whose body is combined of human and animal parts. The Sphinx represents enigma, the undeciphered riddle. It asks a riddle: "Who is the one walking on four legs in the morning, on two legs at noon and on three by evening?" The answer takes us back to the source, to man himself. He is the one who as an infant walks on fours, at adulthood on two legs and uses a stick in old age. Paradoxically, the riddle is trivially simple, but at the same time elusive and difficult to solve. The answer enfolds the meaning of being human. Man undergoes changes and metamorphoses in order to discover the human aspect within himself. Often we are blind to something basic and simple that is right there in front of our eyes. The Sphinx is unforgiving of this blindness, and it crushes all those who fail to answer its riddle in the abyss. Only Oedipus solves the riddle successfully.

Enigmatic messages have a Sphinx-like quality. They are terrifying and associated with violence and traumatic experiences. They relate to the boundary between life and death, which is often a very thin line. According to the myth, Oedipus suffered a trauma a few days after he was born. His father Laius, who wanted to avoid the curse according to which his son would kill him, gave him to a shepherd with the order to abandon the baby on Kitarion mountain. King Laius pierced the baby's ankles with a pin, so no one would pick it up. The baby's legs swelled, hence his name Oedipus ("swollen legs"). The mature Oedipus solved a riddle based on the motif of legs. He had to be in contact with an early traumatic experience, which had a monstrous aspect, and which left its mark on his body. In order to crack the Sphinx's riddle he had to return to the most painful spot, to the cruelty he sustained as an infant.

The person who solves the enigma metaphorically is the leader that society requires. He is the leader who first and foremost is in touch with himself, with his humanity. He is the hero who experiences the social trauma in order to be able to heal the society of its afflictions, and for that purpose he must look inside himself. Perhaps the heroism of the leader in our day and age should be the human heroism of sustaining pain and suffering. Touching the suffering paves the way for being empathic to the other's suffering.

The Sphinx's aspect of the story is total and unyielding. There are only two extreme options—to solve the riddle or to die. The Sphinx will not engage in a dialogue. Its language is one of violence. It can only recognise a glorious victory or a total destruction, with no gradual shades. When Oedipus gives the correct answer, the Sphinx has to commit suicide. The extreme edges are the opposite of dialogue. Oedipus, on the other hand, is gradually becoming more human. Later in the story he will have to discover his true identity, release himself from the perverse act of having had sexual intercourse with his mother, recognise the murder of his father, and thus release society of its afflictions. His own worst affliction as a king was his blindness. He had deluded himself with the delusion of the victor. Victories are grandiose by nature, and the joy of victory is intertwined with the suffering of the vanquished. The Israeli victory in the Six Days War was euphoric, but caused many disasters later on. Victory goes hand in hand with blindness and denial of the price being paid. The circle of victor and vanquished must be broken in favour of humane leadership. In order to see his imaginary victory, in order to see his own delusion, Oedipus had to blind both his eyes and look inside himself. Such perspectives lead to the realisation that the enemy is as human as oneself, and that both sides must break the circle of conqueror and conquered, victor and vanquished. Leaders must discover the oedipal aspect within themselves that has known suffering, pain, and concessions. This may sound naive to those cynically inclined. But on the other hand, it may be society itself that does not allow such a leadership to emerge.

Eyad El-Sarraj was a Palestinian psychiatrist, who died in 2014. He had been the head of mental health services in Gaza. Interviews with him were published in 2000, in *The Washington Post* and *Los Angeles Times*. Sarraj appealed emotionally to the Palestinian people, proposing to leave behind the guns and the stones, and meet the Israeli soldiers with candles and flowers. He blamed the political leaders for lacking vision, and the Muslim religious leaders for encouraging revenge and entrapping the Palestinians in a culture of violence. He spoke also of a kind of double messages exchanged between the two peoples, messages of peace immersed in violence:

> I was brought up to hate Jews. Jews, I was told, had robbed me of my home in Beer-Sheva and forced my people out of Palestine. Jews were monstrous killers. I lived dreading the day when I would meet my first Jew.

In 1956, during the Suez War, when Israel occupied Gaza, I met him. I was twelve. He was a soldier pointing a gun at my back as he ordered me to lead him into our underground dark shelter. I was terrified of the gun but amused that the soldier was apparently frightened too. I asked myself then if they have the same feelings as we do.

The second Jew was shocking. It was in 1971, when I finished my medical degree in Alexandria and was driven by a Red Cross bus across the Suez Canal to serve in Gaza. The Israelis had then occupied Gaza again, along with the West Bank, Sinai desert and Golan Heights following their victory in the Six Day War.

I was sitting in the front seat of the bus facing an Israeli soldier and his gun. I was angry and frightened. It must have shown on my face because suddenly the young Israeli soldier looked at me with a reassuring smile and said, "Have you been away from your family for long?" "Yes," I said, shocked. He then said, "I hope you will find them all safe and in good health." I will never forget his face. I think that I decided then that Jews are humans as we are and that I would never be able to kill.

Living and working in Gaza under the Israeli military occupation for the past thirty years has been a rich but painful experience. I was interrogated many times. I was asked to "cooperate." I was treated with arrogance, fired from my job twice, and listened to hundreds of stories of pain and tears. But I met many wonderful Israelis and some became my friends. I learned much from them.

Israelis who appear as the masters are in fact victims of a history of pain, suffering persecution, and ghettos. They are surrounded by an ocean of hatred as Arabs could not accept defeat, and their rhetoric was fierce.

Palestinians are hurt. They felt betrayed by the Arab regimes and unjustly treated by the Western world. Their anger turned into cycles of defiance and rage. Now they fire bullets of despair on a suicidal path.

For any peace process to succeed, people need to be liberated. Palestinians and Israelis have yet to realise that they are interdependent.

Liberation of the Palestinians from the Israeli occupation of their land, from the humiliation and suffering, will happen when Israelis are liberated from their fear and insecurity. Palestinian bullets only strengthen Israelis' sense of victimisation and paranoia.

Finally I wish to refer to an article published in the Israeli press not long after the breaking out of the second Intifada. It happened just when we seemed to begin seeing the light at the end of the tunnel.

The article in the daily *Yediot Ahronot* (Peri, 2001) described a meeting between the parents of Muhamad A-Dura, the Palestinian child who became a symbol when he was shot dead in his father's arms, and the parents of Bat-Hen Shahak, who was killed by a suicide bomber in Tel Aviv. The joint pain of the parents, and the empathy that each couple felt for the other, made dialogue possible. The parents were photographed together, holding the photos of their dead children. This is a picture stronger than any words. They are holding the photos like citations. The meeting itself is human, with no ceremonies or clichés. The ability to see the other in their natural size and recognise them as human beings, creates humanisation of the enemy. The held-up photos become an incrimination of society.

These citations from 2000 and 2001 are still relevant here and now. There is a forum of bereaved families of the two peoples that tries to voice the hope for peace and for ending the killing. But the leaders of each of the peoples do not listen.

What happens to us when daily we watch pictures of the victims of terror? Do we just see them or do we really observe what we see? In the novel by Jose Saramago (1997), *On Blindness*, a whole society is going blind, and only one woman still sees. She is the one enabling the group of blind people to maintain their human image. She finally asks: "Why have we gone blind?" And answers: "I think we have not gone blind. I think we are blind. We are the blind who see. Blind who even when they see, do not see." Perhaps we too can tell ourselves: "We saw but we did not observe." Our role is to prevent blindness to the best of our ability.

CHAPTER ELEVEN

From possessing to belonging

Martin Buber, in his *I and Thou* (Buber & Kaufmann, 1970), speaks about the human individual as being born from the radiant darkness of the womb, out of universal chaos, into the bright light of creation—a move whose very essence is the statement: I exist, I am here. The human individual, fundamentally, comes to merge with the world and belong to it—not to turn into its owner. Ownership does not settle with being.

Abraham, in the Bible, had a sense of the dangerous side of our drive to conquer. Even before he made his covenant with God, when his name was still Abram, he chose to avoid war with Lot and instead simply divided the land.

> And Abram said unto Lot: "Let there be no strife, I pray thee, between me and thee, and between my herdmen and thy herdmen; for we are brethren. Is not the whole land before thee? Separate thyself, I pray thee, from me; if thou wilt take the left hand, then I will go to the right; or if thou take the right hand, then I will go to the left." (*Genesis*, 13:8)

This unique action is related to Abraham's spiritual side, to his confident sense of belonging to the region, even if he could not actually own all of it.

175

Abraham's position is one of strength and confidence, a position that is directly opposite the omnipotent readiness to kill, to go to the bitter end. The latter is a position that covers up for weakness and insecurity, which stay hidden in the unconscious. This is the attitude of someone who believes that he or she can do and/or know everything. It is the attitude of someone who fails to acknowledge the limits of reality and does not recognise the existence of the other.

Thus, Cain murdered Abel because Abel owned something that Cain did not possess. To Cain, Abel's advantage and his different identity were insufferable. It is omnipotence that generates the need to conquer, to achieve, to control. When a nation's main motive is to conquer territory, we can call this motive "the desire to possess". In the current Jewish–Palestinian conflict, this desire to possess has reached extreme proportions: "It shall be neither mine nor yours, divide it!"—or "Let me die with the Philistines!"

If I do not get what I want, then neither shall you.

Ownership, as an attribute, is total and concrete in character. I want this land to be mine and only mine; or: "Temple Mount is ours" or "Greater Israel"—all of these reflect an omnipotent ideal that does not acknowledge the pain of the other. In such a traumatic situation, with its vicious cycle of violence, there is a need for leaders who are able to transform violence into dialogue. Assassinated leaders like Sadat and Rabin tried to take such a route. What they attempted was to achieve a transition from a political discourse in terms of concrete ownership to one in which belonging featured critically—that is: to translate the motive for ownership into one for belonging. As their respective societies included groups who were not ready for such a transition, these leaders were killed. Making the move from the will to possess to the will to belong is not a simple thing. Belonging occurs on the symbolic level: belonging occurs in a certain spatial realm without actually owning it. A person can feel part of a culture and a region without possessing it. By such a definition each nation is equally in the position to project its own identity and specific nature, as well as its aspirations, on to the very same region. Thus the city of Jerusalem can belong, emotionally or spiritually, to various nations. Each individual can deposit her or his meanings in the very same concrete space. Belonging has no concrete boundaries. We can both dream about Jerusalem. My dream does not need to interfere with yours, because dream-space is infinite. The concrete body does not enclose its spirit. Yehuda Halevi writes: "My heart is in the east, while I am in the remotest west". In English we could say that the word "belong" is composed of two parts: to be and to long, that is. To belong is to be always yearning for something that cannot by definition be attained. No one can rob a person of her inner Jerusalem. Both people, Palestinians and Jews alike, are unable to shift away from a discourse of ownership—which has space for only one subject—to one of belonging that can include two.

Obviously, it is hard to stay on the metaphorical level when paranoid fears are rampant. From fear that the other wants to annihilate me, I hold on ever more tightly to my territory. It is the task of leaders to contain these paranoid fears, to ameliorate them and instigate a movement from ownership to belonging, thus to allow co-existence in the metaphorical realm. Paradoxically, clinging to territory is no solution. A string of armed conflicts and acts of terror renders territory unsafe and psychologically tense. Constant anxiety and harassment, emanating from external reality, corrode internal life and creativity. Thus territorial ownership foregoes the ability to protect mental life.

The Israeli force that conquered the Palestinian territories in 1967 inaugurated an ongoing series of disasters. What the Israelis did not take into account was the fury this unleashed in the Palestinian people. Nor did they foresee the intifadas. In its blindness, the Israeli occupation did not calculate for the energies it would arouse among the Palestinian people who could not accept the occupation's daily humiliation and damage. With time, this fury has only increased. Their territorial imperative tells them to continue the struggle for their rights until the bitter end. The occupation only boosts these energies. Palestinians will continue their struggle in various forms, sometimes using desperate ways, as in the case of suicide bombers. Their war will not end until what has been taken from them is restored. Israelis' territorial imperative, on the other hand, involves fears of extinction, to assuage which they need ever more territory. Some sections of Israeli society, moreover, also refer to an imagined territory in the form of the Biblical Promised Land that they feel impelled to conquer in its entirety. As a result, Israel observes the Palestinian struggle from a position of utter blindness. And it is due to this incomprehension that Israel compulsively repeats the same mistakes, over and over again. Asked what he thought was the difference between a freedom fighter and a terrorist, Amos Keinan answered ironically: "A freedom fighter is one of my own people—a terrorist belongs to the enemy." A Palestinian could give the exact same answer—which illustrates the absence of any dialogue or ability to consider the other side in the conflict. Such a deadlock leads to catastrophe. Why do we go on with our invasions when the likely result is more pain than gain? We must be in the grip of an omnipotence-induced blindness and of a conviction that the entire territory must be ours. Bion calls this "the hate to learn from experience" (Bion, 1962a).

I would like to continue on to Derrida (Bennington & Derrida, 1993), whose ideas have evolved in response to the traumas of the twentieth century—the results of colonialism and totalitarianism, and of course the most horrific trauma of the Holocaust.

Born in 1930 in Algeria, Derrida was thrown out of his *lycee* in El Biar in 1942—as part of the implementation of the new racial laws in occupied France and its colonies. He recollects how he was hurt on being expelled:

> He was a little Jew boy, black and very Arab-looking, who did not understand an iota, whom nobody gave even the slightest explanation, not even his parents or his friends.

Derrida's history is a good example of a life lived on the cusp between territories: between Judaism and Christianity, between Judaism and Islam, between Europe and Africa. Where he lived he had to keep his Jewish identity hidden. As he writes: "In my family, as among the other Algerian Jews, we did not speak about circumcision but about baptism, not about bar mitzvah but about holy communion. I was afraid of events that felt non-Catholic, violent, barbaric, Arab" (Bennington & Derrida, 1993, p. 58).

According to Derrida, the philosopher observes international politics and public and demands explanations. Explanations for injustice, terror, infringement of human rights. Derrida suggests a deconstruction of the notions of territory and the nation state. He believes that the nature of war is changing. The colonialist, imperialist model is vanishing. Wars today are about resources, technological and economic, suggesting that people abandon the model of the nation state. Derrida (2002) proposes instead to build a new cosmopolitan order whose central players will be bodies with many participants and inter-continental collaborations. Derrida aims to reach a true age of enlightenment. This age of enlightenment will be characterised by world citizenship and cosmopolitan rights. Tolerance and forgiveness will be central terms. Forgiveness will be extended even to the unforgiveable. Derrida is aware that this is utopian. Given the current terrorism, exploitation, hunger, and epidemics in the world, he consciously adheres to an optimistic model. He believes that this will happen, though it is hard to tell in how many generations. The world, right now, is plagued by trauma. Much like Winnicott, who discusses the fear of break down as a fear of what will happen to the person in the future, rather than as anxiety about what has already occurred (Winnicott, 1974). Derrida too speaks of terror as creating fear of the future. He claims that if the American people had been told that the terrible death and destruction that occurred when the Twin Towers collapsed would never happen again, it would have been possible to mourn and then return to a regular daily life. The sense of trauma arises, however, with the perspective of the future: there is a perennial threat of chemical, biological, or nuclear attack. Terror, it seems to me, inflicts a deep wound to the living tissue of humanity.

What Derrida's vision suggests, as I understand it, is to build a world of belonging. A world where enlightenment will vanquish violence, where an international discourse will replace terror. Once the concept of the nation is deconstructed, ownership of land will stop being meaningful.

Derrida refers to Kant, who writes : "The community of the future will be a universal society and all of its members will be entitled to present themselves to all others as joint owners of the earth."

According to Kant, once such a sense of community has arisen, a breach of human rights in one part of the world will be felt in all other parts.

Existentialism, too, proposes to strengthen the mutual relations between the human individual and her or his human environment, so that moral and political commitment to the other will be essential to the human subject (Sartre, 1956). Such human relations will act prophylactically vis-à-vis the inhumanity of totalitarian systems. Sartre claims that human beings are condemned to be free. It is up to the individual whether she or he chooses to take the role of the posses-sive master or that of the one who yearns for belonging.

These statements by Sartre lead to immediate associations with the Nazi regime. How few and far between were those who were able to maintain a sense of moral responsibility and come to the succour of the Jewish people. How hard it was to maintain a sense of moral responsibility and humanity under a totalitarian and fascist regime. In his article on courage, Kohut too writes about the few and weak groups that dared to resist the Nazi regime (Kohut & Strozier, 1985). These people, according to Kohut, were able to find their "nuclear self"—in spite of inner doubt, threats, and external temptations. He refers to a small group of resisters that formed in München in 1942, called "The White Rose". Members of this group distributed thousands of news-sheets and leaflets calling for a public struggle against Hitler. They were eventually arrested and executed. The White Rose was led by a brother and sister, Hans and Sophie Scholl. They were twenty-two and nineteen years old respectively when they died. For Hans, the formative event in his life occurred when, as a medical student, he was taken to the Russian front. The train in which he travelled stopped at a station in Poland where he saw a group of women and young girls on the track doing forced labour, their backs bent. They were wearing yellow Stars of David on their uniforms. Hans leaped out of the train and walked up to them. The first person he encountered was an extremely emaciated girl. He observed her very thin arms and her lovely, wise face which, in his eyes, expressed indescribable suffering. He tried to think of something he could give her. Then he pushed his own military ration into her pocket. She threw it back at him. Hans picked a wild chrysanthemum and put it at her feet. Some time later, as the train was pulling out of the station, he saw her from his window, standing, erect, her gaze following him. The white flower was stuck in her hair. This moving episode illustrates the importance of the encounter with the real—the encounter, face to face, with injustice, with a person who has been transformed into an object, with the denial of the basic right to live.

Sophie Scholl met her death peacefully. On the night before her execution she had a dream that she recounted to the woman with whom she shared her cell:

> It was a sunny day and I was carrying a child dressed in a long white baptism robe. The path towards the church wound up a steep mountain, but I held the child tightly and with confidence. Then, suddenly, the ground in front of me rent asunder. I just barely managed to keep the child away from the spot. I succeeded but then I fell into the chasm myself.

Sophie told her cell mate that the child stood for the group's guiding principle that would continue in spite of everything. Sophie's behaviour throughout the rest of that day bore witness to how profoundly her values were assimilated. She was calm and serene all that day. Her face was radiant and in the end she walked up to the site of her execution without a sign of fear.

Acts that clash with our values and conscience are taking place at our doorstep. Oppression, closures, breaches of human rights, children and families are getting killed. But only very few of us actually encounter this injustice face to face as did Hans. Those who have no such experience of reality develop mechanisms of denial and disconnection. Indeed, such disconnection from the harsh reality of the Palestinian people in Gaza is typical of the vast majority of Israelis. Groups that resist the injustices of the occupation are small and they are largely ignored by the general public. Psychologists worry about speaking up. But when it comes to human rights, one's party political persuasion is of no importance. It is our moral obligation as psychoanalysts and as group analysts to protest against injustice. Another form this denial takes is, of course, the way in which Israelis who do not live in the immediate vicinity are disconnected from the citizens of Sderot. There, too, children and adult citizens sustain injuries and are, occasionally, killed.

Communication break-down and spiralling bias are the daily reality of Israeli–Palestinian interrelations. The newspapers present us, again and again, with the same text. Take, for instance, *Ha'aretz* of 23 January, 2008. Israel: "As long as Qassams keep falling, there will no longer be a hundred trucks daily entering the Gaza Strip"; Hamas: "Qassam rockets will go on being launched into Israel for as long as Israeli attacks on the Gaza Strip continue." Half a year on, and this is what we find—on 6 June, 2008—in the same newspaper: "Last week, following the launch of several rockets, the Minister of Defense ordered the renewed closure of the checkpoints between Israel and the Gaza Strip." And, in contrast: "Hamas announced this weekend that it suspends negotiations about a possible deal towards the release of kidnapped IDF soldier, Gilad Shalit until the points of passage between Israel and the Gaza Strip are re-opened." What we have here is the inverted mirror—and what it leads to is a dialogue of the deaf. The assumption that further pressure and further disruption of daily existence will contrive to stop the Qassams from coming, is again and again proven wrong. We could say that both sides are afraid of putting aside their tools of terror. We witness compulsive repetition and an ever increasing number of victims. Information about what makes the other side tick is lacking. What is described here, was repeated exactly in 2014 with many more victims. This tragic failure of communication demands many sacrifices. If this is how things continue, both sides will also continue absorbing deeply traumatic injuries. The inverted mirror and the deaf dialogue evolve from the need to posses out of annihilation anxiety and from no trust in belonging to the same land.

The need to own the land started with the Zionist movement. The Zionist pioneers, however, inaugurated the Land of Israel as a real, existential alternative. Thus they turned what had been a magical object into a total living reality. The soil had an especially central role, more specifically, uninhabited land that could be built on from scratch. This is how the moshavs and kibbutzim evolved. The pioneer saw her or himself as restoring life to the Bible. Then came the first generations of locally born children—they were called *sabras* and they were raised to love the land and the soil. They set up youth movements, trekked the country on foot and absorbed the land with every inch of their body. The *sabras*, too, were the ones who built Israel's army and the country's security-based ethos. Generations of warrior *sabras* put all their energy into the physical conquest of the land. It is through strenuous "know-your-land" treks that a good part of the *sabra* personality was formed. This is how they situated themselves in their native country. And the native country, in return, marked each and every Jewish person who was born in it, as a native.

In 1967, with the Six Day War, a deep rupture showed up in Israeli society. The divide is between the left, which opposes the occupation and wants to return the territories, and the settlers, who have a fervent messianic attachment to the idea of a Greater Israel. The latter are convinced that they are succeeding to reducing any gap that might have existed between the spiritual symbol of the Land of Israel—a mythological place—and the concrete land. They believe they have made a dream come true. The rift between the religious and the secular in Israel is only growing. The different social sectors speak in different languages and act from frequently clashing assumptions. Since they believe that the spiritual space has become concrete, those settlers who have been forcibly removed from their settlements feel that the state has betrayed them, robbing them from their ability to realise the dream that has rendered their lives meaningful. This situation, too, is marked by profound communicational malfunction.

As a result of two intifadas, the status of the occupied West Bank has become weakened and Jerusalem, again, is at the centre of international attention. Jerusalem's Jewish religious population has increased, and the city has become the site of the great struggle for the country.

A Tel Avivan visitor to Jerusalem does not identify with the religious and ultra-orthodox population there. Here, in Jerusalem, this visitor can also meet Palestinians who remind her or him of how this place is not exactly his or hers. This land has always been the land of other peoples: the Pharisees, the Hittites, the Jebusites. Jerusalem encapsulates the memory of the non-ownership of the land. It marks the "land" that will not be contained in the prosaic quotidian life of the city. It pulls Israeli thinking back to the question of place. These days, there seems to be a new possibility for Israel to set itself free from the compulsion to make the place all its own. Gurewitch and Eran (1991) suggest that this may enable us to find the right distance from *the place*. When they say this, they are also referring to the above-mentioned spiritual/religious meaning of the word; however, in their case, as an ideal to which we might belong without having to ally ourselves with the literal soil. This would mean to let go of the feeling that every smallest piece of land must be ours.

There must be a transition from a need for ownership—which speaks in a language of violence—to a need to belong to a group and to society. Belonging acknowledges pluralism and is not violent. My belonging does not get in the way of another person's belonging, and our reciprocal relations make it unnecessary for me to kill her or him. This type of relationship, Bion calls *commensal* relations (1962a, p. 93): they are healthy relations that characterise people who live alongside each other sharing the space. While they can nourish each other, they are also nourished by the resources of their environment. This is a type of co-existence.

The capacity for reverie is the ability to dream of a non-violent future (Bion, 1967). When things are so bad, the leadership must hold on to the dream. The knowledge that things can be different is a form of power that we should not take lightly.

"Reverie" is the leader's special competence during times of distress. It is her or his task to dream of another reality in the future.

The leader's knowledge should also include the knowledge generated by contemporary intellectuals. When this knowledge is absent, leadership becomes hollow, in the words of the author David Grossman.

When we look into the notions of ownership and belonging, I must mention Erich Fromm's *To Have or to Be?* (1976), which has supported me in my thinking about these issues. Fromm's argument is that western society strongly encourages a culture dominated by *having*—the ulterior objective is to amass more and more possessions. It is not easy to move from this type of culture to another that is in the sign of *being*. Intellectuals, however, have always insisted on this issue. Buddha claims that reaching the highest level of human development requires us to give up our material needs. People who need to acquire ever more lose connection with theirselves. Fromm writes that this distinction between having and being, that preoccupied him for many years, is, to him, one of the main questions of human existence. To illustrate the difference between these two positions, he quotes from two poets, the English poet Tennyson who wrote in the nineteenth century, and the seventeenth century Japanese poet Basho (pp. 26–28).

In his "Flower in the crannied wall" Tennyson mentions a flower that is growing from a crack in a wall; this is how the poem reads:

> Flower in the crannied wall,
> I pluck you out of the crannies,
> I hold you here, root and all, in my hand,
> Little flower—but if I could understand
> What you are, root and all, and all in all,
> I should know what God and man is.

Here, on the other hand, is Basho's haiku:

> When I look carefully
> *Nazuna* is blooming
> Beneath the hedge

The difference is striking. Tennyson approaches the flower by way of his desire to *have* it and he picks it "all". By considering it from an intellectual point of view he would like to gain an understanding of the nature of God and man. The flower, however, is dead. Basho, by contrast, approaches the flower in a totally different way. He does not touch it. He only wants to look. He respects life.

According to Fromm, the position of *having* denotes an existential position that relates to the world in terms of ownership. The wish that everything and everyone will be mine. A position of *being*, on the other hand, is vital and authentic in its attitude to the world. Since *being* closely involves notions of process, action, movement, *being* is associated with change, that is, with *becoming*, a state of being in constant flux. Loving, hating, suffering—they are all states of change. Living structures only exist by the grace of change. Change and growth are inherent to life. Bion, too, referred to constant becoming as crucial to anything or anyone alive (1970). According to him, this becoming is infinite in the sense that it will never result in an ultimate reality, to which however it is nevertheless always aspiring. In Buddhism, too, nothing is permanent, including the self. The one real and ongoing thing is becoming, process.

Fromm does not object to the human need to have property and whatever is required to lead a good life. He tries, however, to clarify the psychological position of the person who wants more and more, who needs to have more than everyone else—who needs this so badly that she or he is held in the grip of this need and has to yield being, in which we exist without compulsion and without ulterior goal, enjoying nature, life, the family. Many people in the west only meet their children during their vacations because they cannot quit the race for more.

In times of distress the connection with nature becomes much more powerful. When they are going through hard times, people tend to revert to a state of *being*. At a *Psycho-active* study day we recently heard about a Palestinian man who spent a long time in Israeli prison. He made a connection with a bird that kept appearing at the window of his cell. He talked about the strength he received from this bird, and how it showed him that one day he too would be free again.

When people are destitute they turn to nature. When they are busier getting and owning things, their liberty is curtailed and they become shackled to the material world.

In the current hi-tech era, huge financial transactions are being made, people become extremely wealthy over night—and yet, they find it hard to quit the race. Getting richer seems an endless possibility.

When we look at the difference between ownership and belonging, we should not forget that people sometimes become the property of their society.

This may be hard to accept, but soldiers who are sent to war are nothing but "military force"—they lose their personal identity. A more shocking instance of the same phenomenon is the suicide bomber, the *shaheed*, who becomes an instrument of the intifada. He or she has turned into the property of Palestinian society. Their personal identity as private individuals has thus been taken from them.

In order for such people to maintain themselves as the objects they have become, they must rid themselves of the connection with their real selves. One would assume that in more natural circumstances the *shaheeds* have a will to live like anybody else.

Particular instances of terrorist activity suggest that, before the event, the *shaheed* loses her or himself to the point of losing the connection with her or his body.

Though there is nothing closer to us than our own bodies, the body of the *shaheed*—prompted by his or her master terrorist—becomes alienated. It stops belonging to the person and becomes, instead, a mechanical object, lacking a soul. This psychic position is the opposite of Sophie Scholl's who is strongly connected to her body and her experience, and who concedes her life in full consciousness. The terrorist stops being flesh and blood. He and his body become a thing, a bomb, whose one aim is to put an end to the evil out there, anything out there that is not the terror organisation and, therefore, undistinguishing: the enemy. No matter whether it is a baby, a pregnant woman, a sixteen-year-old girl, or an eighty-year-old man. The suicide bomber does not see people. What she or he sees is an undifferentiated human mass. Much like her or his own individuality has been scrapped, so, too, has the individuality of the other. This is what depersonalisation is about.

When a person transforms into a tool in the hands of a terror organisation, she or he stops seeing life as a value. The one thing they see is the cause they serve.

Israelis watched their TVs in dismay when the mothers of Palestinian *shaheeds* stated they were proud their sons had died for Palestine, and that they were ready to sacrifice their surviving children too. When these mothers participated in group dynamics, it transpired they had been saying what they felt they were expected to say. They did, indeed, continue their children's struggle and justified the cause. But in the group they also expressed terrible pain and mourning, and said: "My son is more precious to me than the whole of Palestine". Behind the mask of the *shaheed* there is a person who has a mother.

To sum up: I have tried to distinguish between two positions—each of them relevant on the personal as well as on the social level. One is the position of ownership that brings along an infinity of catastrophes—the other is the position of belonging that opens up recognition of the other, with all her or his differences, and without the attendant pressure to vanquish or subdue her or himself. The latter position is ethically far more sophisticated, and humanity is unable to choose it as yet. We can hope that as humanity evolves, it will approach this position. This process may take many generations.

Whether such change takes places does in part depend on leadership—and leadership can be attentive to intellectuals. Such leadership may manage to gain access to and create a dialogue with the violent parts of society. It is the task of us, who deal professionally with group processes, to go on investigating reality and hold on to the dream.

CHAPTER TWELVE

The social unconscious and its manifestation in the analytic group

In this chapter I will discuss two traumatic events that occurred in the life of one of my analytical groups. Such events revive past traumas that occurred in the lives of the participants and the group's conductor alike. The revival of an event indicates that a private story occurred within a wider social context, which existed there and then, and returns to life here and now. I will emphasise the role of the social unconscious appearing meaningfully in the life of the group.

I have been conducting the analytic group on the same day and at the same time every week for the past fifteen years. The participants have changed several times over the years. Currently there are eight participants, four women and four men, aged between forty and over fifty, in various occupations.

The first traumatic event was my chronic illness during the past four years. This illness is manifested by acute, continuous pain, which is sometimes unbearable, and is not affected by painkillers. My illness entered the life of the group in various ways, first through interruptions in the group's activity due to my hospitalisation, trips abroad to seek treatment and so forth, and second through my coming to the group sessions while suffering pain that I could not hide. The fact of my being weak and in pain raised a variety of emotions, including fear for the group's future, disappointment, anger, but also compassion.

In this context, a meaningful event took place during the last Hanukkah holiday. I entered the room after everyone was already seated, suffering pain and in a depressive mood. Before I could sit down, I noticed that several large, colourful candles had been placed on a stool in the middle of the room. It turned out that the participants wished to light Hanukkah candles, and brought them to the group session. One of them asked me to leave the room and fetch a plate on which the candles could be lit and so a festive atmosphere could be created. I kept on walking ahead, took my seat, and said "no!" in an unpleasant tone. Silence ensued. A woman participant asked with alarm: "What's the matter?" and I repeated angrily: "I can't see this happening". I was sitting as if frozen, filled with anger at what seemed to me a form of attack on the analytic process. I was particularly enraged by the request to leave the room during the group session, in order to find a plate. Everybody else froze too; you could hear a pin drop. Eventually an attempt was made to turn to other matters, but to no avail. Another woman participant, a veteran, turned to me and said: "I understand you're in pain, Hanni, but you've acted harshly and aggressively. You could have explained why you didn't wish us to light the candles". Later she turned to two other participants adding: "how lucky I stopped you from buying doughnuts; I knew Hanni wouldn't have them in the group". The idea of eating Hanukkah doughnuts during the session made me feel even worse. I thought that all barriers were being broken and that nobody cared about the analytic work. I continued my attack, saying: "we didn't meet here to sing *Ma'oz Tsur Yeshu'ati* [the traditional song accompanying the lighting of the Hanukkah candles]". I felt anger raging in me and became detached and remote.

After a while, it dawned on me that I was the conductor of the group and I went back to work. My earlier stumbling, including the aggressive response, caused important material to surface. The participant who asked me to fetch a plate experienced me as his mother, who was very harsh and often attacked him arbitrarily. His response was one of pain because for him my attack was utterly bewildering. In this session meaningful analytic work was arrived at the hard way. Towards the end of the session I realised that I had wronged the group, and apologised for my behaviour. Simultaneously, the participant who sent me for a plate was able to see his part in the scene, which uncon-sciously invited an attack. On top of that, through the rich material brought up by two women in the group, we identified the informal role they played in their original families, that of the good, giving, nourishing aunt. I believe their emotional experience was unconscious, but was expressed through their behaviour. This had to do with their experience that at that time I was unable to play the good, protective mother to the group; I was the cold mother who made the group work hard, while these two women were playing the good mother who cared for the festive atmosphere and wished to dish out doughnuts in order to sweeten the bitter pill of the analytic work for the participants. There was also a hidden wish to warm and lighten up both the group and me personally. Later I realised they wished to give me a gift, which I had rejected.

Finally, I shared my feelings with the group. I realised that their wish to celebrate clashed with the fact that I had not celebrated Hanukkah at all that year. Every evening I remained secluded in my room, not even realising that there was a holiday. My family avoided mentioning it, out of consideration. The light the participants wished to bring into the group touched the darkness I was in, begetting my response.

The participants who brought the candles were the older ones, of my own generation, in fact. We were all children when the State of Israel was still very young. We were part of the culture in which Hanukkah was celebrated as the holiday of heroism and victory. We all used to sing: "Light up many Hanukkah candles / for the miracles brought about by the Maccabees". We belonged to the age of inno-cence. We believed that from then onwards Israel would always win, and Masada would not fall again. On reflection I realised that the need to celebrate with the group was a remnant from the 1950s, the fine days of Israel as it once was or, alternatively, an attempt to light a memorial candle for those times.

All through the week following the event at the group session, I was engulfed by bright and warm childhood memories. I remembered the whole family gathering every evening of the holiday around the lit candles singing joyful songs, and at school gathered together in the packed hall where every child would be given one, and only one doughnut, and the headmaster would light the candles. Those were exciting and uplifting moments. But all that was gone once I graduated from elementary school and after my beloved father died suddenly when I was fourteen years old. Both the personal and socio-historical backgrounds must have had their unconscious effect on my response that was expressed with: "I can't see this happening". Looking back, it would seem I did not wish to see either the lost childhood, the lost festivity, the protective and promising unity now gone forever, or the trauma of my father's death.

Israeli society in those days was like the great, enveloping mother; everyone was ready to give their life for her, or so it seemed. Nowadays Hanukkah is celebrated as an ongoing tradition, but it has lost the halo of unity and the experience of victory. Israel today is polarised and crumbling.

When dealing with the social unconscious we find that our identity has been formed by social processes that appear in disguise during analytic work. For better or for worse, our culture has changed, and with it the unconscious processes affecting the individual have changed as well. Israel is now part of the global, post-modern, Internet society. The social envelope is no longer a protective one: everything has been broken open and exposed. Quantity has won over quality; you must have a lot of everything, and you must get it fast. We have become a competitive society, characterised by ratings. From a psychoanalytical point of view, ratings are none other than the monstrous mother who is never satisfied. Cultural leaders are no longer those leaders who offer ideology. The numerous reality shows demonstrate that one does not need to have something valuable to say in order to gain a respectable place in society. Due to easily accessed global communication, Israel has been ingested by Western culture, losing its own unique cultural identity.

Against the background of this social culture, the event at the group session resonates of the society that we once knew. It is affected not only by the personal life story of the participants and myself, but also by the socio-historical background that unconsciously infiltrated the life of the group here and now. It is a distant historical background now gone, but its traces appear in the analytic experience.

The past is reconstructed in the present of the transference. From a group analytical point of view, this is a matter of the recursive interplay of the dynamic matrix of the group and the foundation matrix of its contextual society. Lacan says: "History is not the past; history is the past undergoing historization in the present" (Barzilai, 1997). In analysis the sequence of time is a temporality undergoing historisation. Bion would have agreed; historisation, in Bion's language, is the revival during analysis of the empty, frozen, and non-living places. These are places which have once contained life, but now lost it (Bion, 1984, pp. 6–26).

Bion speaks of the emergence of an event during analysis. The new event is unexpected, it is creative, and it disturbs the balance. The event appears unexpectedly, begetting creative effects regarding the past and the future, even if its active space is in the present (Bion, 1984, pp. 27–40).

In retrospect, the picture became clearer. Rationally, I was thinking that I was acting in order to preserve the group's boundaries. Only later did I realise that my reaction was infused with irrational elements that had to do with loss, nostalgia, and all that I miss in the society in which I live. My response was influenced not only by my difficulties here and now; the influence of historisation was not less powerful, and it burst out of me as an undigested element. By the end of the session my feelings towards the group had radically changed; I now felt compassion towards them for being at a loss about what to do with the candles, which one of the men hastily put inside his bag. I felt like the wicked witch who had ruined the celebration. Only later did I realise that no real, lasting harm would have been done had I let them light the Hanukkah candles. On the other hand, my ability to adopt the experience of the wicked figure contributed to the analytic work and caused unconscious material to surface. After all Winnicott regarded the therapist's errors as material for analytic work. The therapist might fail where the parent had also failed, and once the error is rectified a therapeutic experience would emerge (Winnicott, 1982, pp. 158–166).

The term "event" is relevant both externally and internally. Bion uses the term "catastrophic change" in order to distinguish a situation in which a change is experienced as frightening and shaking, but eventually brings about growth and creative development (Bion, 1963, pp. 42–47).

During the celebration of the recent Hanukkah in Israel the celebratory candles were set aside due to the painful social trauma caused by the large-scale forest fire on Mount Carmel. No less than forty-four people lost their lives due to the fire, and huge damage was inflicted on nature and property. Two phenomena that have to do with the social unconscious should be mentioned in this context.

First, not one of the participants in the group or in my private clinic mentioned the horror that was taking place here and now, not even one word. This fact allowed me to experience the mechanism discussed by Earl Hopper, namely encapsulation, which is a social autistic mechanism (Hopper, 2003b). The events on Mount Carmel were so close and frightening, but as long as we are away from the very scene, we manage to feel nothing and push the painful events out of our own private world.

The second phenomenon has to do with the Israeli social unconscious. I refer to the automatic process by which victims become heroes. The halo of heroism blocks out the magnitude of the catastrophe. Heroism gives death some meaning. Hanukkah is the holiday of heroism, and heroism is what we see in front of our eyes here and now. I believe that there is an unconscious process, the purpose of which is to protect us from our leadership's ineptitude and the pointlessness of the death of young people under tragic circumstances. Namely, a dual form of social defence is observed: a protective opaque shell allowing us to avoid feeling on the one hand, and the glorification of death on the other. Both forms of defence are dangerous, because they allow terrible things to go on without protest.

I shall now turn to a different traumatic event, which the analytic group experienced recently. The younger brother of a veteran participant, whom I shall name Eran, contracted a rare and severe form of cancer. Eran spent three months at his brother's hospital bedside, taking turns of duty that included nights and weekends. The group accompanied that process, which was difficult because we experienced pain, but Eran's reports were devoid of emotion and spiked with cynical humour. Eventually, the brother died on a Saturday. Eran did not inform me, but on Monday his chair remained empty. Once the session was over I immediately contacted him. He told me on the phone that he did not wish to bother us with the funeral, but would appreciate visits during the seven days of mourning. (In Israel we visit the mourners in the "shiva", and this duty is above any culture including the analytical culture.)

Eran had joined group therapy due to his lack of ability to have meaningful feelings towards his relatives. He felt that his emotions were flat and that he was not really involved in the life of the people surrounding him. He also felt an acute loneliness, and believed that he had no wishes or expectations whatsoever. For a long period the investigation of childhood remained futile. He described an idyllic household and dedicated parents. On one occasion he recalled a touching childhood experience, albeit while using his typical indifferent tone:

> When I was seven years old, the Six Days War broke out. Father returned from the war with one eye bandaged, but said it was nothing, a trivial wound which would soon heal. And indeed, after a short while the bandage disappeared. My brothers and I loved to horseplay with our father. However, he didn't allow us to throw him a ball, always saying "give me the ball and I'll throw it to you", but we never asked why. When we threw him a bunch of keys, he was unable to catch it. He would say: "don't throw it, put it in my hand". We never asked why.
>
> When I turned twenty-one, right after my military service, Father called over my brothers and me and said he had something to tell us. He said: "since the Six Day War I have a glass eye. I lost my eye not in the war, but due to cancer. We didn't wish to worry you, so we said I was wounded in the war." I looked at him, and for the first time realised: indeed, a glass eye. I then realised why he asked us to hand him objects. Since his field of vision had changed, he lost his hand coordination.

This story is one of the strangest that ever came my way during my career as an analyst. Namely, a child lives with his father for fourteen years without seeing or realising that the father has a glass eye. This remarkable story gave us an insight into what had been missing so far. The glass eye turned into a metaphor for all the things Eran did not wish to, or could not see. The unseeing eye that accompanied his life allowed us to begin seeing the protections placed around him, causing him to lose his curiosity and to avoid asking his parents difficult questions. The door that locked out the pain had blocked the way for warm feelings as well.

The death of Eran's brother, which took place in the group's life here and now, allowed for analytic work in several dimensions. The first dimension was the one of the group. Eran re-enacted his parents' attitude and protected us by preventing our participation in the funeral; ostensibly, he did not wish to bother us. The second dimension was the historisation of the private and public spheres. Eran's father contracted cancer and died a short while after revealing the secret of his glass eye to his sons. Now the younger brother died of cancer at age forty-five, the same age as the father on his death.

Eran grew up in a family that kept religious traditions, and studied in a religious school. While his brothers joined a religious youth movement, he became a boy scout. Politically the family was conservative right wing. His father's brothers were on the *Altalena* [the ship over which a bloody skirmish took place between the Irgun and the newly formed IDF in June 1948]. Family members always talked with admiration about the pre-independence Jewish underground groups and Irgun leader Menachem Begin, and derided the mainstream Haganah for its policy of restraint towards the British and Arabs. It is noteworthy that the father told his sons that he was wounded in the war, having been too ashamed to tell them that in fact he underwent an operation and lost an eye. The atmosphere that encouraged volunteering and fighting for the homeland caused the father to lie, and Eran to internalise forcefully the ideals of his upbringing. Eran enlisted in a fighting unit, and soon after receiving commission led a company in the first Lebanon War (1982). Many of his close comrades died around him. He fought bravely, for this was the ultimate demand. However, on returning from the war his mother said: "I sent off a talkative boy and got back a mute". His reaction to his comrades' death gradually turned into a post-traumatic one. Still, he was unable to feel, and was sad for it. He was envious of people who could demonstrate strong emotions and libidinal heat. Also, Eran was unable to mourn his father, and to this day finds it difficult to read the biographical book published by the family, or to look at his father's photos in it.

The shells around Eran's heart were constructed of personal material, but also of material belonging to the level of the social unconscious. Only recently has he begun to realise the effect of the war on his emotional life. He was one of those on the front line, charging forward. He was not thinking but acting, obeying the unwritten demand passed over from former generations by those who built the state and risked their lives for it. Since the war he would participate in memorial ceremonies for his comrades, but would feel nothing, even while visiting home after home of bereaved parents and widows. He was also unable to fulfil his wish to love a woman and experience intimacy. He relieves his loneliness by constantly continuing his multidisciplinary studies.

Eran's deceased brother, who left behind him a widow and four children, belonged to a protective religious community, that embraced the family during the mourning period, providing food and other necessities. Eran felt even lonelier during that period; witnessing the supportive community he experienced a kind of agoraphobic anxiety. He fled as soon as he could, telling us that he would rather reject such support in time of calamity, because the price to pay was having your privacy constantly violated, and living in a community that was suffocating as well as supportive. However, recently his position became more ambivalent. At the group sessions he brought up macabre scenarios in which he dies at home and is discovered only after several days have passed. He started imagining his own funeral, attended by a mere few participants, contrary to the large crowd at his brother's funeral. Further small changes occurred, that for him were like huge steps. Eran said that his brother avoided talking of his cancer, and would not say his last farewells to his relatives, obeying the family's unwritten law that one must not discuss pain and must hide any distress. Eran said that he was able to feel pain over his dying brother, the kind of pain he previously was unable to feel. On Yom Kippur he joined his brother in prayer at the hospital's synagogue, and he cried, knowing that this was his brother's last Day of Atonement.

The group sessions were often cancelled between May and October of 2010 because of my illness, and I even suggested finding them a different conductor, fearing that I would no longer be able to work. At that time Eran wrote me some moving e-mails, telling me how the fact that I was sharing my condition was positive in his view. His mother never expected his empathy, always projecting a strong figure that could manage on her own. Her need to always seem strong caused the emotional distance between them, and they would always exchange very short, formal, and polite phone calls. Towards me, on the other hand, he expressed warmth, longing, real care, and a strong wish that the group continue under my direction.

Eran said how surprised he was by the strong feelings he suddenly had towards me. Working together, we were able to use this feeling of closeness therapeutically. Through his relations with me Eran gained a deep insight into the fact that his mother loves him and always did. He felt that her ways of expression were different, but that in her own way she needed him after all, and that her love was unconditional. He felt gratitude for what she had always been for him, and shared her terrible pain as a bereaved mother. He realised how much pain was buried inside her as she came daily to care for her grandchildren with dedication and deep love. He began approaching her differently and to seek her company, and currently reports strong feelings towards her. Something inside him has opened, allowing him to understand her way of showing love and dedication.

I believe that the cracks in Eran's shell, manifested in his expressions first towards me and then towards his mother, followed another crack that came from the wider social level. A while earlier Eran found himself going ten consecutive times to watch the film *Waltz with Bashir*, a film expressing the emotional experience of the soldiers during the first Lebanon War. The film had brought back repressed memories, triggering spontaneously painful and mournful feelings, causing a part of him to start softening. He said he no longer needed the memorial days in order to try and feel something; he feels the pain of his comrades' death, and he feels his mother's love.

In Eran's case I find the protective shells grew not only in the private sphere but to a great extent in the wider social sphere as well. I increasingly believe that these two spheres are inseparable. Recently, when Eran was telling about the atmosphere in which he grew up, mentioning his uncles who fought the British, a relative newcomer to the group, whom I shall call Daniel, said he could identify with everything described by Eran. He too grew up in a family of underground warriors, and had a complicated attitude towards religion. It is noteworthy that in Daniel's case the influence absorbed by him from the social level has different characteristics. When he was a child, his father had turned to religion. It happened suddenly and radically, immediately after the death of the father's uncle, who was childless and religiously observant. The father became a copy of the dead uncle in his behaviour and customs. For the family this was difficult and strange; the father became fanatical and imposed strict religious observance on all his family members. One of his customs was to maintain silence one day every month; on such a day no one could talk to him. In the group we viewed this as passive-aggressive behaviour towards his wife and children. Daniel, although as a young boy had rebelled against his father, defended him at the group sessions, supplying various excuses for his custom of silence. Soon after the father's death, about fifteen years ago, Daniel became gradually observant, saying: "my father would have been very happy to see me observe all those rules". Obviously, here was an intra-generational re-enacting: the father following the uncle, the son following the father.

Recently, dramatic events took place in Daniel's family, echoing the social level of a family committed to fighting, as well as the level of fanatical extremism. In recent years Daniel led a large social project, but abandoned it when his principles were compromised. Abandoning the project when it was nearing completion brought him many enemies, and he was turned from a leader to a *persona non grata*. This extreme upheaval only fuelled his belligerence, and he ended up in court, facing several legal suits. He was standing alone, with only his immediate family members who also came under violent threat, feeling he was fighting the war of justice according to the strict principles dictated by the underground warriors of former generations. This is a unique kind of historisation: the battlefield is markedly different, but through his belligerence and brutality Daniel re-enacted the social heritage of the former generation and his father's adhering to his principles. For him, the other people in the project assumed the part of the majority of Labour Party sympathisers who were all wrong, while he played the Revisionist minority who won the battle. The group participants commented on Daniel's belligerent language; even when talking of the relations in his family he used words such as "battlefield", "retreat line", or "ambush".

Eran and Daniel soon established camaraderie, while the rest of the group witnessed with bewilderment their new-found common language. During the group exchange Daniel was asked whether it was really worthwhile to fight constantly; perhaps he deserved some peace and quiet. Immediately Eran came to Daniel's rescue, quoting a line from Beitar Song, written in 1932 by the Revisionist leader Ze'ev Jabotinsky. I was taken aback by the old quote that entered the group's here and now: "silence is filth". Daniel nodded contentedly, his face beaming. After the session I looked up the song and found the longer quote: "For silence is filth / abandon blood and soul / for the sake of the hidden glory". I must confess that I personally cannot fathom that "hidden glory" worth dying for.

Bion emphasises the binocular vision, allowing us to view the personal while placing the social in the margins, and then, moving in the opposite direction, placing the social in focus and the personal in the margins (Bion, 1961, p. 8). This movement is important when we guide an analytic group. Viewing a picture, it is worthwhile turning it upside down in order to discover new elements. Bion and Foulkes used the picture in which we see a vase but alternatively can see two profiles, as a metaphor for psychoanalytical vision. And indeed, in the two events described herein there is a constant movement between the vase—in this case, the personal event that appears in the group, easy to see and occupying the centre of the picture—and the profiles, that are hidden in the background and represent the allusive and hidden social level. However, we soon learn that the two pictures cannot be separated, and that the personal and social spheres are interrelated and inseparable.

When the state of Israel was young, it seemed like the great mother; with its clear ideology, it functioned like a kind of receptacle that allowed its citizens to feel they belonged in it. In this receptacle that was the early state, the contents represented the male or the father function. All the episodes presented in this chapter include a father as a figure that left its mark on the psyche. The personal fathers internalised the great leaders, such as Ben Gurion, Begin, and Jabotinsky. The state raised a generation of warriors, whose shoulders were burdened by their duty to former generations, and the burden was particularly heavy because of the Holocaust. This was the unwritten duty. The state, the great mother, was the land, and her sons were the heroic warriors who fertilised its soil with their sweat, seed, and blood.

The first generations born on this soil internalised the duty of inescapable war. Daniel, of 2010, says he had no choice. The social justice wars in which he fought and was defeated were not his choice: the wars had chosen him.

Indeed, every child born into the traumatic history of wars has but an imaginary freedom to be himself. Such insights lead to recognising the traumas of the second and third generations of Holocaust survivors. Apparently there is no such creature that can be called "self" without the hidden guidance of the social space. Bion (1967, p. 86) likens the early stage of life to the prophecy of the oracle of Delphi. The oracle prophesised what would happen to Oedipus, and Oedipus built his tragic life step by step in accordance with the prophecy, unwillingly and unwittingly. He was governed by immense forces of which he was unaware. In Israel it was once common to say on the birth of a baby that when he grows up he will no longer have to fight. This saying has disappeared from the social sphere. We have given up. We no longer hope or believe. The poet Haim Goury wrote that Israeli-born children "are born with a knife in their hearts". That is the ancient knife that Abraham lifted in order to sacrifice his son Isaac. Abraham did not sacrifice his son, but the terrible image of sacrificed sons remained in the social unconscious. This image is the bringer of misfortune; it allows for the death of the sons prior to their parents.

As I look back on the material that has surfaced while writing this chapter, I see a long continuum of wars and disasters. The Maccabees; the Holocaust; the War of Independence; *Altalena*; the Six Days War; the Lebanon War. The burden of socio-historical catastrophes emerged like some concentrated material in two routine analytic meetings here and now. I feel as if inside me the Hanukkah candles are mixed up with memorial candles; darkness and light, life and death, destruction and construction. The Israeli society is reflected in the individual life, and perhaps requiring that we, the analysts, will again and again mend its broken pieces.

Bion regards the Sphinx as the metaphor for a riddle whose solution lies hidden deep in the social unconscious. The contemporary Sphinx is asking us difficult riddles. It asks how come our leaders no longer believe in peace? How come we are ready to wage war time and again? Why is our society trapped in compulsive repetition? This is the Sphinx who stands over the abyss of the social unconscious, waits for answers, and continues to demand sacrifices.

CHAPTER THIRTEEN

A boy is torn between two realities: looking at his biography in the light of the social unconscious

T here is a problematic issue that is denied and ignored most of the time: how does a psychotherapist treat a patient who belongs to the enemy? A short review of an individual psychotherapy conducted by a colleague reflects the difficulty.

The psychotherapist is a veteran Israeli Jewish woman, who for two and a half years has been treating a Muslim boy, who was at the end of the therapy, twelve years old. This therapy took place in the framework of the Mental Health Services under the Israeli Ministry of Health, at the Community Mental Health Centre in Acco, a town in the north of Israel, which lies on Israel's Mediterranean coast. It has been a joint Arab–Jewish town for generations, but during Israel's 1948 War of Independence, a large part of the Arab population fled the town, and more Jews came in their place. The Arab population is partially Muslim and partially Christian. The Community Centre of Acco serves both Arabs and Jews, but its professional staff—psychologists, social workers, and so on—is more than seventy per cent Jewish.

The boy belongs to a religious Muslim family. In spite of his socio-ethnic background he studies at a Jewish school, that was chosen by his mother, because its standard was higher than that of the Arab schools. This school has only five Arab students, and this boy is the only Arab in his class.

The boy was his father's favourite son. However, about two years prior to the therapy, the father had suddenly left his home and his family and moved to Gaza, where he married another woman. The boy has not seen his father since that time. Gaza is a Palestinian city, that lies outside of Israel's border. Gaza is a part of the Palestinian autonomy. It was the city of Yaser Arafat, the PLO leader, and it was there that the peace agreements between Israel and the Palestinians happened and failed. Gaza is a city politically divided between the forces that support the peace process, and the substantial forces of the extremist religious movements: Hamas and the Islamic Jihad. These movements, which are called "fundamentalist" by their own members, oppose the peace process and carry out brutal acts of terror in the centres of the Jewish population. Dozens of Jews were killed in several such actions. The Hamas adopted the system according to which young men, who identify with its ideas, are sent into crowded Jewish civilian centres carrying a large quantity of explosives on their body, and blow themselves up together with their victims. By so doing, these suicide bombers become martyrs, and the Hamas movement has many youngsters willing to carry out such actions in order to win glory and become martyrs after their death.

This background is important in order to understand the social world in which the psychotherapy of this child took place. As for the therapy itself, it is important to indicate that for a long period the boy used to bury dolls that looked like babies in the sand box during therapy. This game was repeated in every therapeutic hour. Parallel to this ritual at the therapy, aggressive and violent behaviours were manifest at school. The violence against the Jewish teacher was constantly escalating.

The therapeutic method was psychodynamic and psychoanalytic. With a highly sensitive attitude, the therapist mainly tried to relate to the boy's abandonment experience due to his father's disappearance. She related to the great anger towards the father and to the boy's attempts to bury his emotions. It was a correct and admirable therapy, but nevertheless, an unsuccessful one. My guess is that the therapy failed because the therapist ignored the social unconscious (Hopper, 2003b). Perhaps she was afraid to make the social unconscious, conscious. The main problem here is a split and disconnection between the personal culture and beliefs of the therapist, and the culture and beliefs of the society at large, in other words the foundation matrix (Foulkes, 1975a).

Hopper and Weinberg (2011) have enlarged the conceptualisation of the foundation matrix. One aspect of their elaborations is important for the case of this boy: "The matrix of a social system was conceptualized as a source of constraint and restrain on the members of the particular social system" (p. xlvi). It is clear that the boy acted and felt according to the echoes he heard in the Arabic environment, and the therapist did not take this massive influence into account. Penna (2014) emphasises the historical aspect of the foundation matrix. This is relevant to this boy who grew up with a feeling that the land of Israel was in the past a Palestinian land that had been cruelly taken from his ancestors.

The therapist believed that through her humanistic attitude, and through supplying a reformative experience of contact, she would assist the child in growing and overcoming his difficulties. She had faith, which turned out to be a false one, that with the right attitude she could transcend the barriers of society, nation, religion, politics, and territory, and through the contact of one human being to another she would penetrate his soft, vulnerable, childish heart.

Her failure caused her much pain, and it teaches us that it is in fact impossible to transcend all those barriers. It is impossible to have a therapeutic experience, while ignoring the social context. This context penetrates deeply into the therapy. The child was becoming increasingly violent outside, while regarding the therapy room as an isolated space. He was mentally attached to the therapist and appreciated her, but they were cooperating in the performance of a total split between outside and inside, and were living in their own private bubble. I believe that this total split between their personalities as a therapist and a patient inside the therapy room, and their social identity outside it, was harmful to the therapy, and hindered its growth and development. In other words it is harmful to ignore the dynamics of what Hopper (2003b) has called "the there and now".

This split between inside and outside reached its climax in the therapy right after a destructive terror attack in the centre of Tel Aviv, in which more than twenty Jews were killed. The boy arrived for the therapeutic hour happy and laughing, and pulled his finger across his throat saying: "Butcher all Jews!"—disregarding entirely the fact that his therapist was a Jew. The therapist went into an emotional turmoil and was severely shocked. The motion of the finger across the throat took her back to her childhood memories, in which her parents, who were survivors of the Holocaust, told her of their persecution by the Nazis; they too have illustrated the events by the same motion of the finger across the throat, which the Nazis have done when entering Jewish towns. The therapist was looking at her patient and seeing a Nazi in front of her. She was paralysed with disappointment, anger, and pain. The walls that were protecting her, and that distinguished between the interior and exterior of the therapy, collapsed with a bang. Such processes of trauma and countertransference have been discussed by many, but Hopper has emphasised the effects of the social unconscious.

The boy also started to fantasise that his father did not abandon him, but rather went on an exalted mission. According to him, only an exalted idea can justify such abandonment, and he therefore believed that his father went to Gaza in order to join the Hamas and plan the killing of Jews. Right after he started developing this fantasy—that might have contained a grain of truth—the boy started throwing stones at cars belonging to Jews in the streets of Acco. He was beginning to rehearse his identity as a violent child. He was saying that his destiny in life was to become a suicide martyr, and was certain he would be born into a new and better existence. He decided to wait until he grew up a little, and then to go to Gaza and offer himself to the Hamas leaders. His destiny in life was to become a suicide-killer.

In Bion's view (1961, pp. 116–117), this young boy was pushed to take a role. The Palestinian society needs young people to fight the enemy. Out of a pressure that was imposed on him, mainly unconsciously, this boy is chosen by the society to accomplish a role. He takes the role because he has the valency for such a role that evolved from his traumatic biography.

Hopper (2003c) argues that the seed of the idea of taking roles for the entire group is already formulated by Foulkes in his article from 1937 "On introjection". Hopper (2003c, p. 46) also mentions Kernberg who draws on Redl's notion of "role suction". Kernberg writes that there is a spectrum of different types of symbolic leadership, and the one that emerges is a reflection of the degree of regression in the group. I think that acting out and expressions of aggression by this boy point to a regression of the Palestinian society, that chooses killing as the only solution to the conflict created by the extreme helplessness inherent in the situation.

This boy demonstrated to us the process by which a killer driven by an idea is born. He had buried his childhood in the sand, and was willing to turn himself into an explosive charge.

This boy represents a whole generation of children who were born into such tragic dynamics. They grew up learning to hate and be violent. These are children without a childhood. They are vulnerable to manipulation by political movements. They are children with no future. This boy personifies the distress and traumatic experience of his society (Hopper, 2012).

As I have indicated, this therapy was admirable, but its great weakness was its disconnection from its social context. The therapist was representing the occupying people, while the child was representing an occupied people, with no homeland or territory of its own. This remained outside the therapeutic work. Because of the therapist's fear to touch on these painful dilemmas, the child was not given an opportunity to explore in the therapy the insult of being a student in a Jewish school. He had to celebrate the Jewish holidays, which were not his holidays. He even had to celebrate the Israeli Independence Day, that for him symbolised a disaster and the loss of his Palestinian social identity. He actually lived in an abnormal reality in which his religious, ethnic, and national identities were being crushed. He thus lived under mental occupation. In the therapy he did not have the chance to rebel, be angry, or feel pain for the fact that he was living in a territory, that was not his own.

The therapy also ignored the fact that the boy was coming to the community centre, which is situated in a beautiful, large stone building at the city centre, a building that used to belong to Arabs before 1948, but now is a territory "occupied" by Jewish professionals. The boy was coming for therapy in the therapist's territory, which used to be his people's territory. Growing up in a foreign, occupied territory is an unbearable experience. In this social situation the child was in fact the victim of political violence, which was mental rather than physical. This violence was expressed by the fact that he was an alien in an environment that did not care for him. He was among children who would not become his friends. He was uprooted from his natural ground. By a slow and continuous process he had turned from a victim into a perpetrator.

These processes compel us, as professionals who work with groups as well as with individual persons, to relate to the term "self"—which is increasingly becoming central to contemporary psychoanalytical thinking. We must relate to a person's "social self". The self does not grow in the small family cell alone, but it grows also on a ground that is related to a wider identity. Erikson (1951) writes about a third sphere, that he calls a "macro sphere" that represents the world we share with others, and is responsible for our mature identity. Hopper and Weyman (2003) claim that there is no human identity without a social dimension. They point out that human beings share under-standing and a common intellectual and emotional discourse which, as I see it, is the basis for a "social self" or "social identity".

We must investigate closely this wider infrastructure, this social identity, which is passed to the child through his parents since early childhood. This social ground is an important feeding source to the individual self. Uprooting oneself from this ground can be extremely painful. In human history, exile or banishment were considered the worst punishment. Oedipus went into exile in order to atone for his sins. The first human couple was driven out of Paradise. Cain was banished and was sentenced to a life of wandering. Exile is like a mental death, a punishment that might even be worse than death. This mental death is due to the fact that the person is cut off from every-thing that was meaningful in his life. The Jewish people has a long history of exile. The Jews were for many generations a people without a territory, and had to use numerous and sophisticated manipulations in order to preserve their physical and mental existence.

Today we still live in a world full of refugees, homeless people whose territory in which they had their physical and mental existence taken away by force. This act of violence leaves the victims in a state of almost utter helplessness. Their spiritual and social container has been destroyed. After all, a social container is crucial for normal life. Its function is to maintain a routine of daily life, to produce a degree of financial security, and to provide membership in a community.

The population of Gaza, a large part of whom are refugees living in camps, suffers the political violence aimed at them by Israel's bureau-cratic system every day and hour. This is a violence built up by small, daily routines. Not a physical violence, but one that prevents normal everyday existence. This is a kind of stress and cumulative violence, in contrast to the catastrophic violence of the suicide bomber, which is analogous to stress, cumulative and catastrophic trauma (Hopper, 2003b).

The Palestinians in the refugee camps have very large families. They must pass through a daily ordeal in order to get permits, that allow them to work inside Israel. They are always delayed for long hours at the roadblocks. They have to get up in the middle of the night in order to stand in line at the roadblock as early as 4 a.m. and they return home after dark. For this effort they earn very little. The health services they can get are very limited, and often parents who come to the roadblock with sick children in order to go to Israeli hospitals are delayed for days. A whole population of children with serious problems such as cancer or heart conditions is expected to die for lack of an adequate medical treatment. All these things build up gradually and become explosive. A situation of helplessness, the loss of territory, and dependency on the occupier is the principle situation, which fuels violence and revolt. The physical violence and acts of terror carried out by the Palestinians are the outcome of cumulative helplessness.

It is important to indicate that in such an anomalous situation in which an entire people lives under oppression, the social identity becomes increasingly important for the oppressed people, and in extreme situations it swallows the individual identity. In situations of distress people tend to sacrifice their lives for the sake of an ideology or society at large. The extremist Islamic movements offer an alternative that provides great compensation and the opportunity to emerge from a situation of helplessness and inferiority. They offer a new chance to belong. The boy who was mentioned earlier arrived at a situation in which he felt that the only way to find meaning, value, and belonging was to offer himself to the Hamas as a suicide bomber, thus winning admiration. That would be the way to find his true destiny, to change from a misfit boy into a hero and a martyr. This is in fact a strong ecstatic and impulsive experience in which a whole crowd stands behind you, and you feel the grandiose feeling of becoming one with a crowd that has a redemptive mission. As Freud (1921c, pp. 154–155) wrote about this configuration:

> Human groups exhibit once again the familiar picture of an individ-
> ual of superior strength among a troop of equal companions, a picture
> which is also contained in our idea of the primal horde. The psychol-
> ogy of such a group, as we know in form the descriptions to which we
> have so often referred—the dwindling of the conscious individual
> personality, the focusing of thoughts and feelings into a common
> direction, the predominance of the affective side of the mind and of

unconscious psychical life, the tendency to the immediate carrying out of intentions as they emerge—all this corresponds to a state of regression to a primitive mental activity , of just such a sort as we should be inclined to ascribe to the primal horde.

Those people who cover their face and hide their individual identity have renounced their individuality. Their individual identity has been absorbed by their all encompassing social identity. The individual self has become a splinter, a tiny shard of a large mirror, that is duplicated indefinitely until one large social mirror is created. Each and every person as such is anonymous. Each person derives his identity from his reflection in the social mirror. Social violence and social terror are anonymous: it makes no difference who is hitting and who gets hit. In other words a person who is at the same time both a splinter or a shard and covers his face with a mask is a perfect personification of aggregation and massification against the fear of annihilation, which is typical of terror organisations (Hopper, 2003a).

Any social situation in which the only way to maintain a social identity and its boundaries is through trying to liquidate the other while being willing to die with him, is pathological and maybe called "a social psychosis". A social psychosis is characteristic of traumatised societies (Mojovic, 2011, p. 216). Following Hopper's theory of encapsulation, traumatised societies are characterised by negative social psychic retreats. Palestinian and Israelis have been using violence and terror of various forms against each other for more than eighty years.

As psychologists, the cardinal question that we must ask is why is it so difficult to divide a territory and live in coexistence. This question is complex, and may be addressed from various angles. Bion's theory of thinking may shed some light on these distressing social phenomena.

I choose to use the terminology presented by Bion in his book, *Second Thoughts* (1967). This terminology refers to the process of the development of thinking by the individual since infancy. I wish to apply these terms to the study of society rather than the individual.

Bion refers to two principle and different elements in thinking. The first is called "alpha type elements". These are elements that can be thought. The other are the "beta type elements" of which it is not possible to think.

Alpha function refers to the transformation from thoughts that cannot be thought to thoughts that can be thought. Those senses, or impressions, that do not receive a name, a word or a thought, that do not appear in dreams, have not under gone transformation. They remained as beta type elements. Bion calls them"things in themselves". They are like undigested splinters that will usually appear in a form of acting out or as a psychosis.

Beta elements are stored in the collective memory in their crudest form. These are elements upon which time and experience leave no impact. They express the inability to learn from experience, and are repeated over and over again, for example, in terror activity, which is persistent and has recurred in our region for decades. These elements are especially dangerous to society in times of threat, tension, and uncertainty. They are likely to burst out in the form of social violence. They cannot be sublimated. They cannot be transformed to the level of dialogue and they appear as concrete acts. These actions do not undergo mental and emotional digestion, and they recur time and again in the same form. They represent a situation characterised by the loss of hope and a great deficiency in the capacity for reverie. They appear in the most primitive and cruel forms. They do not respond to discourse in any human language.

These ideas led me to realise that, to put the matter very simply, this boy was unable to participate in dialogue about his socio-cultural-political experience. He was living in a state of encapsulated traumatic experiences that remain more alive in his body than in his mind. If he had been able to transform these beta elements into alpha elements in the context of dialogue with another person, he might have been able to learn that terror does not lead anywhere, or more precisely does lead to negative social psychic retreat. On the basis of such dialogue he might even have been able to imagine the idea of coexistence, and believe in the chances that his people now have, no matter how limited they may be. Even those among us who participate in peace talks and believe in peace are afraid of the consequences of their endeavours. Of course they try to contain their anxiety and imagine the realisation of the concept of peace.

The hand motion across the neck saying "Butcher the Jews!" that appeared in the therapy pushed the therapist back into the collective memories of the Jewish people. This phenomenon involves the concretisation of a metaphor. This specific gesture that was registered in memory, opened a drawer that contains a whole world of experiences and memories. This was overwhelming and provoked great anxiety. This gesture, that was registered in collective memory, was transmitted across the generations. The passing years had not reduced the intensity of this image. Actually, it might even have been the case that in her experience of this gesture the therapist regressively transformed alpha elements into beta elements, on the basis of the overlapping social background characterised by massive social trauma.

In this context the difficult question is: what are these social elements that so far cannot be digested? What are those elements that must burst out time after time in the form of violence and terror?

I presume that it is the emotional aspect of terror that remains indigestible. As in cases of primitive hysteria, emotions remain outside of and detached from processes of thought and mental metabolisation. The terror may be likened to a dense object that blows up again and again. Those members of society who carry out these kinds of actions refuse to feel pain for loss, to undergo processes of mourning and be in mental contact with the meaning of a tragedy. Those who do not undergo the processes of mourning remain indifferent to death and disasters.

Social violence is always characterised by what might be regarded as social beta elements. Perhaps it is apposite to quote the French aphorism: "How things have changed, and yet how things are still the same".

Conclusion

In this chapter I tried to integrate clinical thinking about a boy who grew up in a very complex social environment with thinking about the social unconscious. Especially in the context of a traumatised society, social processes penetrate intensively into the consulting room. A therapy does not happen in an empty space. The humanistic attitude of the psychotherapist in the case discussed was not enough. The social envelope was full of holes of rage and violence. In other words, the inner world of the boy was shaped by the foundation of his society.

If we apply Bion's theory of thinking, which was originally developed with respect for individuals, for society itself, we increase our ability to understand the repetition of social violence. When society is severely traumatised, beta elements cannot be transformed through the use of a metaphorical and symbolic language of dialogue and discourse, a point made by De Mare with respect to dialogue in large groups (De Mare, 1972).

CHAPTER FOURTEEN

The unconscious emergence of identity

Introduction

I n this chapter I try to explore some facets of identity that emerge from the social environment, and to describe their importance in the process of building an identity. My exploration is based on my personal experience as a Jew who grew up in Israel, and on my thoughts about the Israeli–Palestinian conflict. My illustrations are from newspapers, literature, and from my experience with the social dreaming matrix. The theoretical background starts with Erikson (1951), who argues that a person is always part of a group and has a social identity, through Fromm (1956, p. 78) who writes about a social character that is the structure shared by most members of the same culture, to Foulkes (1975a), who defines the foundation matrix based on the culturally firmly embedded values and reactions. In our century it is important to mention Hopper (2003b, p. 127), who defines the social unconscious as the existence and constraints of social, cultural, and communication arrangements of which people are unaware. A very interesting way to deal with the issue is suggested by Hadar (2013, p. 74), who writes that the existence of other subjectivities is a necessary condition for subject formation.

During a conference on psychoanalytic systemic thinking, held in Israel in 2005, the coordinators of one of the discussion groups in which I participated asked participants to introduce themselves and state their organisational affiliation. Some of us started by saying: "First of all, I belong to myself".

Freud (1925h, p. 235) was suspicious when it came to answers to questions that were actually not asked. Indeed, the need to state, "I belong to myself", even though we were not asked, is very intriguing. Perhaps the participants who responded correctly to the question did *not* feel that they belong to themselves. Another possibility is that the participants who felt the need to make this statement were anxious and doubtful about whether or not they actually did belong to themselves. They might have been indicating the exact opposite of what they were saying: being part of an organisation is so powerful and absorbing, it is so demanding that, right here and now, I want to remind myself and my colleagues that I am my own person, and please do not take away whatever I have got left of myself. According to Freud (1925h), this is a type of *negation*: stating "I belong to myself" is tantamount to saying "I am afraid that I don't".

In the theatre play *Kineret Kineret* by the famous Hebrew writer Nathan Alterman (1951), the founding members of Kibbutz Kineret convene to sit in judgment over one of the group. This man, under cover of darkness, has opened the Kibbutz treasury in order to put into it a sum of money that he received. By exaggerating the totalising impact of the group, Alterman exposes its absurdity. His play describes how the group, in utter seriousness, accuses the man of treachery and of desecrating the values of the group where every act must first receive common approval. When applied with absolute rigour the paradigm equals "extremism". Here, no room exists for individual action—even when it concerns a major, positive contribution to the desperately poor group's coffers.

In the above example, we witness a group using its power consciously and explicitly. We know, however, that groups often are neither open about nor conscious of their power. The life of a group, of an organisation, or a nation, evolves in such a way that individuals tend to become indistinguishable from the system in question. The dividing lines between group and individual, in this case, may grow so blurred that the latter really does no longer "belong" to her or himself.

An event that took place in a unit of the Israeli army offers an excellent illustration of this . All the excerpts I cite below are taken from *Ha'aretz* newspaper and were published on 16 May 2004 under the title: "Soldiers in Rafah: We are prepared to die to get back our friends' remains".

The article starts:

> The day before yesterday, near Sufa checkpoint, east òf Rafah, the soldiers of the 17th battalion officers training course, were busy getting their armored vehicles ready. None of these soldiers—who were supposed to have officially completed their course that very day—seemed to be impressed by the fact that it was in exactly such armored vehicles that the five soldiers, for whose bodily remains they had been searching on hands and knees for the past two days, were killed.

And a little further on:

> Nearby, scores of soldiers were standing in a tent saying their Shabat prayers. Some of them had recently returned from the Philadelphi route where they had been looking for body parts. "Today, after two of our mates who were covering the search were killed, we talked about this thing, about risking lives to recover body parts," said one of the trainee officers, a paratrooper from the Golan Heights. "They *all* said that they were prepared to die on this mission, so their friends' body parts can get a proper burial. *All* of them, too, expect the others would do the same for them. It's one of those unwritten rules. That the state will do *anything* for its fighters, alive or dead."

And again, a little below:

> Just before they set out on the mission, the officers in command lined up their trainees and told them that those who felt unable to cope with the task should apply to them on a personal basis. No one did.

The article presents a group dynamics characterised by unity and dedication in an atmosphere of apparent freedom. Anyone who wants to, can, after all, turn to his officer and ask to be excused. Clearly, asking for dispensation through an eye-to-eye conversation with the officer presupposes embarrassment, something that requires discretion. Even though whoever wishes to can, on the face of it, opt out, the dominant culture obviously dictates that any soldier who actually does so will find himself an outsider who does not belong in the unit. Whoever chooses to abstain risks excommunication. This is how the group culture or mindset makes it impossible for the individual to look after him or herself and to make a sane distinction between the living and the dead. The difference between life and death has got lost in this context. This incident presents the absurd situation in which so as to save the dead, it has become reasonable and right to sacrifice the living. Here covert totalitarianism presents itself as freedom. The individual, in this case, really does not belong to himself. It is likely that had he been left to make up his own mind he would not have gone out on such a mission.

This event is also an illustration of what both Bion (1961) and Foulkes (1975a) have each claimed, namely, that the "group" pre-exists the "individual". It is within the group that the individual is born. The group was already there when the individual was a foetus. The group, as it anticipated the individual's arrival, spun fantasies, expectations, and wishes around the identity of the yet to be born infant. And belonging is a need that comes and goes during the various life stages of the individual. Group belonging has an almost automatic nature. Thus, Bion and Bion (1992) argue that, much like the word *breast* (because there is no infant without breast) the group also constitutes a cultural layer. Without it, there is no individual—it is from the group that the individual "imbibes" her identity. The adult human looks for nourishment from the group just like the infant looks for nourishment from the breast. Without breast and group, then, human culture cannot exist.

Why do I speak in terms of the group, rather than those of the parents and/or family? Is it not the family that projects its wishes upon the newborn infant? Is it not the family that strives to determine the child's identity even before it is born?

Still, I prefer to use the terms *group* or *society*. Foulkes and Bion, and of course all of those who have tried to direct our attention to society as well as to its members, emphasised the importance of systems thinking. They helped us see that the family is nothing but one possible unit that contains—with greater and often lesser degrees of awareness—the culture, mindset, values, pressure, prejudice, and anxieties of an entire society. In this sense, the family is a microcosm of society at large—and as such it is inextricable from this larger context. It is in this web of unconscious wishes and thoughts that the infant is born.

These thoughts are not spoken. Often, the child who is caught unawares in the unconscious web of historical events of his family, is doomed to realise these unspoken thoughts and turn them into concrete fact. Parental traumas are passed on without words, through unconscious communication to the offspring, who are then fated to enact these unexpressed preconceptions. The poem "Inheritance", by Hebrew poet Haim Guri, shows clearly how this operates. Guri describes Abraham's near-sacrifice of his only son Isaac and looks at the moment when Isaac actually notices the knife. The poem then says that Isaac's offspring are born with a knife in their heart. To me it seems that what this refers to is an image that passes from one generation to the next, unconsciously.

The freedom to be oneself is an illusion for the child who is born into a traumatic history. These insights led to the formulation and recognition of the notion of second and third post-Holocaust generation. A basis for this idea is in Hopper and Weinberg (2011, p. xxxix), who develop the concept of secondary internalisation of collective memories of social trauma.

Bion draws an analogy between the beginning of human life and the prophecies of the oracle of Delphi. The oracle predicts what will happen to Oedipus, and Oedipus, one step at a time, builds his life as a tragic sequence, realising the oracle's prophecy against his will and unconsciously. He is moved by huge forces of whose existence he is unaware.

Of all psychoanalytic thinkers, Bion is the one who took the power of the group to its greatest extreme. But in this context the work of other psychoanalysts should also be mentioned. What they share is the notion that the individual must exert counter-force in the process of individuation. If we want to preserve parts of ourselves, that is to say, we must stand up against the forces that surround us. There is a constant oscillation between conforming to the pressures of the social environment and rebelling against it for being free and unique.

Winnicott (1965) contributed a significant extension of the concept of motherhood. He refers to the *environmental mother*: this is the mother who carries—for better and for worse—her environment's pressures and forces, and passes them on to her child. But this is also the environment itself that carries the projection itself of the infant and that also functions as a mother or in a maternal way. When the early environment provides good-enough support and is responsive to the infant's dependency needs, the latter will develop into an individual who is able to socially integrate while also preserving her autonomous thinking, her ability to express her aggressive and destructive forces in more attenuated ways. When the environment fails to be good enough, neither belonging nor autonomy can mature fully. Disturbances of various kinds, including psychosis, will emerge.

Bollas (2000) elaborated on object relations theory. The mother is the first object. The mother–child dyad is the second object. And the father, who creates a triangle and contains the mother–child dyad, constitutes the third object. According to Bollas, there is a fourth object, namely the family. He regards the family as a group, a microcosm of society. Within the family, various elements reside that pass on to the infant, as soon as it enters the world, myths, tales, history, aesthetics, and visions, as well as facts and rules. The child's development can be configured as the movement of the self within this complex reality. As he internalises these elements, they turn into an internal object. And though the self can reject these contents, it cannot erase their traces. Thus each and every one of us bears within her- and himself the composite elements we have absorbed through our family. The internalisation of the fourth object is developmentally crucial: those who somehow fail to achieve this suffer from both psychological and behavioural disturbances.

Individuals who grew up in a problematic family and internalised a negative fourth object will tend to suffer from, for example, perversions, hysteria, or psychosis.

In contrast to this perspective, but also in sharing certain elements of it, Hopper (2003a), writing within the Foulkesian group analytical tradition, and looking at the social unconscious, emphasises systemic thinking in both social time and social space. He believes that we cannot understand the child's world without reference to the context in which it lives. According to Hopper, *context* is infinite. It can be ecological, social, cultural, psychological, physiological, etc., and an infinity of contexts, in turn, is generated by combining these. The individual exists within the group and the group is an open system. Much of the group's nature is determined by what happens at its borders. It is important to pay attention to what the context provides the group and when it stops providing this sufficiently. The very existence of the group depends on this.

The social unconscious, according to Hopper, consists of social, cultural, and communicational arrangements of which we are not aware. These arrangements exist, but are not perceived as such. And when they are perceived they are denied. And even when they are not denied, they are not taken to be problematic.

The Nazi society seems an extreme example of Hopper's ideas. Arrangements that were horrific and malignant appeared natural and reasonable to the Nazis. Racism seemed sensible and logical. Genocide seemed not only morally unquestionable, but even necessary. The kind of thinking and social processes that enabled this was what Hannah Arendt referred to when she wrote of "the banality of evil". It became possible for people to consider murder in the neutral terms of statistics: a mission that must be carried out like any other industrial project. The social unconscious, especially under totalitarian and fascist conditions, turns monstrous—and those who are members of such a system will not notice that they are under monstrous governance.

Helga Schneider, a German living in Italy, published *Let Me Go* (2004). She was four years old when the Second World War broke out. Her mother joined the Nazi party and volunteered to participate in torture in the form of medical experiments; she was also responsible for sending Jews to the gas chambers in Auschwitz and Birkenau. The daughter wants to set herself free from the mother who abandoned her, for a number of critical years, at age four. During those years her mother preferred to carry out horrific acts in the concentration camps. During the war and following it—when she was imprisoned for war crimes—she failed to make any contact with her daughter who was raised by a stepmother. The daughter only visited her mother twice in the course of her entire life. The second visit occurred when the mother was very old and the daughter was hoping for a consoling, tender meeting before the mother died. Arriving in Vienna, at the retirement home in which her mother lived, in 1998, she found, instead, a determined old woman who still firmly believed in the values of Nazi society and who kept her SS uniform in her closet—neatly ironed and preserved. She met a mother without regrets, without guilt, and without a sense of failure. She repeated that Hitler had been right about the Jews and that it was a shame they had not been eradicated. If he had only been able to complete his work, the whole world would have paid homage to Hitler. Here are some of the mother's words to her daughter:

> I hated all those Jewish women in my barracks. I felt physically nauseous when I saw them. I hated having to see all those perverted faces of that inferior race. Don't be angry with me—hating Jews was obligatory for anyone who belonged to the SS. (p. 125)

If we look at the processes taking place in a fascist society we can get a sense of the power a society can exert on its members. Such impact has this force, that it can cause individuals to ignore their intuitions and to lose their common sense So, for instance, the Goebbels—Hitler's Minister of Propaganda and his wife—had six children. The Goebbels preferred their children (and themselves) not to live in a world that was not purely Aryan. And so, at the end of the Second World War, the mother fed all her children cyanide and then she and her husband took their own lives.

Blind adoration of the leader and ideological fervour came to block parental instincts.

Fromm (1956) did not look for extreme examples to bear out this type of danger. Nationalism and patriotism, by his definition, express love neither for the home country nor for the nation. Once the nation is placed beyond humanity and values of justice and truth, once the nation uses force against another nation, there is no love. Love of one's country that does not include love for humankind as such, is nothing but idolatry.

Building on this notion, we could go further and argue that in such situations not only is love of mankind in general eroded, but also, more specifically, is love of one's self and a person's regard for her or his life and right to live. When ideology reaches its furthest extreme it undoes the self's natural instincts. This phenomenon is exploited by those ideologues who send terrorists on suicide missions. When the soul is trapped in one-dimensional, fanatical thinking, the death instinct gets the better of the life instinct. I am not at all sure whether the suicide bomber really believes in life after death. Perhaps he really believes in what his terror organisation purports to achieve and he wants to please his operators. Young people who carry out these acts have fallen victim to a loss of self and its subsequent merger with the group. The suicide bomber is an extreme instance of someone the boundaries of whose self have been obliterated and who has become fused with the organisation.

Woody Allen's film, Zelig (1983), a comedy with a powerful element of social satire, shows this very well. Zelig is like a chameleon, he merges with his surroundings and becomes one with the person with whom he engages at any given point in time. His own outline blurs to the extent that he becomes indistinguishable from the human landscape in which he happens to be. Under hypnosis he confesses that this is how he feels secure. *Zelig* is a kind of parable about the human need to belong and be one of the group—to the point of losing one's identity. Zelig becomes a media megastar, a celebrity. Paradoxically, as mass hysteria wells up around him, he becomes the most prominent item on the news and features in the headlines. And as they flock to witness this unique phenomenon, the people themselves turn into so many Zeligs, faceless and lacking any personal identity. They are swallowed by the group that dotes on a phenomenon that is nothing but their own affliction. The star-struck crowd loses its own identity and contracts the group syndrome in which they merge and lose their self.

I would like to consider the unconscious emergence of the identity of my generation of Israelis born in the 1950s in a social reality under the sign of nation building, the construction of a state that emerged as a result of persistence and faith. While this wonderful and moving process of creating a state for the Jewish people was underway, however, the rights of another people were being negated. In our youth, though, this fact was denied and we were asked to sacrifice our lives in wars that were called "wars of no choice". That is to say, if we would not defend our country, we would cease to exist. Thus, sacrifice became a supreme value, and here are the origins of the myth of the Sabra-hero, the final answer to the weak and effeminate Diaspora Jew, who went "like a lamb to his slaughter". We all stood to attention, overcome by the fate of the Jewish nation, on remembrance days—whether it was for the victims of the Holocaust or of Israel's fallen soldiers. The boys among us eagerly waited to become paratroopers, and the girls cheerfully joked: "Good guys go to the air force, and good girls go to the good guys in the air force!" If you did not have a boyfriend in a combat unit, you had reason to be ashamed. In 1973, when the October War broke out, thousands of young Israelis, who were studying abroad, flocked back home in a sort of automatic, reflex response. Love of their fatherland was stronger than any personal concern. Many of these young people either were killed or became disabled for life. Dreams of personal growth abroad were put on ice: it was time to save the country. There was the insufferable risk of being perceived as a deserter. Generally accepted, social truths have a way of seeping into us unawares and they come to guide our actions and influence our self-perception. When our self-worth comes under threat we will sacrifice anything to regain social acceptance. These commonly shared truths, that evolve and take root in us over long periods of time, cover up and distract from what is difficult to face and confront. The values with which my generation was raised do not accord with our being a nation that occupies another nation. As a result, there was a long period of denial and a simultaneous clinging to clichés of heroism and sacrifice and wars of no-choice.

Socio-centric cultural narcissism hinges on the love for those who resemble and think like oneself. As ideology becomes more dominating, people's tendency to see themselves as part of a society that is run on values and principles of justice grows too. Such a social narcissism is based on the assumption that whoever is unlike me is inferior, evil, and dangerous. And thus, as social narcissism increases, so does the hatred of the other who gradually turns into an alien and the enemy. At its acme, social narcissism outdoes personal narcissism, and pushes the individual to make sacrifices.

Social narcissism weakened and disintegrated in my generation, making place for personal narcissism. I find it hard to believe that my peers, nowadays, would converge on foreign airports in a bid to save their homeland. Values have undergone a sea change. Intifadas have created a consciousness of the injury and pain of our neighbouring nation. My generation is a traumatised generation, that has suffered too many wars and losses. My generation wants peace and quiet. They want security for their offspring, economic comfort, professional fulfilment and a good life.

Rabin's assassination was a traumatic event that caused the Israeli left to crumble. People turned inward in their frustration and disillusion with social involvement.

It is due to the loss of faith and the above disillusion with a reality that did not act according to the values we were raised upon that we have turned inward to the nuclear family and a small group of intimate friends. What we have here is a post-traumatic society that has preferred withdrawal from the social sphere.

The settlers of Israel's Occupied Territories, by contrast, are an example of a society that has strong faith and principles. In their community, ideology is strong and unifying—social narcissism outdoes its personal counterpart and, correspondingly, people show a great readiness to make sacrifices. Their stable values create a reliable common denominator. These settlers wish to live in their own communities, with their own beliefs.

But when faith is the unifying factor, the other and different is pushed out. Convinced that they are the redeemers of their country, the settlers feel that the state has turned its back on them. They feel that the state, that they have so faithfully served, has become their enemy. Now they have announced that they will no longer volunteer to serve in the army's combat units. In fact, this part of Israel's population has evolved into a cultural enclave that declines to be part of the larger society. In these conditions, this community undergoes severe trauma that obviously will be leaving its marks on the young generation.

My age group, especially those who count themselves among the left, is on the whole unaware of the social trauma we have all experienced. Many try to engage in a form of pseudo social involvement. In his chapter "The Crushed Revolt" Israeli author Gady Taub (1997) calls his own generation, a generation younger than mine, as having fallen victim to what he calls the dictatorship of social posturising. Here are his words:

> A whole age group which considers itself intelligent and sophisticated has created a survival formula for its own use. Mainly, this formula consists of a "correct" political stance. Almost everyone in this group regard themselves as "leftist", but in order not to have to find out for themselves, and instead of a mature political position based on knowledge and familiarity with the relevant detail, they have generated a pseudo-position. This is a general formula which is good for all seasons. One should, generally speaking, be in favour of returning the Occupied Territories in exchange for peace, join a Peace Now demonstration every so often, hate Jewish Orthodox arm-twisting, support recycling, and be aware of ecological issues and AIDS. Once you are equipped with all these, you can be sure you're on the right side of things. You don't need, then, to know what exactly is happening in the mass-detention centers for Palestinians, in the refugee camps, in the army camps, the army's legal courts, in Hebron's Jewish settlement Kiryat Arba, in the development towns of Ofakim and Migdal Ha'emek.

New clichés have thus become moulded into an all-embracing pose that prevents young people to reflect and observe reality from close by. And because they are disconnected from reality, they cannot affect it, so that they turn into the victim of their own disconnectedness. I believe that this non-committal attitude expresses the absence of real social involvement and is the result of trauma—it is a flight into a comfortable bubble.

You can join a leftist demonstration as a form of social narcissism and feel a momentary bond with those who are and think like you.

The notions of "fatherland" and that of the "sabra" have lost their lustre and sound archaic. New forms of social belonging are emerging that are not built on a shared history and from which heroes and leaders alike are absent. What I have in mind here are the virtual, online communities that seem to be a kind of latter day version of the myth of the Tower of Babel. This myth is exceptional because unlike most others of its kind it does not feature an oedipal hero. Nor does it tell a personal, biographical narrative. Instead, the protagonist, or hero, is the group itself. The group that aspired to build a tower that would reach into heaven is punished with multiple languages and consequent dispersal. Bion mentions that it is this story that inspired him to define the idea of attack on linking. He also refers to this narrative in making his distinction between catastrophe and catastrophic change. While the former is terminal, the latter, though it may carry elements that seem catastrophic, actually leads to regeneration and positive change. Thus, though the Tower's collapse appears a disaster, it actually reveals difference in the form of different languages and cultures. The Tower's collapse, therefore, turns out to enrich humanity, opening up spaces unknown at the times of the monolithic, linear, and limited Tower. Bible scholar Cassuto also comments that those who built the Tower intended it to prevent them from becoming dispersed over the face of the earth. They wanted to stick together and around a tower it is easy to gather. Now, here is where they sinned, according to Cassuto, because did not God instruct human beings to "Go and multiply and fill the earth"? They stubbornly insisted, against this injunction, to stay together, and for this reason they were given an ambiguous punishment. They are not destroyed by a second Flood but instead they are forced to stop their effort to stay together. The resulting dispersal leads to pluriformity and variation— the opposite of fascism (Biran, 2014).

Post-modern online communities resemble Babel after the unified group has fallen apart. Each community chooses its language. Each conducts virtual conversations about some shared issue of interest on its forums. What connects between the participants in such communities is a joint problem. Identity, here, is determined through one's connection to one key issue. Members of the community are anonymous, they participate with a code number that discloses nothing about their identity. Personal identity here does not count, what is important is the relevant context. Partners in misfortune, forum members console and support each other.

There is of course an infinity of issues on which people can connect with others, worldwide. In the resulting culture the individual as such is neither known nor important. She or he only appears in so far as they represent the particular aspect under discussion. Forums can be dedicated to pregnancy and birth, to people getting together around certain diseases, motherless daughters, victims of violence, scape-goats, and sharing the pain. These communities illustrate a sort of "Social psychic retreats" (Mojovic, 2011, p. 210). These may well con-stitute the nuclei of future communities. People will meet each other less and will turn to the other more as a source of information and support. I found a message, for instance, on a site for pregnancy and birth, from a woman who is announcing that she has lost her foetus. She writes that she is moving on to another site, one dedicated to loss, but before doing so, she wants to say goodbye. This letter received many responses, such as, for instance: "Be strong, sweet-heart"; "Thinking of you, lovey"; "I'm with you in your pain", etc. Moves from one forum to another are according to issue and the connections are of a new type. Personal identity is almost absent. What matters is the dialogue about the chosen, shared subject. This type of belonging builds on one aspect, not on personal identity. Melanie Klein no doubt would have said that we reverted from being whole objects, to part objects. Significance emerges, substantial help is offered—but all around one axis among people who will never get to know each other or meet each other face to face.

And not only is this virtual discourse among partial objects, it is also among objects about which we cannot know whether they really exist or are invented. The infinite possibilities for imaginary identities and hence fantasised personal narratives lead to a blurring between imagination and reality. But no one cares whether their partner in the virtual conversation really exists or not, the main thing is to keep the electronic conversation going. This type of communication offers an elusive solution to loneliness, a sense of a full life while one exists on the margins of reality.

One might also consider this type of existence as compensatory, and argue that fantasy is stronger than reality and that an entire world can be built on the hatred of a frustrating reality.

The contemporary world creates collective identities through other ways than via the computer, too. Interesting in this context is the commonality created by shared interests. So, for instance, motorbike owners will feel part of a community—a sense of belonging that emerges automatically.

Though they have no personal acquaintance with each other, they will always exchange information and offer each other help. Their motorbikes tell everything about the owners. The bond is even stronger among owners of the same brand of motorbike: common language is instantly available and issues such as year of construction and model, mechanical improvements, etc. Other parts of identity, not directly related to the motorbike will usually remain outside the discourse.

A dramatic illustration of how a joint interest can create a bond is the story of a suicide bomber who failed on his mission and was put into an Israeli jail. Once there, it transpired he was a great football fan. His interviewer asked him if he thought he would be able to detonate his explosives amid a crowd of football fans and he responded that he could not commit such a murder. That is to say, when he becomes aware of a collective identity with which he identifies, total alienation vis-à-vis the victim vanishes and the act of the suicide bomber becomes impossible.

In our attempt to examine the social unconscious as a major influence on identity, it is important to mention the work of Lawrence (2005), who argues that the dream has unconscious aspects that may derive from society at large, from the group, and from the organisation. In current psychoanalytic thinking, social dreaming has taken an important position. Of my various experiences in this field, I would like, here, to relate to one project that was especially elucidating for me in respect of the significance of social identity through dreams.

This project came about as a result of the collaboration between Wolf Werdiger and myself. Werdiger is an Austrian painter who lives in Vienna. Son of a Jewish father, who survived the Holocaust, and a mother who is a non-Jewish German, his complicated identity led him to take an interest in the conflict in our region, and make an attempt to build a bridge between the two peoples. He created an exhibition, "Hidden Images" which is based on interviews he conducted with both Israelis and Palestinians, and in which he asked them to come up with images they had concerning the other nation and about the conflict. The paintings in the exhibition are based on these images and they are emotionally extremely evocative. One thing they evince is a powerful and deep connection between Holocaust-related imagery and images relating to the situation of the Palestinians today.

Between October and November 2003, the exhibition was on show in East Jerusalem, Tel-Aviv, and finally in Ramallah.

Inspired by Gordon Lawrence's ideas, Wolf Werdiger decided to conduct a matrix of social dreaming in the exhibition space and he invited me to host the matrix. A social dreaming matrix is a method of exploring the social aspects that are hidden in personal dreams (Lawrence, 1991). The participants sit in a large room, the chairs are arranged in a shape of a spiral or of a snowflake. They do not see all the faces and their task is to tell dreams and to associate to each others' dreams. The host, together with the participants, tries to find links among the dreams for revealing new thoughts and ideas about the social unconscious.

It turned out that Jewish and Palestinian dreams show much similarity when we look at the social traumas the two peoples have experienced. The social trauma creates a sense of joint fate crossing the boundaries of cultures and mindsets. Dreams reconstructed the images on the paintings. Here, too, the profound and inextricable link between the Holocaust trauma and the conflict with the Palestinians. The Jewish workshop participants, who had experienced trauma that is deeply engraved in the collective memory, were engulfed by Holocaust-related dreams, associations, and memories. The social dreaming revealed how massively the Holocaust has left its marks on the Israeli perception of the Israeli–Palestinian conflict. This is not sufficiently clear to most Israelis nowadays. Dreams, however, show the link between the unhealed national trauma and the deep fears that are leading to military solutions. A nation that lives with the fear of annihilation will have a hard time putting its faith in peace.

At the end of the Tel Aviv workshop, a man told his dream of the previous night. In this dream he felt he was nowhere, he had a sense of being in no-place. He felt he was not in the world. He associated these feelings with ones that he had had as a soldier, at a time of war. Then he fought with a sense of being in no-place, an overpowering sense of homelessness. He felt rootless, not belonging, and that war uproots people from human culture and takes them nowhere.

Earlier, during the East Jerusalem workshop, a Palestinian man had reported on a very similar dream:

> I dreamt I was walking in a street, in a city I didn't know. The build-
> ings were destroyed and people had abandoned them, it was very
> dark, possibly early in the morning. I was completely on my own. I
> jumped over a wall and found myself in a big, white area the size of
> a football field. There was a lot of light there, but I was the only person
> in town. Throughout the dream I was scared and anxious.

Associations that emerged in the wake of this dream bore much resemblance to the ones that occurred in Tel Aviv. A Jew from Tel Aviv and an Arab from East Jerusalem both dreamt of remaining alone in no-place.

In Ramallah, in parallel, someone told a dream that relates to the loss of identity, to the sense of a void, the inability to identify someone's face:

> I dreamt I lost my memory. I could not remember anything or anyone.
> From the other direction one single man was approaching me but I
> couldn't remember him. I remembered his voice, his name, everything
> but his face. I couldn't remember his face.

This dream refers to a traumatic event and shows a great similarity to Holocaust survivors' dreams. Both nationalities come up with encounters with the void—the result of loss that erases place, time, faces—entire lives.

Social dreaming touches on the huge damage that trauma inflicts on the senses of identity and belonging. The traumatic experience creates a hole—emptiness inside and out. The hole in identity is invisible and its existence tends to be denied. Trauma destroys live tissue. It is difficult to build identity on the ruins of a previous identity.

To sum up: I tried, in this chapter, to show how strongly personal identity is affected by society. Society, with its multiple layers, and social history, as it passes from one generation to the next, mould the individual's identity through unconscious processes. Subject to the mastery of the social that insinuates itself quietly and subtly, the individual is not in absolute charge of her or himself.

Some selected facts of my biography

I feel that, in order for the reader to understand and appreciate my interest in people, groups, and society, it would be of value to know something about my personal background and my early formation as a psychoanalyst and a group analyst.

I have used free associations in writing this chapter, revealing my emotional biography. I think that writing about my personal history in a professional book is a kind of homage to Bion who wrote so openly about his life in three volumes of autobiography.

I grew up in one of the first neighbourhoods built in west Jerusalem, the Yegia Kapayim[1] neighbourhood. I was born into a newly-founded state. My neighbourhood had many holocaust survivors, speaking Yiddish, and families of "eastern" origins, like my own, which had come from Persia in 1889. In my family, we spoke Arabic, Ladino, and Hebrew—depending on the context. There was something dark and dismal in the air. As a small child, I took in the feeling that the world was full of agony. I cannot quite recall the assortment of characters around me. Strange figures like Feivele and Rosele haunted me. Feivele and Rosele were made up names for a couple of elderly holocaust survivors, who were the first homeless people I have ever met. They went about searching in trash-cans, dragging along bags full of rags and scraps of food. I had a lot of compassion for the miserable and the outcast. This is where the first seed of my becoming a psychologist was sown.

In addition to this dark atmosphere, when I was only six years old, my world was suddenly shaken: my beloved sister contracted severe polio. Most often, it was the younger children who got sick, but in our family it was the other way around. I was unharmed, while my sister, already fourteen years old, became very ill. During the first week of her illness, I remember hearing my parents and uncles whispering amongst themselves: "how is it that Shulamit got sick and not Hanni?" For many years, I felt guilty about this, as if I had somehow escaped, leaving her to carry the disease by herself. Her agony, my parents' distress, my guilt, and my pain were mixed up with the joy I felt for being well. This encounter with profound distress in my family was one of the landmarks of my life. On the other hand, Shulamit's vitality, her joy in life, and her strength had a great influence on the shaping of my personality. It was my first great life-lesson concerning what Bion termed "catastrophic change". The way my sister had coped with her disaster and the way she built her life out of it was imprinted deep in my mind.

I would like to share with you another memory, one that paints a clear picture of the world that shaped my childhood experiences. This story touches upon my hidden world as a child, helping to explain why I have always been so preoccupied with the attempt to differentiate between my inner world and external reality and especially, much like Bion, with the blurring of the boundaries between the two.

I was in first grade at the "Berl Katznelson" elementary school. My father had been an avid member of the Labour party and he wanted us to get a proper "socialist" education, and that was the school for us. There was a boy in my class, Yossi, whose mother was a Holocaust survivor. Wherever he went, Yossi's mother ran after him with food in her hands, stuffing it into his mouth for fear that he might starve. The other kids mocked him: "Look at Yossi's belly—He's gonna have a baby". He was a victim of their abuse. Because he was fat, he was seen as weird and was treated as if he were stupid. This treatment unsettled him, making him insecure. His failure at school made him feel even more rejected.

I remember his presence in first grade: a fat kid with red, swollen cheeks. He looked like a ripe tomato. Yossi and I were neighbours, and would often walk home together. His exclusion pained me: I always felt the need to protect him.

I had another neighbour who was the same age as I was—his name was Shmaryahu. He went to "Tahkemoni", the religious school for boys. Shmaryahu had a rich imagination and was absorbed in all kinds of fears, that he often instilled in me. I always believed the stories he told me, living them out in utter seriousness.

Every day, at the same time, a man would walk by, standing out against the background of our neighbourhood. He marched in a suit and a tie, looking very European. Whether in rain or shine, he always carried with him an unopened big black umbrella, with a silver tip. He used to play with it at steady pace, swinging it up and down to a special rhythm. I always watched him with terrified curiosity. He never stopped walking. He never spoke to us. We would follow him with our eyes until he was gone.

Shmaryahu said that the man "came out of the Holocaust" and "got crazy". Because the Nazis took away his family, he built a sausage-making machine in his house. He used his umbrella to stab children through the heart, putting them to sleep, and then carried them on his back so he could turn them into minced meat for his sausages. He walked so fast because he was on the prowl for the next victim. Ever since Shmaryahu told me this story, I would run home in terror every time this man appeared.

Once, on my way home from school with fat Yossi, we spotted the man at the other end of the street. I told Yossi, "this man makes kids into sausages", but Yossi laughed and would not run away with me. I left him there to walk at his ease, while I ran home like mad.

The next day, Yossi did not show up in class. I said to myself, "that man must have made him into sausages—Yossi is so fat and plump, he probably makes good sausage . . .". I was frightened. The next day, Yossi was still nowhere to be seen. Our teacher, Carmella, put me in charge of visiting him and giving him our homework assignments. Trembling with fear, I said to her, "Carmella! The Holocaust man made Yossi into sausages". I remember her laughing and insisting that I pay him a visit. That afternoon I walked up the stairs leading to his apartment. Each step took me minutes to climb. After an hour or so, I made it to the second floor. It took all my strength to knock on the door. Yossi's mother opened it: "You can't come in. Yossi is sick with angina". "Ok, I'm just here to bring him his homework . . .".

I think that, together with the intense presence of the Holocaust, this anxiously curious way of looking at the world marked my childhood years. I was especially curious about people: what are they thinking? Are they also afraid? This way of looking is still with me now.

When I was fourteen, my world trembled once again. My father suddenly died of a cerebral hematoma. I loved and admired him and his death was like an earthquake that shattered my world. He was one of a kind. In an article in one of the leading newspapers, Yaron London gave him the nickname "the first Mista'arev".[2] As a young man, he served as the intelligence unit for the "Hagana".[3] He would dress up as an Arab and go out to the Al-Aqsa mosque to listen to the Mufti's speech. He knew where Jews were going to be attacked and gave warning beforehand. In 1947, he chased Nazis in Syria and later he worked for the Israel Security Agency (the Shabak). He was a spy to his very last day. He was not an ordinary father who came home every day, but whenever I met him he was full of warmth, sensitivity, and an endless capacity for giving love and attention. I think that the duality of having a very warm father, who was also absent and unknown at the same time, served as the infrastructure for my imagined conversations with Bion, as a wise old man who would offer comforting thoughts in difficult times.

Only in 1992, Israeli historian Yoav Gelber published a book about the history of Israeli intelligence, entitled *Growing a Fleur-de-Lis*. Most of the first volume is devoted to my father's work. I was especially moved by something my father said, when he was young, about how he got involved in espionage. This is what he said: "I was summoned to the National Committee to see Yitzhak Ben Zvi, where I was told that I had to quit my job and start being a spy. I dressed up as an Arab and went into the old city." I was very moved by his dry, unexcited tone—as if he was being asked to go out for a walk. This automatic consent says so much about the man and the time he lived in. In another testimony that moved me, he describes a time when he was almost captured:

> They ordered me to put my hands in the air, asking who I was and what I was doing there at that hour. They decided to test whether or not I was Arab and told me to recite the Al-Fatiha, the opening verses of the Quran. I recited it fluently, without missing so much as a syllable and they approved of it. Only on my way back to the Dung Gate

[of the Old City of Jerusalem], did I realise how close to death I came; feeling so faint and excited, I passed out and fell to the ground. When I opened my eyes I was in a hospital.

I was moved by the fact that he was not a hero. He was very afraid and despite his fear persevered and performed the tasks he was given.

Several years ago, Israel's national archives finally granted access to materials describing the work of the Jewish Agency's Arab department. Many details concerning my father's career came to light. This is how I discovered what I had already known and remembered of him and his personality: that he was a peace-loving man, actively searching for ways to make peace with the Palestinians.

As a child my father taught me, years before Bion did, to reverse perspectives, to look at the world from different points of view, and to have a dynamic notion of things. As a spy, he had to learn about Arab culture, and part of him fell in love with his study-material. My father spent a lot of time in the Arab towns and villages around Israel, learning to love the Arabs and to see the beauty of their culture. He wrote articles that were ahead of their time: protesting the discrimination of the Arab population, calling it a powder keg, writing about ways to achieve peace. I feel that my father left me an unwritten will, leading me to write about the Jewish–Arab conflict from a psychoanalytic perspective and to take part in the work of "PsychoActive", a movement of mental health professionals struggling for human rights and the end of the occupation. It was my father who shaped this aspect of my professional identity. As you can see, the emotional underpinning of Part IV of this book is rooted in my father's biography and in his colourful personality.

The first two years after his death were very difficult. I could not feel anything. My mother became very depressed, concentrating her attention on protecting my little brother, who was only four years old at the time. My older sisters had already left home. I was alone. At sixteen, I myself sank into depression, feeling alienated and detached from everyone around me. I began psychotherapy at the Jerusalem municipal mental health centre. My therapist was an elderly Yekke[4] woman, named Esther Alexander—I called her Mrs Alexander. I spent one year in her care and my identification with her was immense. During that year, I decided to become a psychologist. I wanted to be just like Mrs

Alexander. To this day, I have kept the notebook containing my dreams alongside Mrs Alexander's interpretations; all my dreams were about my father. I underwent an arduous journey and finally arrived with a lot of strength.

It was only natural for me to enrol in the psychology department of the Hebrew University in Jerusalem. During my masters degree, there were several places available for my practicum; I requested the municipal centre where I was once a patient. It was strange going there for such a different purpose. To my joy, Mrs Alexander was my supervisor. This time, I went to see her at her home, a beautiful house in Jerusalem's German Colony. I continued to admire her as my supervisor. It was an idealisation I just could not grow out of. She was very glad to be my supervisor. I remember only one painful remark. One day, I came in with too deep a cleavage and she said I should not come to sessions with adolescent boys dressed like that. I still remember how overwhelmed with shame I was. I did not meet her again after the end of my practicum. She died about twenty years ago. When I saw the notice in the paper, I burst into tears.

After getting married, I left Jerusalem and moved to the coast. My residency was in Tel Aviv: I got accepted as a resident in a centre for treating children and adolescents, which was run by a strict old-school psychologist. She did not like me and made my life quite miserable. She said that she only accepted me because of my references, but that I was failing to live up to these. This made me more and more insecure. One day, she called me into her office regarding a medical history that I had written. She asked me the reason for one of my conjectures about the patient's father. I told her it was based on my intuition. She reddened with fury, shouting that psychology was a science, not an intuition. That same day, she fired me, after several months as a resident.

It took me a while to recover from this difficult experience at the outset of my professional career. It made it more difficult for me to get accepted as a resident in other places. Eventually, I was accepted at another clinic, and then at a hospital, and my confidence was gradually restored. Still, a deep wound remained, which was waiting to be healed. This healing took place later, through my supervisor, Naomi Huler, who accepted me. She trusted me from our very first meeting and our relationship was full of kindness and growth. Suddenly, someone approved of what I did at the clinic. This was an enormous support, as my supervisor was quite the celebrity—a veritable oracle of psychotherapy. After a short while, I opened my own private practice, where I have been practicing to this day.

Alongside my development as an individual therapist, I was very much drawn to the world of groups. I learned about the nature of group dynamics and of unconscious group processes, as I went along. In those years, organisational consultation was little developed in Israel. Psychologists worked in organisations and concentrated on team-development: what happens in a team working to fulfil its assignment? What takes place between the team and its manager? These were fascinating, challenging issues. This is when I first encountered Bion, through his *Experiences in Groups*.

Throughout all these years, although I had many supervisors and underwent a long analysis, I never tried to apply for membership at the Israeli Psychoanalytic Society. Deep inside, I was certain that this conservative establishment would refuse me and I was afraid of going back to the same insecurity that overshadowed my early years. Moreover, I felt that I could not belong to such a conventional institution that, at the time, required a measure of conformism that was beyond me. It felt good to develop out in the open and the world of groups became more and more important in my life.

Still, there was a paper I found particularly compelling and inspiring. It was published in *Free Associations* in 1992, by an American psychoanalyst by the name of Stephen Kurtz and titled "A brief history of my tears". It was written after a conference held in Los Angeles in 1990 about the subject of "Becoming an Analyst". The paper was written with great associative freedom and from an anti-establishment perspective. Kurtz declared that he was constructing an autobiography that mixed fantasy with fact, in the attempt to reach a different kind of truth, one that was not "dryly" objective, but psychoanalytic in nature. As he put it, psychoanalytic truth and poetic truth are one and the same.

He felt that his work had opened a space inside himself that could perceive things that could not be put into words. He was listening to the music of Bach, which brought him to tears. This divine experience that he found in music is what he was looking for in psychoanalysis. He wanted to feel other people as he did music. He defines his process of becoming an analyst as an evolutionary development occurring through tears.

Kurtz grew up in New York in the 1940s. His grandmother repeatedly told him of her childhood in Vienna. Her stories, though not always sad, brought him to tears. He felt that listening to the world of his grandmother's childhood is what led him to listen to patients relating their own childhood experiences. This is an emotional kind of listening, an attempt to touch the loss embedded in any childhood. He saw his grandmother as his very first patient. At the same time, he saw himself as her patient: he had internalised the way she took care of him and nursed him when he was sick as a child. Kurtz describes how lonely he felt as a child, stating that no one with a happy childhood becomes an analyst. He describes his parents as externally showering him with presents and affection, while incapable of actual love. He felt this as a child, but had no name to give it. Even analysis did not help him distinguish between love and narcissistic relatedness. In his opinion, Freud had also failed to make this distinction. This failure is the foundation of Kohut's theory. About this distinction he says: "When I learned to make it too, it was the beginning of my cure. But a great deal of suffering came first" (Kurtz, 1992, p. 205).

Kurtz mentions several states that he calls "non-ego states". These belong to "the madman, the poet, the mystic and the listening analyst" (p. 214). The differences between these states are quite blurred, but they are all without ego, without concepts, categories, and divisions. In his opinion, in these four states, the eye sees not what it was trained to see, but what is actually there. He sees these states as authentic.

I think that this paper by Kurtz, which I read in 1992, spoke to me so powerfully because it had such freedom of thought, such capacity for learning from the non-verbal world—both that of music and that of tears. I think that as human beings, we are wrapped in layers of words. Reb Nachman of Breslov would say: "when you finish peeling the onion, all you have left is a tear". Bion set out to find the non-verbal world; he learned by observing nature, mathematics, world history. I believe I was touched by this paper by Kurtz long before I came to know Bion's notion of "Becoming O". Today, I can feel this concept as part of myself—feeling moments of elation, of profound insight about a patient; moments that are beyond words, leaving me only with tears, with pain. Those who read Bion and love him know well the wonderful growth that takes place through pain.

While Kurtz was influenced by Kohut, his formulations are very close to those of Bion. Bion, as a theoretician, had the greatest influence over my thinking and my work as an analyst. As the years went by, I gradually turned him into a sort of father-figure, maybe even an ideal-father-figure. As I said before, I had many imaginary conversations with him, which were very personal and brought much joy and light into my life. In 1997, Bion's daughter Parthenope organised an international conference for Bion's followers in Torino. I gave a lecture there, developing the social aspects of α and β thinking. The lecture was also published in the conference book. I was very excited to see his daughter write, in the introduction, that "Bion would have agreed with it". I could ask for no greater gift. I found myself secretly thinking—could she know of the conversations I am having with him?

I find Bion's theories challenging, they force me to think. Nothing is given for granted and the need to think always opens up new paths. I do not know any other theory that enters into such a fruitful dialogue with the reader, sending her to rummage through her unconscious.

Bion's notion of the caesura had a great impact on me. The understanding that things occur in the space between two parts or parties opens up a profound way of thinking about the relations between past and future, and between analyst and patient. The knowledge that any incision is also a possibility for motion, for passing through, brings hope to the analytic work. In the seminar Bion gave in Italy in 1977, two years before he died, he said that the greatest help an analyst can get is not from her analyst, her supervisor, her teachers, or her books—but from her patient. The respect Bion had for the patient always filled me with awe—there is so much humanity in a saying like this!

Bion was once asked: "Do you do anything in analysis other than speak?" He replied, "Yes, I keep silent. I like being silent during the session. It is not easy to be silent for we are under pressure to say something."

Bion talks about writing up the session: we write what we think the patient has said. Bion suggests that we think about the words we use most often in analysis and start getting rid of them, reducing and erasing them. This way, we can reach the purest, most accurate sentence on which the entire session is balanced. Bion was concerned that jargon might take over the session, creating dead metaphors or clichés.

Bion often wrote about the power of the word. Speech is not always communication and Bion was looking for what was behind speech. He saw great importance in putting one's senses to work and would have liked the patient to listen to her own senses. When the patient is constantly, ceaselessly talking, she is making noise, rather than establishing a link with the analyst. Bion calls this kind of speech "noise" because the analyst feels that she is being bombarded with more and more facts. This huge mass of facts makes the analyst feel deaf and blind, as if her senses have stopped working. In such situations, when speech is uncommunicative, we should ask ourselves what is hiding behind the words. In such sessions, the content is of little importance, what is important is to understand why the senses are under attack. This is where Bion's famous oxymoron fits in—"A beam of intense darkness"—when light deceives us, we must find a beam that will allow us to probe the depths of the unconscious. These are only a few examples of ideas from Bion which I resonate with.

In 2000, I was part of a group of professionals that established the Tel Aviv Institute for Contemporary Psychoanalysis. The first analysis I conducted, as part of my training, was a very powerful experience for me. During the analysis, I was diagnosed with breast cancer. My supervisor, Ilan Treves, was very sensitive about my unique condition. During chemotherapy, we started discussing the dilemma of whether or not to tell my patient. She had her own troubled life, which she led in the shadow of a cold and distant mother. She needed so much warmth and protection. My deliberation was intense. My supervisor claimed that the patient felt something that she could not name and that I should tell her. Finally, after being torn apart by the dilemma, I decided to tell her about my illness. I wrote my final paper about this analysis. I chose its title, "The transparent mirror", after something the patient had said: "my mother gave me a transparent mirror. I could not see my reflection in it". The following is one paragraph from my final paper, submitted at the end of my training, in December, 2004:

> I told her, comforting her as I did so. I told her that it was diagnosed early enough and that there is a cure. Her first response was: "well, if you're going through something like this, the last thing you need is me to worry about". Then she kept talking about her own affairs, as

she normally would. I felt grateful that she had let me treat her as usual. I started thinking that maybe she was doing this for me, to make me feel that it is okay that I had told her and that analysis would proceed as normal—that she believed that I have the strength to be her analyst. I picked up a lot of sensitivity and consideration from her: she let me stay in the role of the analyst. Meanwhile, I felt that some real material is surfacing, something we could really work with. I thought that she is repeating her habit of hiding her own pain and emotions. She grew up in a home where no matter how bad things were, everybody always acts as if it's "business as usual": nothing is digested, everything is one more fact of life to adjust to immediately, since "life is no picnic". I remembered how hurt she was when she told me about finding out she is a lesbian—it fell on her like some disaster and she wasn't given any space to work it through. "Nobody understood that I feel like some catastrophe has struck me, everyone tried showing me that it's okay, that nothing happened". The extensive working through of our experiences began at the very next session. It was important for me to let her talk about her feelings. She said: "I was in shock. After I left here, I drove to work. I didn't think about it at all. At night, Nilly fell asleep early. I went to bed with a book, I started reading and then I closed it and began crying. I felt as if I shared your pain. I was touched by the fact that you shared it with me and it also scared me. But there was also something so alive, so warm and real about it. Mother never shared any of her difficulties with me. At home, even as an adult, I felt as if she wasn't taking me seriously, as if I had nothing to give her. Even though a malignant tumor is terrifying, I felt that you treated me as someone who could take it. You didn't treat me like a child." That same night she had a dream: "I only remember a vague image. Something happened to you, you didn't have a daughter. I was there, feeling like I was adopted. When I woke up, my immediate association was to our conversation."

I will not delve any deeper into this analysis, but I wish to stress that my disclosure added depth, authenticity, and strength to our relationship. Re-reading this analysis now, I can feel deeply the meaning of the reversible roles of the container and the contained, and the extent to which the contained can cure the container.

As I was being trained at the Tel Aviv Institute for Psychoanalysis, I was also being trained as a group analyst. I was in the first class of the Israeli Institute of Group Analysis. We studied in concentrated weekend "bursts", with teachers who came to us from the London Institute of Group Analysis. This training formed my identity as a group analyst. I have one long-term group that I regularly treat. There are so many interrelations and mutual influences between these two fields—individual psychoanalysis and group analysis.

Between 2007 and 2011, I suffered from an illness that was accompanied by severe chronic pain. Certain tissues in my body were damaged as a result of the chemotherapy and gradually deteriorated further. This illness was much harder to bear than my cancer. Throughout this period, I underwent various treatments, some of them invasive and excruciating, but found no relief. It was a traumatic period that taught me how much chronic pain can rob us of the joy of living, how much one should take care not to be fooled by certain beguiling healers, how much modesty we need in order to avoid all manner of psychological interpretation that only hurts the sick by blaming their illness on themselves. It is hard for us to accept the mystery of pain and the helplessness it brings about. Only after four long years did I find a cure, in the form of a revolutionary surgery, performed by a brave doctor in Germany. It is a funny feeling: the same Germany that brought such a calamity to my people had saved me from my personal affliction.

In conclusion, I want to say something about inter-generational relations. It is clear to me that without key figures such as my father, my mother who did her best, my sisters with their impressive personalities, my younger and beloved brother who is a scholar and has a deep understanding of Judaism and literature, the psychologist who treated me in my youth, my wonderful supportive husband, my analyst, my supervisors, those who supervised my first analyses, my patients—I would not have become the person I am today. We absorb things and they become inscribed in us while we are unaware of these processes. They trickle in unnoticed. This is how I feel about my sons. I have no idea as to how I am passing on this inter-generational legacy. My elder son is a clinical psychologist. How he chose his profession, in what ways did he identify with me—these are unconscious processes that I cannot account for. My younger son is a film editor and a writer. Something in the atmosphere he grew up in led him to writing. How does such a process take place? Such things seem so mysterious to me, beyond the reach of logic. I feel the same mystery when I think about my two daughters-in-law, who are an integral part of my life, and my three grandchildren who give my everyday life a unique meaning.

In recent years, I have been getting responses from supervisees and patients, showing me that I am passing what I have learned on to the next generations. This transmission is a curious process, occurring differently in every relationship. It is a singular, untraceable experience of growth and becoming. Each person undergoes growth and becoming differently. It is a great privilege to accompany people in their development.

NOTES

1. Literally: labour of one's own hands.
2. Mista'arev, or "arabised", refers to a tactic employed by certain IDF units: it entails disguising the troops so that they appear Arab or Palestinian, in order to carry out arrests or gather intelligence.
3. A Jewish para-military organisation that later became the core of the IDF.
4. The term Yekke refers to Jews of German descent, who were considered strict, meticulous, and austere.

REFERENCES

Allen, W. (1983). *Zelig* (film).

Alterman, N. (1951). *Kineret Kineret*. Tel-Aviv: Hakibbutz Hameuchad.

Anzieu, D. (1989). *The Skin Ego*. New Haven, CT: Yale University Press.

Arendt, H. (1963). *Eichman in Jerusalem, A Report on The Banality of Evil*. New York: Viking.

Barzilai, S. (1997). History is not the past: Lacan's critique of Ferenczi. *Psychoanalytic Review, 84*(4): 553–572.

Behr, H., & Hearst, L. (2005). *Group Analytic Psychotherapy: A Meeting of Minds*. London: Whurr.

Ben-Naftali, M. (2012a). *Spirit*. Tel-Aviv: Achuzat Bayit.

Ben-Naftali, M. (2012b). "Borrowed Memories", a lecture in a conference on *Memories*. March. Tel Aviv University.

Bennington, G., & Derrida, J. (1993). *Jacques Derrida*. Chicago: University of Chicago Press.

Billow, R. M. (2002). Passion in group: thinking about loving, hating and knowing. *International Journal of Group Psychotherapy, 53*(3): 355–372.

Bion, W. R. (1956). Development of schizophrenic thought. *International Journal of Psychoanalysis, 37*(4–5): 334–346.

Bion, W. R. (1958). On arrogance. *International Journal of Psycho-Analysis, 39*: 144–146.

Bion, W. R. (1959). Attacks on linking. *International Journal of Psycho-Analysis, 40*(5–6): 344–346.

Bion, W. R. (1961). *Experiences in Groups, and Other Papers.* London: Tavistock.

Bion, W. R. (1962a). *Learning from Experience.* London: Maresfield.

Bion, W. R. (1962b). A theory of thinking. *International Journal of Psychoanalysis, 43*(4–5).

Bion, W. R. (1963). *Elements of Psycho-analysis.* London: Maresfield.

Bion, W. R. (1965). *Transformations: Change from Learning to Growth.* London: Tavistock.

Bion, W. R. (1967). *Second Thoughts: Selected Papers on Psycho-analysis.* London: Maresfield.

Bion, W. R. (1984). *Attention and Interpretation.* London: Maresfield Reprints (first published by Tavistock Publications Ltd, 1970).

Bion, W. R. (1987). *Clinical Seminars and Other Works.* London: Karnac.

Bion, W. R. (1989). *Two Papers The Grid and Caesura.* London: Karnac.

Bion, W. R. (1991). *A Memoir of the Future.* London: Karnac.

Bion, W. R., & Bion, F. (1992). *Cogitations.* London: Karnac.

Biran, H. (1998). An attempt to apply Bion's alpha and beta elements to processes in society at large. In: B. T. a. Borgagno (Ed.), *Bion's Legacy to Groups* (pp. 95–100). London: Karnac.

Biran, H. (2014). Further thoughts about the foundation matrix, the social unconscious and the collective unconscious: the myth of the tower of Babel. In: E. Hopper & H. Weinberg (Eds.), *The Social Unconscious in Persons, Groups, and Societies (Vol. 2).* London: Karnac.

Bollas, C. (1987). *The Shadow of the Object: Psychoanalysis of the Unthought Known.* London: Free Association.

Bollas, C. (1992). *Being a Character: Psychoanalysis and Self Experience* (1st edn). New York: Hill & Wang.

Bollas, C. (2000). *Hysteria.* London: Routledge.

Bolognini, S. (1997). Empathy and empathism *International Journal of Psycho-Analysis, 78*: 279–293.

Buber, M., & Kaufmann, W. A. (1970). *I and Thou.* New York: Scribner.

Canetti, E. (1979). *The Tongue Set Free : Remembrance of a European Childhood.* New York: Seabury Press.

Canetti, E. (1982). *The Torch in My Ear.* New York: Farrar Straus Giroux.

Canetti, E. (1986). *The Play of the Eyes* (1st edn). New York: Farrar Straus Giroux.

Dalal, F. (1998). *Taking the Group Seriously : Towards a Post-Foulkesian Group Analytic Theory.* London: Jessica Kingsley.

De Mare, P. B. (1972). *Perspectives in Group Psychotherapy*. London: Allen & Unwin.

Derrida, J. (2002). *Des Tours de Babel* (Hebrew Translation). Tel Aviv: Resling.

Derrida, J. (2012). Touch/to touch him. *Edinburgh University Press Journal Online, 16*(2): 122–156.

Douglas, M. (1966). *Purity and Danger: an Analysis of Concepts of Pollution and Taboo*. London: Routledge & Paul.

Eigen, M. (1985). Toward Bion's starting point: between catastrophe and faith. *International Journal of Psycho-Analysis, 66*: 321–330.

Eissler, K. R. (1975). The fall of man. *Psychoanalytic Study of the Child, 30*: 589–646.

Erikson, E. H. (1951). *Childhood and Society*. London: Imago.

Foulkes, S. H. (1971). Access to unconscious processes in the group analytic group. *Group Analysis 4*(1): 4–14.

Foulkes, S. H. (1973). The group as matrix of the individuals' mental life. In: E. Foulkes (Ed.), *S. H. Foulkes Selected Papers*. London: Karnac, 1990.

Foulkes, S. H. (1975a). *Group-Analytic Psychotherapy, Method and Principles*. London: Gordon & Breach.

Foulkes, S. H. (1975b). The leader in the group. In: A. Wolf & Z. A. Liff (Eds.), *The Leader in the Group : In Honor of Alexander Wolf, M.D., for His 35 Years of Outstanding Teaching, Supervision, Writing, and Clinical Practice* (pp. 83–94). New York: Aronson.

Foulkes, S. H. (1990). The group as a matrix of the individual's mental life. In: *Selected Papers* (pp. 223–233). London: Karnac.

Foulkes, S. H., & Anthony, E. J. (1957). *Group Psychotherapy: The Psychoanalytic Approach*. Harmondsworth: Penguin.

Freud, S. (1900a). *The Interpretation of Dreams. S.E., 4–5*. London: Hogarth.

Freud, S. (1911b). Formulations on the two principles of mental functioning. *S.E., 12*: 213–226. London: Hogarth.

Freud, S. (1914c). On narcissism: an introduction. *S.E., 14*: 73–102. London: Hogarth.

Freud, S. (1915c). Instincts and their vicissitudes. *S.E., 14*: 109–140. London: Hogarth.

Freud, S. (1916–1917). The development of the libido and the sexual organization. *Introductory Lectures on Psycho-analysis. S.E., 16*. London: Hogarth.

Freud, S. (1921c). *Group Psychology and the Analysis of the Ego. S.E., 18*: 67–143. London: Hogarth.

Freud, S. (1925h). Negation. *S.E., 19*: 223–239. London: Hogarth.

Fromm, E. (1956). *The Sane Society*. London: Routledge.

Fromm, E. (1966). *You Shall Be as Gods; a Radical Interpretation of the Old Testament and its Tradition* (1st edn). New York: Holt.

Fromm, E. (1976). *To Have or to Be?* (1st edn). New York: Harper & Row.

Gampel, Y. (1992). Thoughts about the transmission of conscious and unconscious knowledge to the generation born after the Shoah. *Journal of Social Work and Policy in Israel, 5*: 43–50.

Gampel, Y. (1999). Between the background of safety and the background of the uncanny in the context of social violence. In: E. Bott Spillius (Ed.), *Psychoanalysis On The Move* (pp. 59–74). London: Routledge.

Gampel, Y. (2005). *The Parents Who Live Through Me*. Tel-Aviv: Keter.

Green, A. (1981). Projection. In: *On Private Madness* (pp. 84–103). Madison, CT: International Universities Press.

Gurewitch, Z., & Eran, G. (1991). *About the place* Alpaim. Tel Aviv: Am Oved.

Ha'aretz (2008). Daily newspaper, 23 January and 6 June.

Hadar, U. (2013). *Psychoanalysis and Social Involvement*. London: Palgrave Macmillan.

Halperin, S. (1979). Who is the murderer or who am I? *Aley Siach, 7–8*: 80–95.

Hopper, E. (2003a). Incohesion: aggregation/massification. The fourth basic assumption in the unconscious life of groups and group like social systems. In: R. M. Lipgar & M. Pines (Eds.), *Building on Bion—Roots: Origins and Context of Bion's Contributions to Theory and Practice*. London: Jessica Kingsley.

Hopper, E. (2003b). *The Social Unconscious: Selected Papers*. London: Jessica Kingsley.

Hopper, E. (2003c). *Traumatic Experience in the Unconscious Life of Groups*. London: Jessica Kingsley.

Hopper, E. (2005). Countertransference in the context of the fourth basic assumption in the unconscious life of groups. *International Journal of Group Psychotherapy, 55*(1): 87–114.

Hopper, E. (2009). Building bridges between psychoanalysis and group analysis in theory and clinical practice. *Group Analysis, 42*(4): 406–425.

Hopper, E. (Ed.). (2012). *Trauma and Organizations*. London: Karnac.

Hopper, E., & Weinberg, H. (2011). *The Social Unconscious in Persons, Groups and Societies, Vol. 1*. London: Karnac.

Hopper, E., & Weinberg, H. (Eds.) (2015). *The Social Unconscious in Persons, Groups and Societies: Volume 2: Mainly Matrices*. London: Karnac.

Hopper, E., & Weyman, A. (2003). A sociological view of large groups. In: E. Hopper (Ed.). *The Social Unconscious* (pp. 42–71). London: Jessica Kingsley.

Kaniel, R. K.-I. (2013). Therapist from the depths: a conversation with Mike Eigen. *Tikkun*, 21 May.

Klein, M. (1975a). *Envy and Gratitude & Other Works, 1946–1963*. New York: Delacorte.

Klein, M. (1975b). *Love, Guilt, and Reparation & Other Works, 1921–1945*. New York: Delacorte.

Klein, M. (1975c). *The Psycho-Analysis of Children* (revised edn). New York: Delacorte.

Kohut, H., & Strozier, C. B. (1985). *Self Psychology and the Humanities: Reflections on a New Psychoanalytic Approach*. New York: Norton.

Kristeva, J. (2005). *The Power of the Terrifying* (Hebrew translation). Tel-Aviv: Resling.

Kurtz, S. A. (1992). A brief history of my tears. *Free Associations*, 3(2): 199–218.

Lanzmann, C. (2012). *The Patagonian Hare: A Memoire*. London: Atlantic Books.

Lawrence, W. G. (1991). Won from the void and formless infinite: experiences of social dreaming. *Free Associations*, 2(2): 259–294.

Lawrence, W. G. (2005). *Introduction to Social Dreaming*. London: Karnac.

Levin, C. (2008). The sibling complex: thought on French–English "translation". *Canadian Journal of Psychoanalysis*, 16: 262–274.

Lintott, B. (1983). Mind and matrix in the writing of S. H. Foulkes. *Group Analysis*, 16(3): 242–251.

Lipgar, R., & Pines, M. (Eds.) (2003a). *Building on Bion: Roots*. London: Jessica Kingsley.

Lipgar, R., & Pines, M. (Eds.) (2003b). *Building on Bion: Branches*. London: Jessica Kingsley.

Mojovic, M. (2011). Manifestations of psychic retreats in social systems. In: E. Hopper & H. Weinberg (Eds.), *The Social Unconscious in Persons, Groups, and Societies* (pp. 209–234). London: Karnac.

Molino, A. (1997). *Freely Associated: Encounters in Psychoanalysis*. London: Free Association.

Neumann, E. (1991). *The Great Mother: An Analysis of the Archetype*. Princeton, NJ: Princeton University Press.

Nitsum, M. (1996). *The Anti-Group*. London: Routledge.

Oz, A. (2002). *A Tale of Darkness and Love*. Tel Aviv: KeterS.

Penna, C. (2014). Collective memories in traumatized societies. Paper panel, Voices in the Wake of Collective Traumas, 16th Symposium in Group Analysis, Lisbon, August, 2014.

Peri, S. (2001). Solidarity of parents, a meeting of Israeli and Palestinian bereaved families, Shahak and A-Dura. *Yediot Ahronot* (daily newspaper), 24 April 2001.

Pines, M. (Ed.) (1985). *W R Bion and Group Psychotherapy*. London: Routledge & Kegan Paul.

Rickman, J. (2003). *No Ordinary Psychoanalyst: The Exceptional Contributions of John Rickman* (P. King, Ed.). London: Karnac.

Sandler, J. (1960). The background of safety. *International Journal of Psycho-Analysis*, 41: 352–356.

Saramago, J. (1997). *On Blindness*. UK: Harvill Press.

Sartre, J.-P. (1956). Existentialism is a humanism. In: W. Kaufmann (Ed.), *Existentialism from Dostoyevsky to Sartre* (pp. 345–368). London: Penguin.

Scharff, J. S., & Scharff, D. E. (2005). *The Legacy of Fairbain and Sutherland*. Hove: Routledge.

Schneider, H. (2004). *Let Me Go*. New York: Walker & Co.

Scholem, G. (1974). *Kabbalah*. Jerusalem: Keter.

Sontag, S. (2003). *Regarding the Pain of Others* (Hebrew Translation). London: Penguin.

Sophocles (1982). *The Three Theban Plays*. New York: Viking.

Sophocles (2007). *Three Theban Plays: Oedipus the King, Oedipus at Colonus, and Antigone*. New York: Barnes & Noble Classics.

Taub, G. (1997). *A Dispirited Rebellion*. Tel-Aviv: Hakibbutz Hameuchad.

Werbart, A. (2000). Our need of taboo: pictures of violence and mourning difficulties. *Free Associations*, *8*(2): 21–48.

Winnicott, D. W. (1949). Hate in the counter-transference. *International Journal of Psycho-Analysis*, 30: 69–74.

Winnicott, D. W. (1982). *The Maturational Processes and the Facilitating Environment; Studies in the Theory of Emotional Development*. London: The Hogarth Press (first published 1965).

Winnicott, D. W. (1974). Fear of breakdown. *International Revue of Psycho-Analysis*, 1: 103–107.

INDEX